Open Data in Developing Economies

Toward Building an Evidence Base on What Works and How

Stefaan G. Verhulst and Andrew Young

AFRICAN
MINDS

Published in 2017 by
African Minds
4 Eccleston Place, Somerset West, 7130, Cape Town, South Africa
info@africanminds.org.za
www.africanminds.org.za

Cover photograph: Doug Linstedt—Unsplash

ISBNs
978-1-928331-59-9 Print
978-1-928331-60-5 e-Book

Copies of this book are available for free download at www.africanminds.org.za

ORDERS
For orders from Africa:
African Minds
Email: info@africanminds.org.za

For orders from outside Africa:
African Books Collective
PO Box 721, Oxford OX1 9EN, UK

Email: orders@africanbookscollective.com

TABLE OF CONTENTS

ACKNOWLEDGEMENTS

The authors would like to thank our partners at USAID: Mark Cardwell, Samir Doshi, Priya Jaisinghani, Merrick Schaefer, Vivian Ranson, Josh Machleder, Brandon Pustejovsky, Subhashini Chandrasekharan; and at FHI 360: Hannah Skelly and Abdul Bari Farahi who provided essential guidance and input throughout the project.

We would also like to acknowledge the great team responsible for the case study research that informs this book: Michael Canares and François van Schalkwyk from the Web Foundation; and Anirudh Dinesh, Auralice Graft, Juliet McMurren and Robert Montano at the GovLab. Editorial support for this book was provided by Akash Kapur and David Dembo. The members of our Advisory Committee were a great resource to the project for which we are grateful.

Special thanks to the stakeholders we interviewed to gain on-the-ground and expert perspectives on the use of open data in developing economies, as well as the peer reviewers who provided input on a pre-published draft. Finally, we would also like to acknowledge our gratitude to African Minds, the publishers of this book whose mission to foster access, openness and debate exemplifies the core values behind open data, and thus provided the perfect setting to share our findings among a broader audience.

LIST OF ABBREVIATIONS

BBW	Banana Bacterial Wilt
BODI	Burkina Open Data Initiative
CIAT	International Center for Tropical Agriculture
DFID	Department for International Development, United Kingdom
EITI	Extractive Industries Transparency Initiative
ELOG	Elections Observation Group
EOSDIS	Earth Observing System Data and Information System
ESM	Electricity Supply Monitor
ESMI	Electricity Supply Monitoring Initiative
EITI	Extractives Industries Transparency Initiative
GODAN	Global Open Data Initiative for Agriculture and Nutrition
IDRC	International Development Research Centre
IEBC	Independent Electoral and Boundaries Commission, Kenya
IMCO	Mexican Institute for Competitiveness
MERC	Maharashtra Electricity Regulatory Commission
MPR	Medicine Price Registry, South Africa
MPRApp	Medicine Price Registry Application
NERC	National Ebola Response Centre
NGO	Non-Governmental Organization
OD4D	Open Data for Development
ODC	Open Development Cambodia
ODI	Open Data Institute
OGP	Open Government Partnership
OSM	Open Street Map
PEG	Prayas Energy Group
PHC	Primary Health Care Centre
PII	Personal Identifiable Information
RBF	Results Based Financing
SDG	Sustainable Development Goals
TAP	Transparency, Accountability and informed Participation
UNICEF	The United Nations Children's Fund
USAID	United States Agency for International Development
WOUGNET	Women of Uganda Network

CHAPTER 1

Introduction

In 2009, the United States launched the data.gov portal. Since then there has been a rapid increase in the systematic opening of government data around the world. The 2016 Open Data Barometer,[1] published annually by the World Wide Web Foundation, found that 79 of the 115 countries surveyed had official open data initiatives, and many others indicated imminent plans to establish such initiatives. Similarly, as part of the Open Government Partnership (OGP), a multilateral network established in 2011, some 70 countries have now issued National Action Plans, the majority of which contain strong open data commitments designed to foster greater transparency, generate economic growth, empower citizens, fight corruption, and more generally enhance governance. Approximately half of these countries are from the developing world,[2] suggesting the uptake of open data is happening not only within economically advanced countries, but also in those less developed. All of this is part of a general move toward more transparent and innovative governance mechanisms, as emblematized by rising interest in notions of open government and open development.

The growing enthusiasm for, and use of, open data in developing economies leads to several questions about open data's role in fostering development.[3] Can open data bring about economic growth and social transformation? Can open data truly improve people's lives in the developing world—and, if so, how and under what conditions? This book's goal is to take stock of what is known about open data's use and impacts in developing economies, and to distil a theory of change based on existing theory and practice that can inform future open data use and research. This book neither serves as a booster nor as a skeptic regarding the potential of open data in developing countries. Rather, it aims to sift through the evidence, draw out cross-cutting signals and insights from practice across developing economies when present, and start identifying

---

1   World Wide Web Foundation, *Open Data Barometer*, Fourth Edition, 2016, http://opendatabarometer.org/.

2   See Open Government Partnership website, http://www.opengovpartnership.org/, accessed November 30, 2016.

3   Andrew Young, Stefaan Verhulst and Juliet McMurren, "The GovLab Selected Readings on Open Data for Developing Economies," August 1, 2016, http://thegovlab.org/open-data-for-developing-economies/.

the conditions under which open data appears able to work best, as well as those conditions that impede its potential.

Methodology

To formulate answers to the above questions and devise a theory of change, the authors undertook an extensive research effort that comprised a desk review of existing literature and identification of dozens of active open data projects around the developing world. From among these projects, the research team selected 12 case studies based on geographic and sector relevance. Each case study included further document review and consultations and interviews with project stakeholders over the course of three months. The outputs of these efforts were reviewed and informed by an advisory group of open data for development experts and a group of open data peer reviewers. Throughout the book, examples from these case studies are employed to illuminate the real-world impacts of open data, when they exist, as well as the enabling and disabling conditions that play a role in determining whether such impact is positive, negative—or negligible.

In developing a change theory and identifying meaningful answers to the above organizing research questions on the impact of open data, this book builds upon existing studies and analyses about the relationship between open data and development.[4]

Limitations

The primary objective of this research was to capture the universe of current narratives and evidence of open data for developing economies. We found that the literature remains largely focused on the potential of open data to bring about positive impacts. In many instances, the benefits of open data are celebrated despite little concrete evidence to prove that opening data has in fact created positive on-the-ground impacts at a meaningful scale. In addition, when evidence is being presented, little distinction is made between intent, implications, and impact. As such, this book does reflect the positive narrative provided by the literature on open data for developing economies, but does so to help identify a meaningful signal in the noise, and provide an analytical framework to enable others to build on our work and further crystallize the

---

4   See Appendix D online for an annotated selection of the key readings: http://odimpact.org/files/odimpact-developing-economies-appendices.pdf.

true impacts and drivers of successful open data initiatives in developing economies. Our aim is to enable the field to move from ideology to evidence; we see this book as an initial step toward that end.

Before considering the (variable) evidence, it is important to note that "developing economies" are not uniform or monolithic. Our analysis focuses particularly on low- and medium-income countries, spread primarily across Africa, Latin America, and Asia. We do believe that some of the examples and evidence presented could be helpful in informing discussions and efforts underway in other contexts and countries. But questions of replication and scalability are complex—particularly when considering technological interventions—and we make no claims that the lessons offered here are universal, or even universally applicable across the diversity of countries that could be classified as low or medium income. So, although this book seeks to provide a set of testable research-driven premises and useful recommendations for open data practitioners and funders working across the developing world, it remains essential to always consider a country's local context and needs when seeking to replicate success stories or implement recommendations found in this book.

Book contents

In essence, the book seeks to answer the following key questions:

- What makes open data uniquely relevant to developing economies?
- How can the impact of open data in developing economies be captured and evidence be developed?
- How can open data be leveraged as a new asset for development?

Toward that end the book begins, in Part I, by providing examining the use of open data for development. This includes a brief assessment on the theories and narratives of open data in development; a change theory and a logic model to capture and develop evidence on open data in developing economies; and an examination of open data's impacts across various development sectors. In Part II, we present the 12 open data in developing countries case studies, organized according to the four different types of open data impacts. The book concludes in Part III with a set of key takeaways and recommendations for aid organizations, governments, private sector entities, and others that are considering replicating or using open data as an asset for development.

PART 1
Open Data for Development

CHAPTER 2

The Relevance of Open Data for Developing Economies

What is Open Data?

In this book, open data is defined as follows:

> *Open data is publicly available data that can be universally and readily accessed, used and redistributed free of charge. It is structured for usability and computability.*[5]

Not all forms of data shared actually possess all the attributes included in this definition, nor do they necessarily conform to all the principles found in the Open Data Charter.[6] In many ways, this is a gold-standard definition of open data, an important target to work toward. In fact, the openness of data exists on a continuum, and many forms of data that are not strictly "open" in the sense defined above are nonetheless shareable and usable by third parties. It is this broader sense of "open" that is used in this paper.

Open data exists in a wide variety of fields and domains. Three sectors in particular are responsible for producing the bulk of open data: governments, scientists, and corporations. In this paper, we focus mainly on the release and use of government data. We acknowledge, however, the importance and often untapped potential of more open access to science data and corporate data. Those other data sources, as well as crowdsourced data collection are also often mashed up with open government data, supplementing official public datasets to create new insights, opportunities, and impacts as a result. In what follows, we deconstruct the main reasons why open government data matters to developing economies.

---

5   GovLab, "Open Data: What's in a Name," January 16, 2014, *GovLab Blog*, http://thegovlab.org/open-data-whats-in-a-name/.

6   Open by Default; Timely and Comprehensive; Accessible and Usable; Comparable and Interoperable; For Improved Governance and Citizen Engagement; For Inclusive Development and Innovation. http://opendatacharter.net.

The literature on open data reflects considerable enthusiasm about the potential for open government data in development. For example, a recent report published by the Open Data for Development Network suggests that open data is central to the development community's goals of "enabling widespread economic value, fostering greater civic engagement and enhancing government transparency and accountability to citizens." The report goes on to argue that "open data is increasingly recognized as a new form of infrastructure that is transforming how governments, businesses, and citizens are organized in an increasingly networked society."[7] We do find some evidence to support such enthusiasm: across sectors, we see signs that open data can indeed spur positive economic, political, and social change. On the other hand, we also find grounds for caution; the impacts of many of the projects we examined remain largely aspirational or speculative, and some cases even led to harms (or potential harms). Although the real-world impacts of open data in developing economies remain emergent, it is important to distil these early lessons and develop a frame of analysis to support the current window of opportunity to increase access to data sources—a window that is likely to close absent any further evidence of open data's impact or a better, more targeted description of the value proposition and change theory driving the field.

What makes open data uniquely relevant to developing economies?

We live in an era of big data. Every day, an unprecedented amount of information is being generated by an ever-increasing diversity of devices and appliances. Today, a growing consensus exists that this data, if applied correctly, and with attention to the attendant risks, can help spur positive social change. Sometimes called the "data revolution,"[8] this new paradigm often fails to distinguish between the benefits of data per se and the complementing benefits of *unlocking government data*.[9]

---

7   Open Data for Development Network, *Open Data for Development: Building an inclusive data revolution, Annual Report, 2015*, 11, http://od4d.com/wp-content/uploads/2016/06/OD4D_annual_report_2015.pdf.

8   See United Nations Independent Expert Advisory Group on a Data Revolution for Sustainable Development, "A World That Counts, Mobilizing the Data Revolution," 2014, http://bit.ly/2am5K28.

9   At the same time, there is a growing recognition of open data's potential to meet the Sustainable Development Goals (SDGs). The World Bank, for instance, has explored the various ways in which open data could help to make progress toward the SDGs. Similarly, a recent White Paper by the Open Data Institute (ODI) concludes: "Open data can make an impact across the globe. Its role in combating development challenges of the next 15 years, both as a tool for measuring progress and in finding solutions, is becoming more clear." See The World Bank, "Open Data for Sustainable Development," Policy Note, August 2015, http://bit.ly/2aGjaJ4; and Open Data Institute, *Supporting Sustainable Development with Open Data*, 2015, 3, http://theodi.org/supporting-sustainable-development-with-open-data.

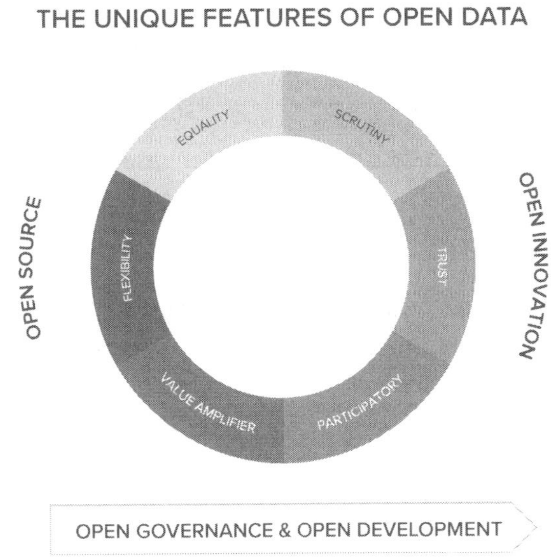

THE UNIQUE FEATURES OF OPEN DATA

Figure 1. The Unique Features of Open Data

Based on our examination of the narratives and evidence provided in the existing literature, six distinguishing features seem to be credited to open data. Although these characteristics are unique to open data, in many cases, they would not be possible without a broader data, technology, and innovation ecosystem. Across our case studies, we've seen that the existence of a strong information and communication technology for development (ICT4D) sector in a country, for example, tends to result in higher impact, more quickly developing open data efforts.

With the understanding in mind that open data must exist in a strong ecosystem, the six distinguishing features that are most quoted with regard to open data in a development context include:

- *Scrutiny*: Because open data is subject to greater scrutiny and exposure than inaccessible institutional data, there is potential for enhanced review and improvement of government data quality (e.g., by data-literate civil society groups or other crowdsourced methods). This can result in more useful data—again, a benefit that is relevant in less developed countries and societies, where data is scarce, and of limited quality and usefulness.[10]

---

10   Tim Davies, for instance, notes that, "researchers and other users outside of government may highlight inaccuracies and inconsistencies between datasets" as a result of access to open data, and thereby improving data quality and usefulness. Tim Davies, "Open Data in Developing Countries: Emerging

- *Equality*: Open data can lead to an inherently more equitable and democratic distribution of information and knowledge. This is a key intended benefit in all countries, but particularly salient in many developing economies that struggle with large socioeconomic and digital divides.[11] It is important to keep in mind, however, that the lack of Internet penetration and access to tools for using and accessing open data still present challenges in many contexts—and, indeed, such technological inequities can be further entrenched through open data in some cases.

- *Flexibility*: Open data is open with regard not only to the information it contains, but also to its format. This means that, when released in a usable manner, open data can be easier to repurpose and combine with other pieces of information than data institutions fail to make accessible, which in turn means that it is more flexible, with secondary uses that are likely to yield innovative insights. This is true of data from all sectors, but perhaps especially of government data, which often exists in vast, untapped silos; opening that data (turning it "liquid") can play a key role in generating new insights and policies.[12] Such liquidity can only become a reality if data, and the tools used to manipulate it, are interoperable and adhere to agreed upon standards. Creating such technical capacity can, however, lead to opportunity costs and require significant upfront resource allocation on the supply side, potentially slowing progress at the outset.

- *Participation*: By facilitating citizen participation and mobilization, open data can allow a wider range of expertise and knowledge to address and potentially solve complex problems. This quality of "open innovation" can allow resource-starved developing economies to access and benefit from the best global minds and expertise. It can offer a more participatory way of solving complex public dilemmas, with pathways toward more easily tapping into previously inaccessible knowledge (e.g., those related to social and economic development).[13]

---

insights from Phase I," *Open Data Research*, July 15, 2014, http://opendataresearch.org/sites/default/files/publications/Phase 1-Synthesis-Full Report-print.pdf.

11 Aspasia Papaloi and Dimitris Gouscos, "Parliamentary Information Visualization as a Means for Legislative Transparency and Citizen Empowerment," *Journal of Democracy and Open Government*, 2013, http://www.jedem.org/index.php/jedem/article/view/222/183.

12 "By using common open repositories, public administrations can save time and money from the automisation of internal data exchange," Raimondo Lemma, Federico Morando and Michele Osella, "Breaking Public Administrations' Data Silos: The case of Open-DAI, and a comparison between open data platforms," *Journal of Democracy & Open Government*, 2014, http://www.jedem.org/index.php/jedem/article/view/304.

13 Jae-Nam Lee, Juyeon Ham and Byounggu Choi, "Effect of Government Data Openness on a Knowledge-based Economy," *Procedia Computer Science*, 91, 2016. http://www.sciencedirect.com/science/article/pii/S1877050916312364.

- *Trust*: Because it increases transparency and avenues for citizen oversight, unlocking data can lead to higher levels of accountability and trust throughout societies and countries.[14] This "sunlight" or "trust" quality of open data can have powerful ripple effects, including incentives for better government practice, and the enhancement of the quality of public life and citizenship. Such increases to trust and accountability rely on meaningful data being made open, however, rather than governments participating in "open washing" where largely useless datasets are made accessible toward boosting institutional reputation.

- *Value amplifier*: Finally, it is now widely recognized that data is a new kind of asset or knowledge is a form of wealth. The opening of government datasets in a flexible and equitable manner can amplify the value of data thanks to data filling important data gaps felt in society. Though this attribute is important across the world, it may have a particularly important role to play in developing economies. In its 2016 *World Development Report*, The World Bank pointed out that technology can play an "accelerator" role in developing countries.[15] But while the inherent scarcity of resources (data and otherwise) in the developing world increases the apparent value and potential impact of open data, cultural and political barriers to timely and well-targeted open data provision efforts could slow progress.

These narratives surrounding the open data movement reflect those associated with the cross-sector paradigm shift from closed processes to open ones, and how it applies to governance and development. Software, for example, is increasingly developed in an *open source* manner. With the rise of the collaborative coding platform GitHub, a notable driver,[16] the open source movement, similar to open data, is seen to be providing for more equal and flexible ways to create and access code—resulting in distributed coders, not just tech company employees, creating and improving exciting new products. Similarly, businesses and governments alike are embracing *open innovation* techniques, posing opportunities to the crowd to provide input on important challenges and absorbing the best ideas—providing for enhanced participation

---

14 Ali Clare, David Sangokoya, Stefaan Verhulst and Andrew Young, "Open Contracting and Procurement In Slovakia," GovLab, Accessed October 25, 2016, http://odimpact.org/case-open-contracting-and-procurement-in-slovakia.html.

15 World Bank, *World Development Report 2016: Digital Dividends*, World Bank, 2016, 4, http://documents.worldbank.org/curated/en/896971468194972881/pdf/102725-PUB-Replacement-PUBLIC.pdf.

16 Laura Dabbish, et al., "Social Coding in GitHub: Transparency and collaboration in an open software repository," *Proceedings of the ACM 2012 Conference on Computer Supported Cooperative Work*, February 11, 2012, http://dl.acm.org/citation.cfm?id=2145396.

and scrutiny, other features of open data.[17] The emerging fields of *open governance* and *open development* are also built on similar principles and techniques (see text box below).

OPEN GOVERNMENT AND OPEN DEVELOPMENT

Open Governance/Government[18]

Definitions of open governance or open government vary not only across sectors but within them. Definitions focus to varying degrees on the key elements of transparency, citizen participation, and collaboration, among others, depending on the context. Some illustrative examples of "open government" definitions[19] include:

- *Wallace Parks, "Open Government Principle: Applying the right to know under the Constitution" (1957)*—"The general availability of government information is the fundamental basis upon which popular sovereignty and the consent of the governed rest, subject to several important restrictions on this general rule (i.e., to allow for the carrying out of the constitutional powers of the Congress and the President; to protect the personal and property rights of individuals, corporations and associations; to acknowledge administrative complications as to whether to release, to withhold, or to partially release particular types of information under particular conditions; to protect confidentiality of communications internal to government; to acknowledge the difficulty of segregating information when parts of a document should be released and parts withheld)."[20]

- *White House, "Transparency and Open Government: Memorandum for the Heads of Executive Departments and Agencies" (2009)*—"Open government is defined as a system of transparency (information disclosure; solicit public feedback), public participation (increased opportunities to participate in policymaking), and collaboration (the use of innovative tools, methods, and systems to facilitate cooperation among Government departments, and with nonprofit organizations, businesses, and individuals in the private sector)."[21]

---

17 Dietmar Harhoff and Karim R. Lakhani (eds.), *Revolutionizing Innovation: Users, communities, and open innovation,* Boston: MIT Press, 2016.

18 See GovLab, "Open Data: What's in a Name," January 16, 2014, *GovLab Blog,* http://thegovlab.org/open-data-whats-in-a-name/.

19 See also (in Spanish), Silvana Fumega, "Algunas Ideas para 'Debates Conceptuales sobre el Gobierno Abierto,'" September 25, 2016, http://silvanafumega.blogspot.fr/2016/09/algunas-ideas-para-debates-conceptuales.html.

20 *George Washington Law Review* 26, no. 1 (October 1957), http://heinonline.org/HOL/Page?handle=hein.journals/gwlr26&div=10&id=&page=&collection=journals.

21 At: https://www.whitehouse.gov/the_press_office/TransparencyandOpenGovernment.

- *Open Government Partnership, Open Government Partnership Declaration (2011)*—"Open government involves: Increasing the availability of information about governmental activities; Supporting civic participation; Implementing the highest standards of professional integrity through: Increasing access to new technologies for openness and accountability, information sharing, public participation, and collaboration."[22]

Open Development[23]

In the wake of open government taking hold as an organizing concept for improving and innovating governance, open development has evolved as a more networked and innovative pathway to improving international aid and development efforts. In a book on the topic, the International Development Research Centre (IDRC) seeks to gain clarity on the contours of the field of open development.[24] Their assessment of the theory and practice involves a number of key elements present in open development work, including:

- The power of human cooperation
- Sharing ideas and knowledge
- The ability to reuse, revise and repurpose content
- Increasing transparency of processes
- Expanding participation
- Collaborative production

Based on the examination of these strands of openness in development efforts from the World Bank, ONE, African Development Bank, and others, the IDRC authors conclude that the central idea behind open development is: "harnessing the increased penetration of information and communications technologies to create new organizational forms that improve the lives of people."[25]

---

22 Open Government Partnership, "Open Government Declaration," http://www.opengovpartnership.org/about/open-government-declaration.

23 See Matthew L. Smith and Katherine M.A. Reilly, eds., *Open Development: Networked innovations in international development*, MIT Press, 2013, http://idl-bnc.idrc.ca/dspace/bitstream/10625/52348/1/IDL-52348.pdf.

24 Ibid.

25 Ibid.

The Data Life Cycle

An important insight from the emerging research and practice is that data is not "a thing" but involves a "process"—what we call a "data life cycle."

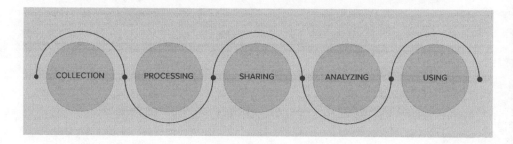

Figure 2. Data Life Cycle

How each stage of the data life cycle is implemented—from collection to processing and sharing; to analysis and using; and back to the start of the cycle again—will determine the value of data and who ultimately benefits. Disparities among those who collect and have access to data or have the capacity to make sense of the data can reinforce existing imbalances in power or influence. This is especially true in a developing economies context where the number of data holders and data scientists is more concentrated, and this smaller group is disproportionately empowered to make meaningful use of data. Within that context, opening datasets is often characterized as a force for democratization—engaging private and civil society actors, and, often indirectly as a result of intermediation, citizens themselves in analyzing and using data.[26] As such, open data provides for unique efficiencies by leveraging civic-minded technologists (government and nongovernment), as well as entrepreneurs, to analyze, disseminate, and/or use data in a new, sometimes profitable way, as discussed more below.

On the other hand, each stage of the data life cycle contains risks. Risks are often the result of technological weaknesses (e.g., security flaws); individual and institutional norms and standards of quality (e.g., weak scientific rigor in analysis); legal confusion or gaps; or misaligned business and other incentives (e.g., companies seeking to push the boundaries of what is socially appropriate). Although there are common elements across these risks, it is useful to examine them by separately considering each stage of the data value cycle.

---

26 Jonathan Gray, "Five Ways Open Data Can Boost Democracy Around the World," *The Guardian*, February 20, 2015, https://www.theguardian.com/public-leaders-network/2015/feb/20/open-data-day-fairer-taxes.

When risks are not addressed at the initial stages of the value cycle (e.g., when dirty data is not cleaned at the collection stage) they may accumulate and lead to additional risks downstream (e.g., making flawed inferences from the data analysis due to inaccurate data). Therefore, it is important to consider potential risks not just at the points of opening data, but also at the data collection stage and evaluate those risks vis-à-vis the (potential) value of releasing the data. As such, to prevent harm, there may be a legitimate case—especially when there is a clear understanding of the purpose of the use and user—to share certain government datasets with those targeted audiences in a more protected manner to generate necessary insights while limiting the risks. We examine the risks introduced by open data efforts in developing economies in more detail in Part II.

The Impact of Open Data on Developing Economies

Capturing impact and developing evidence

Many studies of open data are concerned with proving a case—either that open data can spur rapid social transformation (the positive case), or that it has a negligible or harmful effect (the negative case). In truth, the evidence is mixed and emergent; the impact of open data is, in fact, far more ambiguous. Rather than just asking *Does open data spur development?* we seek in this paper to also ask, *How and under what conditions can it work?*

To answer this question, we've examined a wide and variable range of attempts to provide evidence to develop a plausible "theory of change" that would explain the role of open data in development. Theories of change are important. A recent report from the United Kingdom's Institute of Development Studies points to "the persistence of poorly articulated theories of change that fail to specify realistic causal pathways at the outset" in relation to transparency initiatives.[27] Weak theories of change can lead to a variety of false assumptions and misconceptions when it comes to understanding how open data works; these, in turn, can lead to missed opportunities, spending inefficiencies, and a general failure to live up to open data's potential.

A review of the literature shows that numerous pathways and theories of change have in fact been proposed. For example, a recent study conducted by IDRC, the World Wide Web Foundation, and the Berkman Klein Center for Internet and Society at Harvard University cites at least thirteen "theories of change," including open data's ability to reduce transaction costs, generate new forms of economic growth and prosperity, generate new revenue models, and disrupt traditional business models.[28] Others point to the social and environmental benefits of open data. For example, Martin Hilbert draws

---

27 Duncan Edwards and Rosie McGee, eds., "Opening Governance," *IDS Bulletin* 47, no. 1 (January 2016), https://opendocs.ids.ac.uk/opendocs/bitstream/handle/123456789/7686/IDSB_47_1_10.190881968-2016.103.pdf?sequence=1.

28 José M. Alonso, "Measuring Impact of Open Government Data—Open Data Research (South) Meeting Report," May 24, 2012, http://webfoundation.org/2012/05/odrs-meeting1-report-available/.

attention to the potential of opening geospatial-, education-, and housing-related information. Based on a review of 180 pieces of literature related to Big and Open Data, he concludes—with caveats we discuss further below—that open data does in fact contain true opportunities for development.[29]

Open Data in Developing Economies Logic Model

In what follows, we describe a change theory for open data using the Open Data in Developing Economies Logic Model (Figure 3).[30] This model suggests that:

Open data (supply), when analyzed and leveraged by both governmental and non-governmental actors (demand), can be used in a variety of ways (actions and outputs), within the parameters established by certain enabling conditions (and disabling factors), to improve government, empower citizens and users, create economic opportunity and/or solve societal problems (impact).

It is important to reiterate, however, that these positive impacts are always subject to certain local, context-sensitive enabling conditions and disabling factors. While this logic model presents a general outline of how open data can work, Table 1, below, presents a more detailed explanation of how it interacts with various sector-specific opportunities and challenges to create genuine impact on the ground.

The logic model is built around the premise (informed by the case studies and primed for further experimentation and research) that higher impact open data projects are the result of matching the supply to the demand of data actors who can operationalize open data toward specific activities and outputs. These outputs and activities can, in turn, serve a broader and more diverse group of users and objectives.

Having a logic model allows for a more detailed analysis within and across sectors of open data toward providing a number of highly specific lessons about actors and conditions, opportunities and challenges.

---

29 Martin Hilbert, "Big Data for Development: A review of promises and challenges," *Development Policy Review* 34, no. 1 (January 2016), http://onlinelibrary.wiley.com/doi/10.1111/dpr.12142/full.

30 See also Andrew Young, Stefaan Verhulst, and Juliet McMurren, "The GovLab Selected Readings on Open Data for Developing Economies," August 1, 2016, http://thegovlab.org/open-data-for-developing-economies/.

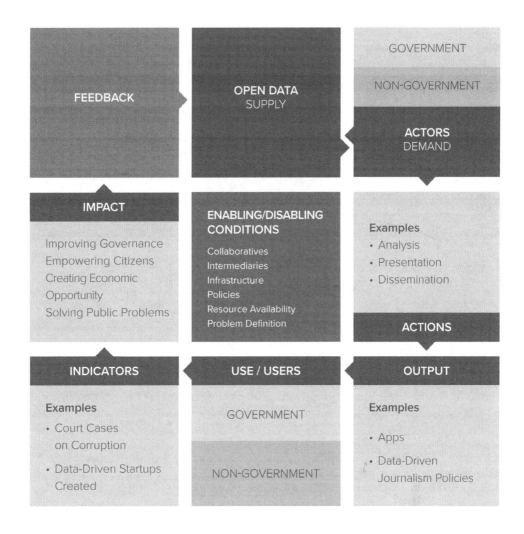

Figure 3. Open Data in Developing Economies Logic Model

Examining the Open Data in Developing Economies Logic Framework

The logic model presented in Figure 3 above describes the elements in place across the lifespan of an open data initiative, from the initial input or supply of data through its use and impact, with several enabling conditions and disabling factors influencing impact. We explore each of the elements introduced in the table in more detail below, with attention to the types of impact and the enabling conditions and disabling factors that inform the Periodic Table of Open Data Elements.

Table 1. In-Depth Logic Framework

Input (Supply)	Actors (Demand)	Activity	Output	Use/Users	Indicators	Impact
Open Government Data "Open data is publicly available data that can be universally and readily accessed, used and re-distributed free of charge. It is structured for usability and computability." Including, for instance: • GIS Data • Observed Data (e.g., weather) • Financial Data • Administrative Data • Statistical Data • Audit Data	NGOs & Interest Groups Researchers and Academia Journalists and Media Outlets Donor Organizations Private Sector—Entrepreneurs and Corporations Government Officials	*Data Analysis (Methods)* *Presentation (Visualization)* *Aggregation and Commingling (Mashups)* *Dissemination—*toward, for instance: • Benchmarking • Hotspotting • Comparing services and performance • Resource allocation • Diagnosis and assessment	Decision Trees Maps Apps and Platforms Dashboards Process improvements Data-driven journalism Infographics Searchable databases Policies Advocacy Alerts	*Other Government Agencies and Officials* *Nongovernment Actors including, for instance:* • Citizens • Researchers • Entrepreneurs • Corporations • Service providers • NGOs & interest groups • Media outlets • Donor organizations	The outputs of open data have had several real-world effects, which can be assessed according to a number of indicators, for instance: *Accountability* • Court cases on corruption *Improved service delivery:* • Increase in citizens receiving services *Increased information sharing:* • Collaborations between public entities *Enhanced decision-making capacity and choice:* • Satisfaction among citizens *Social mobilization:* • Data-driven advocacy efforts *Job creation:* • Employment in data-driven fields *Frugal innovation:* • Data-driven startups *Economic growth:* • Industry-level growth figures *Improved situational awareness:* • Time saved responding to emerging situations and crises *More expertise and knowledge brought to bear:* • Number of disciplines engaged in decision-making processes *Targeting interventions and tracking impact:* • Assessment of change against baseline indicators	*Improving Government* • Accountability • Improved service delivery • Increased information sharing *Empowering Citizens* • Enhanced decision making capacity and choice • Social mobilization *Innovation and Creating Economic Opportunity* • Job creation • Frugal innovation • Economic growth *Solving Public Problems* • Improved situational awareness • More expertise and knowledge brought to bear • Targeting interventions and tracking impact

Enabling Conditions and Disabling Factors
• Problem and Demand Definition: whether and how the problem to be addressed and/or the demand for open data are clearly defined and understood
• Capacity and Culture: whether and how resources, human capital and technological capabilities are sufficiently available and leveraged meaningfully
• Partnerships: whether collaboration within and, especially, across sectors using open data exist
• Risks: whether and how the risks associated with open data are assessed and mitigated;
• Governance: whether and how decisions affecting the use of open data are made in a responsive manner

Input (Supply)

A diversity of data types make up the supply side of open data in developing economies and, as the input, plays a key role in determining the ultimate impact. Data types being made available in developing countries range from information about the planet, such as geospatial and weather information, to information about the workings of government itself, like financial and administrative data. Of importance within a developing country context, involves data that is collected and potentially supplied by international (donor) organizations and civil society (often through crowd-sourced means) that may complement the supply of domestic government data. Much of the focus in the early days of open data (in both developed and developing economies) has fallen on improving the supply side of open data, with the Open Data Charter and Open Government Partnership, for example, pushing government data holders to make certain types of data accessible according to a number of principles and in a standardized way.

Actors (Demand)

As the global open data ecosystem matures, a greater focus is being placed on understanding the demand side of open data—the actors who will make use of the information the governments released. As the supply side of open data continues to improve thanks to international standardization efforts, including the Open Data Charter and advocacy at the national and regional level, the demand side stands to benefit through greater engagement of existing demand-side actors, and the identification of additional stakeholders who could make use of that information. Some of the key yet distinctive segments or constituencies (often with different interests and needs) on the demand side of open data include nongovernmental organizations (NGOs), including not only government watchdog groups but also service providers, researchers and scholars, data-driven journalists, entrepreneurs and businesses, and government officials themselves who benefit from more liquid data that has escaped internal silos.

Activities

The activities enabled by access to open data are in many ways only limited by the imagination and skills of the actors on the demand side of the equation. Some of the most common ways that open data is used include data analysis to uncover new insights, presentation and visualization to make the information more comprehensible, aggregation and commingling of multiple datasets to gain a more multi-faceted view of an issue, and eventually dissemination of processed open data toward benchmarking efforts, hotspotting (e.g., data-driven crime or healthcare maps), or informing future resource allocation decision making.

Output

Like the activities open data enables, the output of processed open data can take any number of forms depending on the problem or opportunity the data is meant to address and the priorities of the actors on the demand side. Although the output of open data initiatives is often some form of data or technology—such as searchable databases, information dashboards or smartphone applications—they can also take the form of evidence-based policies, advocacy, or activism efforts or data-driven journalism pieces.

Use/Users

The existence of actors on the demand side of open data and users of the open data-driven outputs those actors create complicates the lifespan of open data and makes clear the need for responsiveness and feedback loops on the supply side. In many cases, the types of actors representing the demand side of open data are also present as users of open data outputs—such as NGOs or journalists. The community of user includes a broader swath of the population, however, with individuals and entities that lack any data science capabilities still able to make use of the outputs of open data—whether in the form of smartphone weather applications, data-driven infographics in the newspaper, or government process optimizations.

Indicators

In many ways, open data is a double-edged sword. How open data is made accessible to the public ensures that anyone can use open data for any reason. It also means that identifying those usages and capturing their impacts is extremely challenging, especially for resource-strapped governments. To gain some meaningful sense of the impact of open data releases, data holders can seek to develop indicators tied to the problems open datasets stand to address. After the release of open data on the financial dealings of government officials, for instance, an uptick in court cases on corruption could provide a window into open data's impact on accountability. Similarly, the creation of more data-driven startups, increased investment from international donors, or increases in hiring among technology companies that use (or are likely to use) open data can act as indicators of open data's effect on economic development. Especially in developing economies where government resources are often limited, meaningfully capturing the impacts of open data through indicators of success will likely prove essential for maintaining the political will needed for open data efforts to be sustainable.

Types of Impact

As reflected in Table 1, our research indicates that open data has four main types of impact, and that each type of impact requires different indicators. Although the four types of impact described below provide a framework of analysis, it is also important to understand that these types of impact can manifest in different ways, and some projects might seek to achieve more than one type of impact. In the discussion below, we point to a diversity of open data initiatives aimed at having a positive effect in one or more of these impact areas, but in some cases, impact remains largely aspirational; in others, impact was negligible, or in fact, negative. Rather than focusing exclusively on gold-standard open data projects with unquestionable and consequential on-the-ground impacts—like the oft-referenced Global Positioning System or opening of weather data in the United States—we examine initiatives across the spectrum of impact to develop a more detailed understanding of the current reality for open data in developing economies, and more importantly, to provide testable premises of how to create an impact based on lessons learned from efforts to date, even some efforts that have not (yet) created major positive impacts.

To be sure, much of the evidence provided below is emergent, and in some cases largely speculative. Collecting and organizing these signals of what is known (and believed) about open data for development, however, provides for a systematic understanding of the current field, and informs more strategic, analytical assessments of open data's impact going forward. So although the evidence here is unquestionably variable—ranging from concrete, clearly demonstrable on-the-ground impacts to largely ideological assertions of impact—they provide a frame for understanding the field and taking the next step toward meaningful impact assessment.

Improving governance

One of the most consistent ways in which open data has an impact on development, across countries and regions, is in ***improving governance***. This impact manifests in several ways:

22

- Greater transparency and citizen involvement can make governments *more accountable* to their citizens.
- A focus on data use and data-driven decision making engendered by the institutional process of opening data (i.e., cleaning and making liquid government datasets) can result in *better and more efficient service delivery.*
- In addition to making data accessible to entities outside of government, open data efforts can *increase information sharing* between departments and agencies within government, improving coordination and knowledge-sharing.

Emergent evidence:

- *Elections in Burkina Faso:* To ensure elections in Burkina Faso were conducted fairly, poll results were made available in real time via an official election website, which tracked candidates leading in each of the provinces. This project, run by the Burkina Open Data Initiative (BODI, http://data.gov.bf/about) with the support of the ODI, sought to promote democracy and trust between Burkina Faso's citizens and elected officials. For a country in transition like Burkina Faso, opening electoral data was seen as an important first step toward establishing longer term political stability and citizen trust in the electoral process, though the number of citizens or organizations who actually accessed and acted upon the data is unclear.[31]
- *Elections in Indonesia:* In a similar initiative, Indonesia's Kawal Pemilu ("guard the election," in Indonesian) was launched in the immediate aftermath of the 2014 presidential elections, as the country was riven by political polarization and the two leading contenders for the presidency traded allegations of vote rigging. A globally dispersed group of technologists, activists, and volunteers came together to create a website that would allow citizens to compare official vote tallies with the original tabulations from polling stations. These tabulations were already made public as part of the Elections General Commission's commitment to openness and transparency. Kawal Pemilu's organizers, however, played a critical role in assembling a team of over 700 volunteers to digitize the often-handwritten forms and make the data more legible and accessible.

---

31 The author of a case study from the participating Open Data Institute, which disseminated the results of the effort, notes that, "Whether or not the improved information flow and accessibility to results— enabled by the application of open data—led to increased trust in the election process, or even an improved process, is not something that we can or indeed set out to prove or show empirically, although the outcome of this case study is certainly supportive of that conclusion." Anna Scott, "Case Study: Burkina Faso's open elections," Open Data Institute, October 2016, https://theodi.org/case-study-burkina-fasos-open-elections#1.

The site was assembled in a mere two days, with a total budget of just $54. Not only did the site enable citizen participation in monitoring the election results, but Kawal Pemilu's vote tallies also played an important role in court hearings confirming the election winner.[32]

- *Data Journalism in Kenya*: In Kenya, journalists leveraged open data to report on a "freeze" in the dissemination of welfare support to the elderly and disabled. The freeze was traced back to a government failure to build an effective system for distributing such funds and, as a result, a significant amount of public money went missing. Media attention and public pressure that grew out of this open data-driven journalism effort led to an audit of the program and the implementation of reforms.[33]

Empowering citizens

Open data also has a powerful role to play in *empowering citizens*. This role is evident in several ways:

- With more access to information in hand (including information on, for example, health care or education choices), citizens can have *improved decision-making capacity and choice.*
- As a result of increased transparency, open data can act as a *social mobilization* tool when information made available to the public can inform advocacy efforts, including those related to corruption or perceived corruption, consumer advocacy, or health care and other service delivery.

Emergent evidence:

- *Follow the Money Nigeria*: In Nigeria, a consortium of activists, journalists, researchers and NGOs use open data to track and visualize government expenditures. Based on knowledge drawn from open data regarding current spending practices, the group successfully pushed the Nigerian government to allocate $5.3 million to help address a lead poisoning crisis in the village of Bagega that affected thousands of children. Follow the Money Nigeria in fact demonstrates how open data can both improve governance (as a result of enabling better, more evidence-

---

32 Auralice Graft, Stefaan Verhulst and Andrew Young , "Indonesia's Kawal Pemilu—Elections: Free fair and open data," The Governance Lab, http://odimpact.org/case-indonesias-kawal-pemilu.html.

33 Third International Open Data Conference (IODC), "Enabling the Data Revolution: An International Open Data Roadmap," http://1a9vrva76sx19qtvg1ddvt6f.wpengine.netdna-cdn.com/wp-content/uploads/2015/09/IODC2015-Final-Report-web.pdf.

based policy decisions) and empower citizens to have an impact on their communities.[34]

- *Seeking to Improve Voter Turnout in Kenya with Open Data*: Kenya's national Independent Electoral and Boundaries Commission (IEBC) released information about polling center locations on its website in the lead up to Kenya's 2013 general election. The information, however, was difficult to access and reuse. Seizing on the gap between opening government data and citizens' actual ability to use that data, two Code 4 Kenya fellows conducted an experiment in unlocking government data to make it useful to the public. The fellows scraped the released IEBC data and built a simple website where it could be more easily accessed. The result was the initial version of GotToVote! a site that provided citizens with voter registration center information, and also helped them navigate the sometimes complex world of registration procedures. This first version was developed in just 24 hours at minimum cost, garnered over 6,000 site visits in just its first week of existence, and has since been replicated across sub-Saharan Africa.

- *Social Movements in Brazil*: The availability of open data has helped to inform the community organizing and advocacy efforts of several social movements in Brazil. Efforts to fight the use of pesticides latched onto the fact that "each Brazilian citizen is exposed to [5.2 litres] of pesticides every year." Similarly, an effort to fight school closures has rallied around the 24,000 schools that open data shows have been closed over the last 10 years. Efforts to fight violence against women and the consolidation of land ownership are similarly using open data to aid in their advocacy. There's little causal evidence that these efforts directly created significant policy impact, however, though the resignation of the Minister of Promotion of Racial Equality is credited to open data-driven reporting and advocacy.[35] So although these advocacy efforts demonstrate how open data can empower citizens and advocates through access to important factual information, more work needs to be done (and responsiveness in the public sector must be engendered) to create more direct, tangible impacts. [36]

---

34 Jonathan Gray, "Open Budget Data: Mapping the Landscape," https://github.com/okfn/research/blob/master/research/OpenBudgetData.pdf.

35 "Credit Happy Brazilian Minister Admits Mistake and Resigns," *Merco Press*, February 3, 2008, http://en.mercopress.com/2008/02/03/credit-happy-brazilian-minister-admits-mistake-and-resigns.

36 Alan Freihof Tygel, Maria Luiza Machado Campos and Celso Alexandre Souza de Alvear, "Teaching Open Data for Social Movements: A research strategy, *Journal of Community Informatics*, 11, no. 3 (2015), http://ci-journal.net/index.php/ciej/article/view/1220/1165.

Creating economic activity

Under the right conditions, open data can help *create economic activity*. If harnessed properly, this is a particularly important form of impact in developing economies. Our case studies indicate that open data can have a positive impact on economic activity in the following ways:

- As the global economy becomes increasingly reliant on data and information, the accessibility of open data can enable *business creation, foreign investment*, and meaningful *job creation*.
- Open data is increasingly seen as a new business asset but, unlike many such assets, it is available free of charge, opening the door to more *frugal innovation* efforts in the private sector.
- More than just an asset to individual businesses or entrepreneurs, many predictive analyses have pointed to open data's potential for creating more systemic and far-reaching *economic growth*, particularly when commingled with proprietary data held by private sector entities.[37]

Emergent evidence:

- *Market Research in Kenya and Nigeria*: Sagaci Research is a market intelligence firm based in Kenya that works across countries in Africa. The firm's strategic knowledge offerings—spanning sectors like consumer goods, agriculture, and telecom—are built from researchers and field surveyors active across Africa and, importantly, open census and national statistical data from the Kenyan and Nigerian governments. According to the Sagaci website, 90 percent of its clients have pursued follow-on work with the firm, demonstrating the value of its open data-driven offerings.[38]
- *Data Mapping Consultation in India*: Excel Geomatics is a private consultancy firm that leverages open data to provide geospatial insights to private and public sector clients. The company's offerings—including ward maps of more than 700 towns and cities and satellite image-enabled population distribution maps—would not be possible without access to data from the Indian census, as well as publicly accessible village and

---

37 See, for example, James Manyika, et al., "Open Data: Unlocking innovation and performance with liquid information," McKinsey & Company, October 2013, http://www.mckinsey.com/business-functions/business-technology/our-insights/open-data-unlocking-innovation-and-performance-with-liquid-information.

38 Open Data Fact Sheet, "Business, Research and Consulting," Fall 2016, http://opendataimpactmap.org/Bus_Factsheet.pdf.

district boundary maps. Importantly, Excel Geomatics uses the Earth Observing System Data and Information System (EOSDIS) and ASTER database from NASA for its products and services—demonstrating how the opening of data in developed countries often creates impacts far afield. [39]

- *Open Data to Benefit Tourism in Jamaica*: Like much of the Caribbean, the Jamaican economy is strongly dependent on the health of its tourism industry. Influenced by the rise of all-inclusive resorts and a general disincentive for tourists to stray far from a few highly trafficked areas, tourists rarely experience much of Jamaica's unique culture, and the economic benefits of tourism are often concentrated in a few areas. To increase tourism, spread its positive impacts and provide useful skills to citizens, a community mapping project[40] combined open government data with crowdsourced, volunteer-collected mapping data to enable the more participatory development of the tourism sector. Built around open tourism data and the engagement of government agencies, civil society organizations, developers, and an interested group of community mappers, the initiative has created new artefacts aimed at better spreading the economic impacts of the tourism industry in Jamaica, though impact remains primarily aspirational.[41]

Solving public problems

Finally, open data's impact is evident in the contribution it makes to *solving public problems*. Open data can help address complex problems in the following ways:

- Especially in crisis situations where geospatial information can prove essential,[42] open data can play a role in *improving situational awareness*.
- In some developing countries, government is the primary data holder and data user, limiting the number of people capable of creating value with data. The accessibility of open data can help to bring a *wider range of expertise and knowledge* to bear on public problems.

---

39 Open Data Fact Sheet, "IT and Geospatial," http://opendataimpactmap.org/IT_Factsheet.pdf.

40 See http://icm.msbm-uwi.org/.

41 Empowering Local Communities with Open Data and Interactive Community Mapping," Caribbean Open Institute, http://caribbeanopeninstitute.org/node/133.

42 Evangelia Berdou, "Mediating Voices and Communicating Realities: Using information crowdsourcing tools, open data initiatives and digital media to support and protect the vulnerable and marginalised," Institute of Development Studies, 2011, http://bit.ly/2aqbycg.

- In many cases the result of improved situational awareness and more expertise brought to bear, open data can play an important role in *targeting interventions* and meaningfully *tracking impact*.

Emergent evidence:

- *Stopping Deforestation in Brazil and Indonesia*: To monitor deforestation in Brazil and Indonesia, Global Forest Watch consolidates satellite imagery datasets to monitor global deforestation in real time. Monitoring on this scale has produced several observable positive effects. For instance, data from the project has been used in legal proceedings related to illegal logging. Although causation cannot be proved directly, deforestation has declined in both countries—deforestation in Indonesia is at its lowest levels in a decade and has declined by 18 percent in Brazil.[43] It is important to note that prior to this project, deforestation levels were consistently rising in both nations. The Indonesian government also uses GFW to monitor forest and peat fires and target response.[44] In Brazil, firefighters have reduced their response time to forest fires from 36 hours to 4 hours. This project is a forceful demonstration that intelligent use of open data can be used for successful advocacy—and could even provide additional benefits that may not have been anticipated.
- *Fighting Ebola in Sierra Leone*: In the parts of West Africa affected by the Ebola epidemic, roads, village names, and villages were missing on many online maps. OpenStreetMap (OSM), a free, crowdsourced mapping tool provided critical mapping information to Sierra Leone's National Ebola Response Centre (NERC), the United Nation's Humanitarian Data Exchange, and to the Ebola GeoNode to assist them in coordinating public health strategies in response to the epidemic. The OSM data was then often mashed up with open data from affected governments and international organizations. Although the direct impact of open data in the Ebola response was difficult to empirically measure, those working on the ground during the response made clear that providing missing data in open formats played an important role in fighting a complex epidemic and coordinating relief efforts of those working in a chaotic, fast-developing context.[45]

---

43 Open Data Watch, "Real-time Data for Mapping Forest Change Worldwide," Data Impacts Case Studies, http://dataimpacts.org/project/forest-watch/.

44 Victor Montoro, "Satellite-based Forest Mapping Platform Hits Its Stride," *Mongabay*, June 26, 2015, https://news.mongabay.com/2015/06/satellite-based-forest-mapping-platform-hits-its-stride/.

45 Andrew Young and Stefaan Verhulst, "Battling Ebola in Sierra Leone: Data sharing to improve crisis response," GovLab, http://odimpact.org/case-battling-ebola-in-sierra-leone.html.

- *Targeting Disaster Risk Funding in the Philippines:* The Philippines was one of the eight founding members of the Open Government Partnership launched in 2011, endorsing an Open Government Declaration to commit to open data. As part of its commitment, in 2014 the Philippine government launched data.gov.ph, which publishes data from government agencies for the public to access. Though some federal agencies have been hesitant to disclose their data in an open and accessible way, at the local government level the open data initiative is making more headway. The disclosure of spending data in Bohol province, for example, allowed civil society groups to notice that insufficient funds were allocated to disaster risk reduction projects. As a result, organizations are now drafting new disaster-reduction proposals to lobby the government to provide more support to this area.[46]

- *PakReport Crisis Mapping:* In the wake of the worst flooding in Pakistan in decades, several crisis mapping organizations (led by PakReport) teamed with relief organizations to map affected areas in real time. This project was a piece of a broader trend toward crisis mapping, particularly after natural disasters. Collaboration of this kind allows aid organizations to survey areas that may be difficult to landscape because of the disaster and correctly understand where needs are greatest and what kind of assistance populations across the affected area require. The efforts of the PakReport team demonstrate the complicated nature of international disaster relief and the need for comprehensive and proactive data responsibility assessments. Pointing to the risks and unintended consequences of open data, PakReport was forced to restrict access to its crowdsourced maps, which were intended to be open and freely accessible, after the Taliban threatened to attack foreign aid workers in the country, whose presence they deemed "unacceptable."[47]

Enabling Conditions and Disabling Factors

Based on the existing literature and case studies, we have developed a Periodic Table of Open Data Elements (Table 2) detailing the enabling conditions and disabling factors that often determine the impact of open data initiatives.

---

46 Michael P. Canares, "Opening the Gates: Will open data initiatives make local government in the Philippines more transparent?" Open Data Research Network Report, 2014, http://www. opendataresearch.org/content/2014/672/opening-gates-will-open-data-initiatives-make-local-governments-philippines-more.

47 "UN Reviews Security after Pakistani Taliban 'Threat,'" *BBC News*, August 26, 2010, http://www.bbc.com/news/world-south-asia-11095267.

Problem and Demand Definition	Capacity and Culture		Governance		Partnerships	Risks
U User Research						**Pr** Privacy Concerns
C Causes and Context	**Di** Data Infrastructure		**Od** Open by Default	**Dh** Data Holders		**Ds** Data Security
Rf Refinement	**Pu** Public Infrastructure	**Se** Skills & Expertise	**Fi** Freedom of Information	**I** Intermediaries		**Dm** Poor decision-making due to faulty information
Bg Benefit and Goals	**Lp** Tech Literacy & Internet Penetration	**Fl** Feedback Loops	**M** Performance Metrics	**Dq** Data Quality	**De** Domain Experts	**Pa** Entrenching power asymmetries
Da Data Audit and Inventory	**Rb** Cultural/ Institutional Roadblocks	**Rs** Resource Availability & Sustainability	**Rm** Risk Mitigation	**R** Responsiveness	**Co** Collaborators	**Ow** Open washing

Table 2: Periodic Table of Open Data Impact Elements

Although the importance of local variation and context is, of course, paramount, current research and practice shows that the elements included in five central issue categories—Problem and Demand Definition, Capacity and Culture, Partnerships, Risks, Governance—are likely to either enable or disrupt the success of open data projects when replicated across countries.

As discussed above, there is a large variability as it relates to evidence of open data's impact, so we provide these enabling conditions and disabling factors not as a concrete, certain drivers of success or failure, but as an aggregated set of premises to be tested as the field of practice and research of open data in developing economies continues to expand and mature. We examine these enabling conditions and disabling factors in more detail below.

Problem and Demand Definition

Particularly in developing economies, where resources to put toward data release or data use can be in short supply, a clear, detailed understanding of the problem to be addressed by open data can help to ensure that efforts are targeted and optimized. Some of the most effective open data projects examined here are laser-focused on a specific user group (e.g., smallholder farmers in Colombia or Ghana), or identified gap (e.g., the lack of power quality in the Indian energy sector). Clearly defining the problem can also aid in the development of metrics of success and a strategy for monitoring progress against a well-defined baseline. Many of the initiatives studied as part of this project lacked such a monitoring strategy, making assessments of impact, evidence-driven iteration, and the demonstration of return on investment more challenging.

U Users and Audiences

Open data initiatives tend to be more successful and avoid the notion of, "if you build it, will they come," when they are clearly optimized for an intended audience or user base from the start. The upfront identification, mapping and understanding of relevant constituencies, and a similar examination of their needs can enable more targeted open data-driven interventions.

C Causes and Context

In many open data initiatives, and in governance innovation efforts more generally, practitioners can find themselves addressing symptoms rather than the root causes of problems. Open data projects, such as the effort to predict dengue outbreaks in Paraguay, tend to be more successful when they seek to address underlying problems (mosquito breeding and transmission) rather than the symptoms of those problems (high levels of dengue fever).

Rf Refinement

To move from a well-understood problem area, to a granular, actionable, and quantifiable path forward, successful practitioners often look to refine their understanding of the problem to be addressed by seeking to understand, for instance, *why* the problem exists in its current form, what contributing factors could be at play, what potential knock-on effects of addressing the problem might be, and why the problem has not yet been solved by some other interested party.

31

Bg Benefits and Goals

Open data projects often fail to build an audience or continue to evolve and expand successfully over time if they do not successfully define the intended benefits of the open data use and set clear target goals. These deficiencies often can create difficulty in the development of metrics and indicators—important drivers of iteration and impact.

Many of the projects studied, including notably Kenya's GotToVote! project did not have a clear baseline against which to measure the success of the project. Without an understanding of the current baseline, measuring progress toward identified goals and demonstrating whether and how open data efforts actually benefited the public remains a challenge.

Da Data Audit and Inventory

Once the problem and value proposition are in place, practitioners are able to explore the availability of datasets, both in the form of open government data, and from other potentially useful and relevant data sources, like NGOs, the private sector, or crowdsourcing efforts. A clear problem definition can help to uncover which data sources could add value and inform strategies for collecting or accessing that data. Colombia's Aclímate Colombia, for instance, identified the types of data it needed for its agriculture algorithms and engaged the semi-public industry groups that had it. The Prayas Energy Group in India, on the other hand, found that no one collected or stored the type of energy usage information it needed for its power quality monitoring efforts, so it launched its own (open) data collection effort across 18 Indian states.

Capacity and Culture

The lack of available resources, insufficient human capital and immature technological capabilities can create major challenges to achieving meaningful impact with open data projects. These challenges can exist both within a country's open data ecosystem—that is, the capacity of government, civil society, tech community, and the general public—as well as within the actors on the demand side using open data toward certain objectives and the donor organizations funding them.

Open Data Ecosystem Elements

Di Data Infrastructure

On the supply side of open data the lack of a strong data infrastructure—that is, hardware and software platforms to make data consistently accessible and machine-readable in a timely manner—often creates major challenges to positive impact.

Burundi's OpenRBF platform is an example of working around issues related to data infrastructure. Burundi provided access to data on its results-based financing efforts around healthcare through the OpenRBF platform, a digital infrastructure for collecting and publishing such data. The existence of an "out-of-the-box" tool for making results-based funding (RBF) data public in reusable formats catalyzed the widespread opening of RBF data across many developing countries in Africa.

Pu Public Infrastructure

Similar to the ICT4D environment, much of the literature and practice[48] of open data in developing economies points to the importance of a strong public infrastructure—human capital (including data science and statistical knowledge), public services (including education and libraries), and civil society—to ensure that data is collected, cleaned, and released in a usable manner and that updates and feedback are seamlessly incorporated into open datasets. Supply side efforts to leverage these public infrastructures can increase the demand for open data and establish touchpoints with users.

An active ecosystem of data users and international open mapping platforms and individuals helped to ensure that Nepal's open data-driven crisis response efforts could be quickly developed and put into practice. The challenges experienced by Ghana's Esoko platform as a result of unreliable electricity access in the country, on the other hand, shows the many ways that public infrastructure can affect the success of open data projects.

Lp Tech Literacy and Internet Penetration

Even as access to the Internet continues to expand across the developing world, especially through smartphones and other portable devices, many open data projects are being launched into communities that suffer from low Internet penetration and a persistent digital divide. Several of the initiatives studied struggled to achieve their transformative potential, particularly when practitioners failed to engage intermediaries or civil society groups capable of reaching unconnected audiences.

Stakeholders involved in South Africa's Medicine Price Registry Application (MPRApp) and Tanzania's open education dashboards pointed to low Internet penetration rates, and the related challenge of low tech literacy, as major barriers they confronted to achieving greater positive impacts.

---

48   See Andrew Young and Stefaan Verhulst, "Kenya's Open Duka: Open data for transactional transparency," GovLab, http://odimpact.org/case-kenyas-open-duka.html.

Rb Cultural/ Institutional Roadblocks

As is often the case in developed countries, too, cultural and institutional roadblocks can limit the impact of open data. These roadblocks can manifest in the form of an institutional culture that remains skeptical of openness, or the absence of well-trained individuals and professionals capable of recognizing and acting on the potential of open data (readiness)—beyond the prevalence of engaging volunteers in the development of open data initiatives. In all cases, a more concerted culture- and capacity-building effort is often necessary to create an impact.

In Burundi, for instance, efforts to create transparency and accountability around its results-based financing efforts were slowed and complicated by a lack of readiness for technology-enabled openness within key institutions. Jamaica's open data tourism efforts relied on the readiness of outside volunteers to supplement open data through crowdsourcing—with the impact of the project dependent on their capacity to collect data and information in a strategic, usable manner.

Open Data User/Donor Elements

Se Skills and Expertise

Especially for more technical uses of open data—such as sophisticated data analytics—actors on the demand side of open data need to possess certain skills and expertise. Employees at CIAT, the organization behind Aclímate Colombia, for instance, possess high-level data science capabilities that enabled them to leverage open data to create sophisticated algorithmic tools to inform agricultural decision making. Other projects, like crowdsourcing efforts from Jamaica and Nepal, relied on the skills of a few important institutional actors on the demand side and the less-technical efforts of volunteer data collectors.

Fl Feedback Loops

Open data initiatives tend to be less successful when they do not create mechanisms for users and beneficiaries to provide input to demand-side practitioners. Tanzania's open education dashboards are a notable example. The platforms were launched into an environment with low Internet penetration and digital literacy, with seemingly little opportunity for the intended users and beneficiaries of the tools, like parents or education advocates, to suggest ways to make the platforms more usable (and useful) for the community.

Rs Resource Availability and Sustainability

The availability of funding and resources are a key variable of success on both the supply and demand sides of open data. Focusing on the demand side, although many open data projects can be stood up quickly on a tight budget (such as Kenya's GotToVote! an initial prototype of which was created for only $500), sometimes with a very small team (Paraguay's dengue prediction efforts were championed by researcher Juan Pane and a small team under his direction), establishing sustainability and scaling use often requires more sustained funding and/or well-defined business models. This was the dynamic at work for example in South Africa, where the MPRApp relied almost entirely on the time and effort of a single person. Likewise, in Uganda, CIPESA, the developers of the iParticipate open health data and citizen engagement effort, struggled to proactively elevate health service delivery concerns to relevant government officials because of funding issues affecting both data collection and outreach efforts.

The agriculture information tool Esoko, on the other hand, has managed to take hold in Ghana in large part due to its for-profit, largely business to business (B2B) model, as well as significant investments from foundations and international organizations.

Partnerships

In many high-impact open data projects, partnerships within and especially across sectors play a key role in enabling success. Whether creating touchpoints with citizens through partnerships with civil society, informing the public through media partnerships, or filling important data gaps through partnerships with private sector entities, open data suppliers and users often improve outcomes through collaboration.

Dh Data Holders

Although open data is meant to provide value to data users without any direct engagement with data holders necessary, partnering with entities on the supply side (including government) can help to fill data gaps and enable higher impact data use.

Aclímate Colombia is a strong example of the potential of such partnerships. The initiative, aimed at providing farmers with a better ability to plant crops in a way that is resilient to the effects of climate change, would not be possible without collaboration between the driver of the initiative (a civil society organization), key data holders (government ministries and agencies), and a second group of key data holders (private and semi-private crop growers' associations). GotToVote! in Kenya, on the other hand, did not establish such cross-sector partnerships, and its long-term sustainability is now in question.

I Intermediaries

In many developing economies, as mentioned above, Internet penetration and, especially, data literacy are low among the citizenry. The presence of intermediaries—including journalists and others with relevant skills—can help to determine whether or not the available open data-driven outputs reach a community of users, and the intended impact is achieved.[49] The continued advancement of open data intermediaries can be seen as a key area of capacity building in developing economies.

To encourage the use of Code for South Africa's MPRApp, doctors and pharmacists played an important intermediation role with citizens. These trusted advisors—with nothing to gain from helping patients spend less money on their prescriptions—helped to alert citizens to the database and the potential for identifying much cheaper generic drugs to treat their ailments.

In addition, the open data-driven offerings of Open Development Cambodia are often presented on the initiative's website in a comprehensible manner (similar to data-driven Wikipedia articles on topics of public concern, like forest cover or development aid spending), but reach a much wider audience when taken up by journalists in the country and abroad in reporting on conditions in the country.

Both of Tanzania's open education dashboards, on the other hand, failed to attract a regular user base, likely as a result of a failure to engage consistently with intermediaries that could make the sites' offerings useful to an intended audience with low digital literacy and access.

De Domain Experts

In many cases, demand-side open data actors' expertise lies in technology or data science rather than the problem areas they seek to address through the use of open data. Tapping into the knowledge of stakeholders with relevant sector-specific expertise can improve efforts to optimize and target open data efforts based on a true understanding of needs, opportunities, and barriers. Nepali NGOs and businesses using open government data and crowdsourced data during the response to a major earthquake in the country, for instance, engaged with on-the-ground experts in crisis response who came to Nepal from around the world to help target its offerings.

---

49   See François van Schalkwyk, et al., "Open Data Intermediaries in Developing Countries," *Journal of Community Informatics* 12, no. 2 (2016), http://ci-journal.net/index.php/ciej/article/view/1146.

Co Collaborators

Open data practitioners can extend their capacity by collaborating with like-minded organizations, institutions, or individuals, including foreign actors. Ghana's Esoko agricultural information service, for example, is part of the Global Open Data for Agriculture and Nutrition (GODAN) network, enabling the company to tap into the knowledge of similar organizations from around the world seeking to leverage open agriculture data for business development and/or public benefit.

Risks

The release and use of open data in developing economies are not without risks. An upfront mapping and consideration of risks associated with intended uses of open data can allow practitioners to design programs from the outset in a way that is well-positioned to overcome or mitigate those risks. The risks listed here, however, should not be considered arguments against using open data in development. Rather, they are reasons for taking a more fine-grained approach that pays close attention to the empirical evidence, sifting out what works and what does not, and identifying conditions for scaling and replication.

Pr Privacy Concerns

Privacy concerns probably rank among the most commonly cited worries over opening up data. Especially in conflict-stricken regions, individuals' anonymity can be of life-or-death importance. Potential privacy harms can arise even from the release of ostensibly anonymized personally identifiable information (PII).[50] Although the vast majority of open data efforts seek to anonymize or otherwise limit the release of PII, it is important to recognize that a lack of sophistication in anonymization or aggregation efforts can result in the inadvertent release of sensitive information.[51] In addition, in some instances information that itself poses no privacy concerns can be combined with other openly available datasets; the aggregated and linked information can lead to unexpected disclosure of personal data, such as bringing together open data on political activities with separately accessible information on a person's location or place of work, for example.[52]

---

50 See, for example, Alexandra Wood, David O'Brien, and Urs Gasser, "Privacy and Open Data Research Briefing," 2016, https://papers.ssrn.com/sol3/papers.cfm?abstract_id=2842816.

51 See, for example, Ira Rubinstein and Woodrow Hartzog, "Anonymization and Risk," 2015, https://papers.ssrn.com/sol3/papers.cfm?abstract_id=2646185.

52 Stefan Kulk and Bastiaan van Loenen, "Brave New Open Data World?" *International Journal of Spatial Data Infrastructures Research*, 7, 2012, https://www.researchgate.net/profile/S_Kulk/publication/254811532_Brave_New_Open_Data_World/links/0c96053a43af7ceb94000000.pdf.

Ds Data Security

Because much government data contains sensitive information regarding individuals, industries, and national security, opening that data often leads to quite reasonable questions about data security. Cybersecurity remains a challenge across the world, and perhaps especially so in developing countries, which may lack the technical expertise to adequately protect information from sophisticated hackers and other intrusions.[53] At the same time, though security concerns are very real and important, they must be balanced against the opportunity cost or risk of not sharing data; often, government decision makers can lean on tenuous security concerns to justify keeping data closed and restricting access, potentially limiting the solution space.

Dm Poor decision-making due to faulty information

Whether related to humanitarian efforts, crisis relief, or the livelihoods of vulnerable populations, data-driven efforts in developing economies can be literally life-or-death affairs. Given the many challenges and obstacles involved in open data projects, it is important to recognize the risks inherent in basing such life-and-death decisions on information that could be incomplete, out-of-date or otherwise faulty. The broader point is this: insights generated from data are only as good—and their impacts only as positive—as the quality of the underlying data.[54]

Pa Entrenching (power) asymmetries

Although data can be empowering, it can also consolidate or reinforce existing privileges and authority inherent in societies. This problem is closely linked (though not restricted) to digital divide challenges; when only the elite of a society have access to data and/or data science capabilities, releasing data is likely to disproportionally benefit that elite.[55] We found numerous examples,[56] and they are important reminders that open data projects need to work hard to ensure that their social and economic benefits are widely, and evenly, distributed.

---

53 David Burt, et al., "The Cybersecurity Risk Paradox: Impact of social, economic, and technological factors on rates of malware," Microsoft Security Intelligence Report Special Edition, January 2014.

54 See, Michael Canares and Satyarupa Shekhar, "Open Data and Sub-national Governments: Lessons from developing countries," Open Data for Development, 2016, http://od4d.com/wp-content/uploads/2016/01/ODDC-2-Open-Data-and-Sub-national-Governments.pdf.

55 Michael Gurstein, "Open Data: Empowering the empowered or effective data use for everyone?" *First Monday*, February 2011, http://firstmonday.org/article/view/3316/2764.

56 See odimpact.org.

Ow Open washing

The term *"open washing"* has taken hold in practitioner circles over recent years describing the risk that governments may seek to leverage the enthusiasm for open data to avoid more difficult and potentially transformative openness and transparency efforts.[57] The Extractives Industries Transparency Initiative, for instance, is a laudable effort to push for more energy-related openness around the world, which has had demonstrable impacts on accountability. There is a growing belief, however, that a subset of still largely closed governments is joining the initiative only "in order to increase their international reputation and bolster their access to foreign aid."[58]

Governance

A diversity of governing decisions affect the use and impact of open data efforts. Issues of governance exist at both the ecosystem level—especially related to standards and policies of data release—and on the demand side, with questions of risk mitigation and impact assessment leading the way.

Open Data Ecosystem Elements

Od Open by Default *(and other principles)*

Given the level of government resource allocation and time investment required to implement strong open data initiatives, high-level political buy-in and codified open data policies (reflecting the International Open Data Charter principles[59]) are needed to provide the incentives and flexibility to government officials to meaningfully advance open data goals.

The ESMI effort in India, for example, is an industry- and NGO-driven effort to create and open useful data on power quality in the country. This effort, which has had relatively little discernible impact to date, is only necessary because of the lack of energy data being opened by government—an issue

---

57 See, for example, Christian Villum, "Open-Washing"—The Difference between Opening Your Data and Simply Making Them Available," Open Data International Blog, March 10, 2014, https://blog. okfn.org/2014/03/10/open-washing-the-difference-between-opening-your-data-and-simply-making-them-available/; and "#openwashing...anyone?" Web Foundation Blog, October 31, 2016, http:// webfoundation.org/2016/10/openwashing-anyone/.

58 Benjamin Sovacool and Nathan Andrews, "Does Transparency Matter? Evaluating the governance impacts of the Extractive Industries Transparency Initiative in Azerbaijan and Liberia," *Resources Policy* 45 (2015), https://eiti.org/sites/default/files/documents/Sovacool%20%26%20Andrews%20 %5B2015%5D%20-%20Does%20transparency%20matter%20-%20%20Evaluating%20the%20 governance%20impacts%20of%20the%20Extractive%20Industries%20Transparency%20Initiative%20 %28EITI%29%20in%20Azerbaijan%20and%20Liberia.pdf.

59 See the Open Data Charter website, http://opendatacharter.net/.

that could be resolved with a commitment to openness by default and other internationally accepted principles.

Fi Freedom of Information and other Policies

Clear policies pushing forward access to information and data can act as important drivers for open data initiatives. Without explicit policy backing, the sustainability of open data efforts can be called into question, and access to necessary data can dry up at any time. The existence of Freedom of Information policies can also provide means for accessing relevant information, though often at a much slower pace than open data.

A key enabler for the MPRApp open data initiative, for example, was South Africa's legislative framework that promotes and enacts transparency in medicine pricing. Such a framework compels the Department of Health to collect and publish data on medicine prices in South Africa, ensuring that the supply side of the MPRApp will continue to be made accessible, allowing Code for South Africa to focus on improving the tool and getting it into the hands of its intended users.

Dq Data Quality

A widely prevalent challenge to positive impact arises from poor data quality. Data quality is an issue in developed countries, but often presents even greater barriers to success in developing countries. Quality issues can manifest in a number of ways, like inaccurate information, a lack of completeness in official datasets, out-of-date data, or otherwise corrupted datasets.

Aclímate Colombia, for example, experienced challenges gaining access to the most complete and up-to-date information sets for its agriculture tools, slowing their development. Open Development Cambodia's efforts are consistently challenged by not only strong restrictions in terms redistribution, reproduction, and reuse on some datasets, but also by the inconsistency and unpredictability of when updates to important official datasets occur.

In South Africa, the MPRApp was hurt by a lack of interoperability; that is, open data was not made available in standards that allowed for aggregation and manipulation. Likewise, Kenya's GotToVote! experienced major challenges when one of its central data sources crashed unexpectedly, rendering the platform temporarily unusable.

R Responsiveness

Just as open data is unlikely to create a major impact without demand-side actors to act upon released data, a lack of responsiveness, often characterized by a lack of commitment to take up data-driven insights within governing institutions, can limit the impact of open data. Often, governments succumb to the temptation to open wash data, nominally opening it up but failing to create feedback loops to ensure that users are actually using the data or that data is being released to meet a genuine demand.

In Jamaica, for example, an interactive community mapping project is supplementing open datasets with a crowdsourced effort to improve tourism in the country; the project's clear potential has not yielded major impacts yet in part because tourism authorities have not yet acted on the generated insights. The researchers who used open data to predict dengue fever transmission in Paraguay also experienced ongoing challenges wresting the most useful data for their algorithms from government data holders; there has been little indication that their insights will be meaningfully taken up by institutional authorities.

Open Data User/Donor Agency Elements

M Performance Metrics

Open data projects are better positioned for success when practitioners develop and monitor metrics of impact to inform management and iteration.

The vast majority of the open data initiatives studied in this series lacked clearly defined performance metrics. Not only does this create major challenges for iterating upon early efforts, it calls the sustainability of these interventions into question, with a demonstration of success and impact a likely requirement for continued funding and investment.

Rm Risk Mitigation

In some cases, open data projects can be advanced despite some level of risk. In such cases, practitioners must ensure that projects that deal in information that is potentially personally identifiable (including anonymized data) have outlined and implemented a clear, upfront strategy for addressing risks created by open data use.

Many of the projects studied in this series dealt in potentially sensitive information—e.g., health, energy consumption, political, and education data. Although each project took steps to ensure that no personally identifiable information was released to the public, all would benefit from a clearly defined—and, preferably, openly available—risk mitigation strategy to ensure that no harms inadvertently fall on data subjects.

The Challenge of Scaling and Replication

Much of this paper, including the above, seeks to identify cross-cutting lessons for open data projects—either in the form of opportunities or challenges.

41

As noted, however, it is important to keep in mind the diversity that exists within the broad category of "developing economies." Differences in culture, economic, and political environments, as well as many other variables, can have a profound effect on the success or otherwise of open data projects.

In many ways, this is another challenge facing stakeholders—and perhaps the most intractable: the difficulty of finding an appropriate balance between universal lessons and certain, locally embedded conditions, when seeking to *scale and replicate open data projects*. The preceding discussion and the sector-specific examples detailed in Section III do suggest that certain enabling (and disabling) conditions have wide applicability—e.g., the need to include intermediaries and civil society groups,[60] or the paramount importance of capacity and resources.

Perhaps the most critical element for scaling and replication found in the Periodic Table is *Metrics*: the need for open data projects should be evidence based, with clearly defined metrics and standards to evaluate performance. Only with those metrics in place can the applicability or appropriateness of lessons or principles be determined—and only then can the success or failure of projects be established. When making any funding or design decisions, it is essential to take a fine-grained approach that pays close attention to the empirical evidence, sifting out what works and what does not. That is a key goal of the 12 case studies that accompany this landscaping paper; we have tried to build a ground-up, highly empirical picture of open data projects in the developing world.

---

60 See François van Schalkwyk, et al., "Open Data Intermediaries in Developing Countries," *Journal of Community Informatics* 12, no. 2 (2016), http://ci-journal.net/index.php/ciej/article/view/1146.

CHAPTER 4

The Impact of Open Data in Developing Economies across Sectors

The preceding section has described a logic framework that examines the different components that determine how open data could create an impact. It identifies both enabling and disabling factors for open data initiatives that seek to create four different types of impacts, and expands on them in a practitioner-focused Periodic Table of Open Data Elements. This in effect allows us to create more particular or fine-grained theories of change for each sector and area of impact. In this section, we consider the emerging (and again, variable) evidence of open data's impact on specific sectors that are relevant to the development context. We focus on six sectors: Health, Humanitarian Aid, Agriculture and Nutrition, Poverty Alleviation and Livelihoods, Energy, and Education.

For each sector, we describe illustrative examples of open data's use in developing economies. The cases described here are provided to offer a glimpse into the current field of practice. Some sectors have seen more notable (and novel) applications of open data than others, and some of the examples described here have had little impact to date, or represent instructive failures. But even these lower impact initiatives can aid in identifying testable premises to guide future practice and experimentation. Considered together, these over-arching and sector-specific theories of change build a more complete and detailed matrix of how and under what conditions open data impacts development, providing a set of hypotheses for further research and experimentation.

Health

Improving Governance	Empowering Citizens	Innovation & Creating Opportunity	Solving Public Problems
The health sector is a major recipient of public funds and international aid, particularly in developing countries.[61] Increasing the transparency of this large area of government expenditure in turn increases accountability, helping ensure resources efficiently and adequately target public health needs.	Accessing quality-of-care information for different health care providers can bolster citizens' ability to make informed choices regarding their service providers.[62] Data on corruption or malpractice in the health care system can particularly enable evidence-based advocacy efforts for patients.	As the health sector becomes increasingly data-driven, open data can help spur job creation and the establishment of new service models as a result of both making more information available on the supply side, and using newly accessible health data on the demand side. Though concerns regarding the potential for technology and automation to negatively impact employment also exist.	Especially in the wake of health crises (such as the Ebola outbreak in West Africa or mosquito-borne epidemics in India, for example[63]), access to data across institutions on the availability and location of health resources and on emergent health outcomes can play an important role in addressing major epidemics or ingrained public health concerns.

Predicting Dengue Outbreaks in Paraguay with Open Data

Logic Framework Components:

- Input: Open health, climate, and water data
- Actors: Researchers and academia
- Activity: Data analysis
- Output: Process improvements, alerts
- Users: Government officials, researchers
- Indicators: Accuracy of data-driven predictions
- Intended Impact: Solving public problems

Description: Since 2009, dengue fever has been endemic in Paraguay. Recognizing the clear problem at hand, and the lack of a strong system for communicating dengue-related dangers to the public, the National Health

---

61 Organization for Economic Cooperation and Development, "Aid at a Glance Charts," http://www.oecd.org/dac/stats/aid-at-a-glance.htm.

62 Tawnya Bosko and Matthew Briskin, "Transparency in Healthcare: Where does it stand?" *Management in Healthcare* 1, no. 1 (2016): 83–96.

63 Like similar efforts in Paraguay and Singapore, researchers in India demonstrated how open data can be analyzed using statistical modeling and machine learning to determine how transmission of dengue (or other mosquito-borne illnesses like Zika) could be minimized through increased citizen awareness and/or more strategic allocation of resources. Vandana Srivastava and Biplave Srivastava, "Towards Timely Public Health Decisions to Tackle Seasonal Diseases with Open Government Data," *World Wide Web and Public Health Intelligence: Papers from the AAAI-14 Workshop*, June 18, 2015, http://www.aaai.org/ocs/index.php/WS/AAAIW14/paper/view/8728/8221.

Surveillance Department of Paraguay opened data related to dengue morbidity. Leveraging this data, researchers created an early warning system that can detect outbreaks of dengue fever a week in advance. The data-driven model can predict dengue outbreaks at the city-level in every city in Paraguay. Importantly, the system can be deployed in any region as long as data on morbidity, climate, and water are available.

Code for South Africa Cheaper Medicines for Consumers

Logic Framework Components:

- Input: Open medicine data
- Actors: NGO
- Activity: Dissemination
- Output: Searchable database
- Users: Citizens, health service providers
- Indicators: Money saved by individuals
- Intended Impact: Empowering citizens

Description: In 2014, Code for South Africa, a South Africa-based nonprofit organization active in the open data space, took a little known dataset from the national Department of Health website and created the Medicine Price Registry Application (MPRApp), an online tool allowing patients (and their doctors) to make sure that they aren't being overcharged by their pharmacies. With no marketing or promotions to speak of, MPRApp has had an impact on the lives of a few South Africans; with a more sustainable model and increased awareness of MPRApp, particularly among trusted intermediaries in the health sector, it could provide more patients access to cheaper medicines.

Open Health Data in Uganda

Logic Framework Components:

- Input: Open health data
- Actors: NGO, media
- Activity: Aggregation and commingling, dissemination
- Output: Apps and platforms, dashboards
- Users: Citizens
- Indicators: Improved health service delivery, increased public participation
- Intended Impact: Empowering citizens

Description: In Uganda, open data initiatives are being used in an attempt to improve health outcomes and revolutionize a health care industry marred by staff shortages, lack of resources and corruption. The Kampala-based organization CIPESA has collaborated with a local media organization, Numec, to create the iParticipate project (http://cipesa.org/tag/iparticipate/), which analyzes open government data, and trains citizens and intermediaries to use that data toward empowering citizens to play a bigger role in health governance. Similarly, the Women of Uganda Network (http://wougnet.org), which trains women to use information technology, created an online platform to collect and document information relating to poor health care services. Both these initiatives allow citizens to scrutinize and lobby the public health care sector, aiming to improve its efficiency and ensure that services respond to the needs of citizens in a robust manner.

Open Health Data in Namibia

Logic Framework Components:

- Input: Open health and climate data, private data
- Actors: Researchers and academia
- Activity: Aggregation and commingling, dissemination
- Output: Maps
- Users: Government officials
- Indicators: Distribution of mosquito nets
- Intended Impact: Solving public problems

Description: An effort by the government of Namibia to eradicate malaria in the country was bolstered by the use of satellite and cell phone data. Researchers were able to draw "maps of environmental factors like vegetation density, population, and rainfall that affect mosquito and parasite populations and the likelihood of transmission" and identify areas where citizens were at high-risk.[64] Cell phone data provided by Namibia's largest telecommunications provider assisted researchers to track human movement—and thus the spread of malaria. As a result, the Ministry of Health distributed 1.2 million bed nets to the communities that needed them most.

---

64 Open Data Watch, "Data Impacts Case Studies: Using satellite and cell phone data to eliminate malaria in Namibia," http://dataimpacts.org/project/malaria/.

Open Results and Performance Based Financing

Logic Framework Components:

- Input: Open results-based financing data
- Actors: NGOs, government officials
- Activity: Dissemination
- Output: Process improvements, searchable databases
- Users: NGOs, government officials
- Indicators: Decreased instances of corruption
- Intended Impact: Improving governance

Description: As part of efforts to improve health outcomes and health system functioning, Burundi was one of the first African countries to introduce RBF. RBF is an instrument that links development financing with pre-determined results. Payment is made only when the agreed-upon results are shown to have been achieved. Open RBF—a platform for opening data related to RBF initiatives—was first delivered in Burundi in response to the Burundian Ministry of Health's efforts to improve health care functioning at the national level and strengthen accountability mechanisms. By opening RBF data, it was believed that increased accessibility and scrutiny of the data could lead to improvements in data quality and engender more accountable data practices. Early returns appear to be positive—Ministry of Health staffers played a role in pushing their peers toward making information on results accessible, for example—though not transformational, and Open RBF engaged in a longer-term partnership with the government. Open RBF was concurrently applied to the education and AIDS awareness programs in Burundi; as another sign of impact and scalability, since its launch in Burundi, Open RBF has scaled across 15 countries.

Open Data and Open Contracting for Nigerian Health Care Centres

Logic Framework Components:

- Input: Open budget and contracting data
- Actors: NGO
- Activity: Dissemination
- Output: Apps and platforms, dashboards
- Users: Citizens, NGOs and interest groups
- Indicators: Decreased instances of corruption
- Intended Impact: Improving governance

Description: In Nigeria, primary health care centers (PHCs) are often located far away from the people who need them most—namely the greater than 50 percent of Nigerians living in poverty. As a result of open data and open contracting efforts, the platform Budeshi enables citizens and watchdogs to actively monitor and unearth financial discrepancies and inefficiencies in the construction of badly needed PHCs around the country. In addition to increasing the transparency of these health care providers, Budeshi positions itself as an advocacy tool, aiming to push the Nigerian government to make a fuller-scale commitment to open contracting principles.[65]

Humanitarian Aid

Improving Governance	Empowering Citizens	Innovation & Creating Opportunity	Solving Public Problems
The misuse of international aid has a long history, with money targeted for specific development efforts failing to be put to use in the expected way. For developing countries that receive a significant amount of aid funding from international organizations, tracking how that money is being used can help root out corruption and catalyze better spending practices in government.	When funnelled through institutional bureaucracies, humanitarian aid can often overlook the micro-level needs of citizens and their communities. By opening aid allocation data to the public, citizens can provide valuable feedback to governments on how aid is being used, and become active co-partners, rather than mere recipients, of the aid industry.[66]	In a field commonly disabled by inaccurate data, where guess-work is rife,[67] open data in humanitarian aid allows NGOs and other civil society organizations to create innovative strategies based on new and accurate information, for example, to help communities in conflict areas or recovering from natural disasters.	Open data initiatives, when built on high-quality, accurate data, can help organizations better identify where and how to invest humanitarian aid to most effectively solve social problems, allowing governments and humanitarian actors to better coordinate relief efforts[68] (for example, through the Humanitarian Data Exchange[69]) and identify sectors that most urgently require humanitarian assistance.

Open Development Data in Cambodia

Logic Framework Components:

- Input: Open government data and open NGO data

---

65 Seember Nyager, "Can Data Help Us Attain Healthier Lives?" Budeshi, May 15, 2016, http://www.budeshi.org/2016/05/can-data-help-us-attain-healthier-lives/.

66 Regarding the discursive attributes related to the terms "participation," "empowerment" and "citizenship" in aid, see Andrea Cornwall, *Beneficiary, Consumer, Citizen: Perspectives on participation for poverty reduction*, Stockholm: Sida, 2000, http://www.alnap.org/resource/10271.

67 Vanessa Humphries, "Improving Humanitarian Coordination: Common challenges and lessons learned from the cluster approach," *The Journal of Humanitarian Assistance* 30 (2013).

68 Eleanor Goldbert, "Open Data Platform Lets Aid Groups Respond More Efficiently to Crises," *Huffington Post*, May 31, 2016, http://www.huffingtonpost.com/entry/open-data-platform-enables-aid-groups-to-respond-more-efficiently-to-crises_us_574876fee4b03ede4414a6a4.

69 The Humanitarian Data Exchange, https://data.humdata.org/.

- Actors: Researchers, NGOs
- Activity: Data analysis, presentation, aggregation and commingling, dissemination
- Output: Infographics, maps, apps, and platforms
- Users: Government officials, citizens, researchers, NGOs, media
- Indicators: Decreased instances of corruption
- Intended Impact: Improving governance

Description: Developed by the East-West Management Institute, and part of the broader Open Development Initiative, Open Development Cambodia (ODC) seeks to improve public awareness and information-sharing around development data. ODC uses data aggregated from a diversity of governmental and nongovernmental sources to provide visualizations, maps and other data-driven products and tools to provide the public sector, private sector, civil society, data-driven journalists, and the general public with a view into the workings and impacts of development efforts, with news reports drawn from its information offerings representing its most apparent benefit to date.

AidData in Africa

Logic Framework Components:

- Input: Open development funding data
- Actors: NGOs
- Activity: Dissemination
- Output: Searchable databases
- Users: Media, NGOs, and interest groups
- Indicators: Decreased instances of corruption, improved allocation of aid money
- Intended Impact: Improving governance

Description: The open data initiative AidData (http://aiddata.org) tracks international development funding and can be used by developing countries to track and scrutinize their government's foreign aid spending. The project is housed at the College of William & Mary in Virginia; its database has already revealed that China appears to provide more foreign aid to African countries that support their vote in the United Nations General Assembly.[70] Information made available through AidData has also allowed journalists in Africa to chart

---

70 "Diplomacy and Aid in Africa," *The Economist,* April 14, 2016, http://www.economist.com/blogs/graphicdetail/2016/04/daily-chart-10.

levels of foreign investment to their countries, owing to the discovery that China has become Tanzania's single largest trading partner, and that Chinese firms receive the lion's share of Tanzanian engineering contracts.[71] The project makes clear that access to aid data can transform the way aid is targeted, and provides citizens and watchdogs with information needed to monitor and give feedback on development projects in their communities.

Response to Nepalese Earthquake

Logic Framework Components:

- Input: Open geospatial data, crowdsourced data
- Actors: NGOs, private sector
- Activity: Presentation, dissemination
- Output: Maps, process improvements
- Users: Government officials, citizens
- Indicators: Lives saved
- Intended Impact: Solving public problems

Description: In the wake of the devastating earthquake that struck Nepal in 2015, so-called "digital humanitarians"—both local and international volunteers—took it upon themselves to create detailed maps in the most affected areas.[72] One such platform, Quakemap.org, allowed citizens to report needs to organizations that provide relief—with 434 of 551 actionable reports acted upon.[73] This response built upon an already robust mapping project in Nepal and demonstrates how open data efforts can work in collaboration with humanitarian relief efforts at both the local and international level.

Open Aid and Budget Data in Nepal

Logic Framework Components:

- Input: Open aid and budget data
- Actors: NGOs
- Activity: Data analysis, dissemination

---

71 Mzwandile Jacks, "China Emerges as Tanzania's Major Investor," *Ventures Africa*, January 29, 2014, http://venturesafrica.com/china-emerges-as-tanzanias-major-investor/.

72 "Open Data's Role in Nepal's Earthquake," ICT.govt.nz, 2015, https://www.ict.govt.nz/assets/Uploads/Case-Study-Nepal-Earthquake2.pdf.

73 Nirab Pudasaini, "Open Source and Open Data's Role in Nepal Earthquake Relief," OpenSource.com, June 8, 2016, https://opensource.com/life/16/6/open-source-open-data-nepal-earthquake.

- Output: Searchable databases
- Users: Citizens, NGOs and interest groups
- Intended Impact: Improving government

Description: The early impact of a project in Nepal to open aid and budgetary data held by the government has shown limited impact to date, likely due to the political and economic reality of the nation, which is rebuilding from decades of civil unrest and governance breakdown. Political, legal, and technical realities present significant challenges to advocates of greater digital transparency, key stakeholders interviewed demonstrated widely-varying perceptions of what "open data' meant, stakeholders viewed themselves more as facilitators than end-users, and government data quality was called into question by several experts.[74]

Agriculture and Nutrition[75]

Improving Governance	Empowering Citizens	Innovation & Creating Opportunity	Solving Public Problems
Open data can make agricultural agencies and implementing organizations more accountable, by making information accessible on whether or not financial resources provided were used according to contractual obligations; and whether they serve people and farmers they are supposed to be supporting.	A major problem in developing countries is the different levels of food access across populations, with research pointing to the emergence of "food deserts" in Africa's urban centers.[75] Open data that pertains to regional food access can allow citizens to identify these disparities in nutrition and food access, empowering citizen groups to lobby government institutions for more equitable food policy. In addition, smallholder farmers could be full participants in defining, implementing, and evaluating projects intended to improve their farms and lives when provided access to data.	An increased awareness of weather trends, models of crop yields and other relevant datasets can help inform more strategic, evidence-based agricultural decision making and increase the viability of individual farms.	On a micro level, open data can play a role in both predicting potentially damaging conditions for crops, and informing more strategic planting choices following, for example, a catastrophic weather event. At the macro level, the increased availability of usable data on climate change can help governments to advance a forward-looking sectoral approach to the end of ensuring food security in the future.

---

74 Krishna Sapkota, "Exploring the Impacts of Open Aid and Budget Data in Nepal," *Freedom Forum*, August 2014, http://www.opendataresearch.org/sites/default/files/publications/Open%20Aid%20 and%20Budget%20Data%20in%20Nepal%20-%2015th%20Sept-print.pdf.

75 See also the Agriculture Open Data Package developed by GODAN, http://AgPack.info.

76 Jane Battersby and Jonathan Crush, "Africa's Urban Food Deserts," *Urban Forum* 25, no. 2, Springer Netherlands, 2014.

Uganda's Banana Bacterial Wilt Solution

Logic Framework Components:

- Input: Open international organization data, crowdsourced data
- Actors: Government officials, international organization
- Activity: Aggregation and commingling dissemination
- Output: Apps and platforms, data-driven journalism
- Users: Citizens, media
- Indicators: Crops and money saved
- Intended Impact: Solving public problems

Description: Faced with a crisis caused by the spread of banana bacterial wilt (BBW), the Ugandan government turned to open data included in U-Report (http://ureport.ug), UNICEF's community polling project. U-Report helped spread awareness of the disease, mobilized a network of nearly 300,000 volunteers across the country, and also provided vital information to the government about the disease and its pattern of spreading. Using U-Report, the government was able to disseminate information (via SMS) about treatment options and actionable crop-protection strategies to some 190,000 citizens.

Colombia and the Cultivation of Rice

Logic Framework Components:

- Input: Open climate and agricultural data, semi-public agricultural data
- Actors: NGOs and researchers
- Activity: Data analysis
- Output: Decision trees, apps and platforms, searchable databases
- Users: Citizens, Industry groups
- Indicators: Money saved by smallholder farmers
- Intended Impact: Creating opportunity

Description: The production of rice is in a state of continual decline, adversely affecting local farmers. These trends are often blamed on the shifting climate. Researchers analyzed climate and meteorological data alongside measures of rice production and found that the most commonly planted rice in the region, Cimarron Barinas, is highly sensitive to changes in temperature. As a result, farmers adjusted when they planted the crop. Farmers were thus able to improve their yield and protect themselves from the environment. It is estimated that $3.5 million in potential losses were avoided as a result.[77]

Improving the Global Farming Knowledge Base

Logic Framework Components:

- Input: Open agriculture data, open science data, open international organization data
- Actors: NGOs
- Activity: Data analysis, aggregation and commingling, dissemination
- Output: Apps and platforms, advocacy
- Users: Citizens, industry groups
- Indicators: Crops and money saved
- Intended Impact: Empowering citizens

Description: To combat the pests and diseases responsible for killing 40 percent of the world's planted crops each year, Plantwise (https://www.plantwise. org) combines a diversity of relevant global and local databases, government data, and research publications in an openly accessible platform to improve decision making related to pests and disease. This tool has been accessed by over 600,000 farmers from 198 countries, who have contributed to over 900,000 factsheets on crop pest prevalence and best practices to help manage and prevent potential crop loss from pests and diseases.[78]

Empowering Smallholder Farmers in Ghana

Logic Framework Components:

- Input: Open agriculture data, crowdsourced data
- Actors: Private sector
- Activity: Data analysis, dissemination
- Output: Decision trees, process improvements
- Indicators: Crops and money saved by smallholder farmers
- Intended Impact: Creating opportunity

---

77 "Big Data, Big Prospects: Crunching data for farmers' climate adaptation," *CCAFS Annual Report 2015*, https://ccafs.cgiar.org/blog/big-data-big-prospects-crunching-data-farmers-climate-adaptation#. WFBRtKOZORu.

78 CABI, "Plantwise Knowledge Bank Wins Open Data Award for Social Impact," *Plantwise Blog*, November 5, 2014, https://blog.plantwise.org/2014/11/05/plantwise-knowledge-bank-wins-open-data-award-for-social-impact/.

Description: Esoko is a for-profit company, with close relationships with the public sector, offering a simple communication tool for businesses, government, NGOs, and others to connect with farmers. Managed from its main office in the capital city of Accra, Esoko is principally directed at businesses, while individual farmers only constitute its secondary group of interest. Nevertheless, the information that Esoko provides to farmers by repackaging data from different sources (including government and crowdsourced data) and disseminating the information via mobile phones with call-center support in local languages gives smallholder farmers a new addition to their toolkit— that is, if they are made aware of the opportunity to the extent needed for a meaningful impact. In addition, Farmerline, a mobile communications organization, offers similarly data-driven offerings to smallholder farms in Ghana.[79]

Poverty Alleviation

Improving Governance	Empowering Citizens	Innovation & Creating Opportunity	Solving Public Problems
Identifying and addressing corruption through open data can lead to resources being reallocated toward public services that are better suited for addressing systemic poverty.	An improved understanding of how government allocates resources can enable public mobilization around issues that are being under-addressed according to official datasets, including issues related to poverty.	Whether enabling job creation, frugal innovation efforts, or more systemic economic growth, as developing economies begin to leverage data as an economic asset, poverty alleviation can accelerate as a result.	Open data can improve intervention programs that seek to alleviate poverty and improve quality of life by enhancing the understanding of cities, organizations, and donors as to where the needs are the biggest, and why, as well as evaluating what intervention is most appropriate.

Code for Africa

Logic Framework Components:

- Input: Open budget data
- Actors: NGOs
- Activity: Data analysis, presentation, dissemination
- Output: Apps and platforms, process improvements
- Users: Media, researchers
- Indicators: Decreased corruption in extractives industry
- Intended Impact: Improving government, empowering citizens

---

79 Business Call to Action, "Empowering Farmers Through Mobile Communication in West Africa," *The Guardian,* October 15, 2014, https://www.theguardian.com/sustainable-business/2014/oct/22/empowering-farmers-through-mobile-communication-in-west-africa.

Description: Unlike North America and Europe, countries in Africa often have limited access to open government data, and are consequently also limited in their ability to harness technology and use it as a driver of growth. Code for Africa (https://codeforafrica.org) aims to nurture skills in technology and coding from within communities to create opportunities for citizens to act as watchdogs for governments, corporations and public institutions. Fundamental to this is seeing civic technology and open data as potential public assets, and Code for Africa has developed a Data Fellowship program that embeds people trained in data skills to work on projects in a variety of media and nonprofit organizations. School of Data offers a similar fellowship program aimed at increasing data skills and literacy and putting them to use in local partner organizations around the world.[80] By nurturing this burgeoning field, Code for Africa's projects have in turn interrogated public expenditure, as seen in the platform 'Where My Money Dey?'[81] which tracks open data on public revenues received from mining companies. This effort is aimed at providing citizens, NGOs, and watchdogs with information that can help ensure communities benefit from large industrial projects on their land.

Bhoomi Project

Logic Framework Components:

- Input: Open land record data
- Actors: NGO
- Activity: Dissemination
- Output: Searchable database
- Users: Citizens
- Indicators: Increased use of land record information by the poor
- Intended Impact: Empowering citizens

Description: This project in Karnataka, India, was intended to install kiosks in local communities that would provide access to newly digitized land records and democratize the flow of information, reduce inequality, and empower the poor. The system, however, was widely exploited by richer members of society, which weakened the social standing of poorer citizens, exactly the opposite of the goal of the project. Despite its good intentions, the project largely resulted

---

80 "Fellowship Programme," School of Data, http://schoolofdata.org/fellowship-programme/.

81 http://wmmd.codeforafrica.org.

in the transfer of wealth from poor to rich in those communities due to pre-existing inequalities in access to information.[82]

Energy

Improving Governance	Empowering Citizens	Innovation & Creating Opportunity	Solving Public Problems
Like the health sector, energy is the subject of significant public money expenditures, and government sponsorship and procurement (especially in the extractives field). Improving the transparency of a country's energy budget could potentially identify and prevent corruption. In addition, open datasets such as open address data, can improve service delivery by providing energy companies and government with a better understanding of current conditions.	By providing more information to citizens about energy consumption—including perhaps individualized information about their own habits, as offered by GreenButton in the United States[83]— citizens can make more informed decisions regarding usage and, as a result, decrease their energy spending. Open data on utility services and pricing can also be used to identify the best-priced service.	The use of open energy data to bolster predictive capabilities and reel in energy expenditures could have wide-ranging economic impacts for both the public and private sectors.	An improved understanding of energy consumption patterns (at the aggregate and/or individual level) can help individuals, organizations, and policymakers take concrete steps toward decreasing consumption and addressing climate change's impacts. Open data from various sources can help decision makers prioritize investments in energy production and delivery.

India's Electricity Supply Monitoring Initiative

Logic Framework Components:

- Input: Energy provider data
- Actors: NGO
- Activity: Data analysis
- Output: Dashboards, searchable databases
- Users: Citizens, corporations, researchers, government officials
- Indicators: Improved power supply, increased citizen advocacy around energy

---

82 Michael Gurstein, "Open Data: Empowering the empowered or effective data use for everyone," *First Monday*, February 2011, http://journals.uic.edu/ojs/index.php/fm/article/view/3316/2764; Kevin Donovan, "Seeing Like a Slum: Towards open, deliberative development," *Georgetown Journal of International Affairs* 13, no. 1, April 26, 2012, https://papers.ssrn.com/sol3/papers.cfm?abstract_id=2045556.

83 http://www.greenbuttondata.org.

- Intended Impact: Empowering citizens

Description: The poor quality of energy infrastructure in India results in frequent shortages, blackouts, and interruptions. The Indian government does not consistently provide open data on these energy issues. In response to this, the Electricity Supply Monitoring Initiative (ESMI) was launched in 2014 by the Pune-based non-profit Prayas Energy Group. ESMI collects information from cities across 200 locations in India through electricity supply monitors (ESMs)—devices installed in key sites to record voltage data, which log this information with a central server. This data is then made publicly available through the website watchyourpower.org, where users can monitor their power supply and compare this with other regions. ESMI has collected one million location-hours of data, and already found that rural areas experience four to five times more power disruptions than cities or districts. ESMI has already surfaced important evidence about the Indian power supply, but whether and how the capture of this evidence will create meaningful change remains an open question, dependent on an institutional willingness to act upon insights generated—a willingness that has not yet surfaced.

Azerbaijan's Extractive Industries Transparency Initiative Efforts

Logic Framework Components:

- Input: Open extractive industry data
- Actors: NGO
- Activity: Dissemination
- Output: Searchable databases
- Users: NGOs and interest groups, researchers, government officials
- Indicators: Reduced discrepancies between government and contracting business receipts
- Intended Impact: Improving governance

Description: The Extractive Industries Transparency Initiative (EITI) is a global partnership that requires member countries to provide open data and information on the governance of oil, gas, mining, and other extractives. Though questions remain about the line between true impact and positive public relations (see "open washing" discussion above), Azerbaijan, one of the earliest compliers to the EITI standards, saw its "double-digit discrepancies between corporate receipts and government intakes"—an indicator of corruption—essentially disappear between 2003 and 2009. The World Bank

Independent Evaluation Group went on to rate the country's EITI efforts as "highly effective."[84] This example, however, also points to the frequency of backsliding in open initiatives, and the challenges created by the political contexts in which open data initiatives are launched. In 2015, Azerbaijan's EITI membership status was downgraded due to crackdowns on civil society, political opponents, and the media. In 2017, the country's membership was suspended entirely.[85]

Education

Improving Governance	Empowering Citizens	Innovation & Creating Opportunity	Solving Public Problems
Low quality in public education can often point to corruption or more ingrained problems in public expenditure. By opening education data and allowing this data to be scrutinized by the public, governments are encouraged to weed out vested interests that may overdraw the public educational fund.	More information on the expenditures and performance of schools can help parents make more informed decisions about school choice, and mobilize citizens to demand changes to any identified deficiencies.	Like other sectors, the world of education is increasingly data- and technology-driven. More accessible data on schools and on the subjects taught in schools can spur the creation of a data-driven "ed-tech" industry.	Analyzing open data through learning analytics can improve the often poor quality of the education sector in developing countries by, for instance, sharing insights on how teaching can be improved or how the education environment can be designed to support both teachers and students.

Tanzania's Education Dashboards

Logic Framework Components:

- Input: Open education performance data
- Actors: NGO, private sector entrepreneurs, donor organizations
- Activity: Aggregation and commingling, dissemination

---

84 Benjamin Sovacool and Nathan Andrews, "Does Transparency Matter? Evaluating the governance impacts of the Extractive Industries Transparency Initiative in Azerbaijan and Liberia," *Resources Policy* 45 (2015), https://eiti.org/sites/default/files/documents/Sovacool%20%26%20Andrews%20%5B2015%5D%20-%20Does%20transparency%20matter%20-%20%20Evaluating%20the%20governance%20impacts%20of%20the%20Extractive%20Industries%20Transparency%20Initiative%20%28EITI%29%20in%20Azerbaijan%20and%20Liberia.pdf.

85 "Azerbaijan Suspended from the EITI – a Bankwatch and Counter Balance statement," *Bankwatch*, March 9, 2017, http://bankwatch.org/news-media/for-journalists/press-releases/azerbaijan-suspended-eiti-%E2%80%93-bankwatch-and-counter-balance-.

- Output: Dashboards
- Users: Citizens, media
- Indicators: Education advocacy efforts
- Intended Impact: Empowering citizens

Description: Two recently established portals in Tanzania tried to improve low national examination pass rates, providing the public with more data on education and Tanzania's schools. The first, the Education Open Data Dashboard (educationdashboard.org), is a project established by the Tanzania Open Data Initiative, a government program supported by the World Bank and the United Kingdom Department for International Development (DFID) to support open data publication, accessibility and use. The second, Shule (shule.info), was spearheaded by a lone programmer, entrepreneur, and open data enthusiast who has developed a number of technologies and businesses focused on catalyzing social change in Tanzania. Although these projects initially encouraged citizens to demand greater accountability from their school system and public officials, both are in a state of near abandonment resulting from the lack of a clear sustainability and long-term management strategy.

Mexico's Mejora Tu Escuela

Logic Framework Components:

- Input: Open education performance and budget data
- Actors: NGO
- Activity: Data analysis, aggregation and commingling, dissemination
- Output: Dashboards, research report
- Users: Citizens, media, NGOs and interest groups, government officials
- Indicators: Reductions in education corruption, education advocacy efforts
- Intended Impact: Empowering citizens

Description: Founded by the Mexican Institute for Competitiveness (IMCO), with support from Omidyar Network and others, Mejora Tu Escuela (http://mejoratuescuela.org) is an online platform that provides citizens with information about school performance. It helps parents choose the best option for their children, empowers them to demand higher quality education, and gives them tools to get involved in their children's schooling. It also provides school administrators, policymakers, and NGOs with data to identify areas that require improvement and hotbeds of corruption, in the process raising the overall quality of education in Mexico. Some of the data used to create the Mejora Tu Escuela platform was also instrumental in identifying widespread corruption in the education sector and targeting public outrage regarding "phantom" teachers on school payrolls, unchecked teacher absenteeism, and misappropriated funds, among other issues.[86]

Brazil and Education Monitoring

Logic Framework Components

- Input: Open education performance and budget data, census data
- Actors: NGOs, researchers
- Activity: Aggregation and commingling, dissemination
- Output: Searchable databases
- Users: Citizens, NGOs and interest groups, government officials
- Indicators: Money saved in education, education advocacy efforts
- Intended Impact: Empowering citizens and improving government

Description: The development of QEdu[87] in Brazil highlights the link between improved educational standards and open data initiatives. The database—which monitors state, county, and school performance based on metrics like test scores, census data, and educational spending—is easily searched and freely accessible. Reliable data can allow school managers to implement more targeted reforms and allow parents to understand the system that is educating their children. Similar projects have been undertaken in Mexico, Kenya, Tanzania, and the Philippines and appear to be meeting with success.

---

86   Andrew Young and Stefaan Verhulst, "Mexico's Mejora Tu Escuela: Empowering citizens to make data-driven decisions about education," GovLab, http://odimpact.org/case-mexicos-mejora-tu-escuela.html.

87   http://www.qedu.org.br.

PART 2
Case Studies

Open Data's Impact on Improving Government

CHAPTER 5

Burundi's Open RBF

Making health spending and performance transparent

Auralice Graft, Andrew Young and Stefaan Verhulst

Summary

As part of efforts to improve health outcomes and the functioning of health systems, Burundi was one of the first African countries to introduce results based financing (RBF) in the health care sector. RBF is an instrument that links development financing with pre-determined results. Payment is made only when the agreed-upon results are shown to have been achieved. Open RBF, a platform for opening data related to RBF initiatives, has been central to the Burundian Ministry of Health's efforts to introduce RBF methodology and more generally strengthen accountability in health care. Open RBF was first introduced in 2014. Early returns were positive and Open RBF entered into a longer-term partnership with the government. Open RBF has also been applied to education and AIDS awareness programs in Burundi.

Context and Background

Problem Focus/Country Context

Burundi is a low-income nation with a population of 10.5 million. It is one of the world's poorest countries, with development and economic indicators that are among the weakest. Burundi ranks 166th out of 169 countries on the United Nations 2010 Human Development Index,[88] and the national GDP per capita was under USD 210 in 2015.[89] Health outcomes are poor, with a heavy disease burden characterized by infectious and communicable diseases, primarily HIV/AIDS, malaria and diarrhea. Life expectancy in 2016 was just 50 years (for both men and women).[90,91] National healthcare expenditures are estimated at 9 percent of GDP.[92] In addition to low public health expenditures, Burundi's national healthcare system faces significant challenges, including a scarcity of health professionals, poor quality of health services, poor access to essential medicines throughout the country, and a weak health information system.[93]

Results Based Financing (RBF)

Results based financing (RBF) is a method that links development financing with pre-determined results.[94] Payment is made only when the agreed-upon results are shown to have been achieved, an approach that seeks to shift the focus from inputs to results. According to one report that outlines the benefits of RBF: "By only paying for results once they have been achieved, we partly avoid the risk that the donor contribution is not used effectively."[95]

RBF is used across developing countries in cooperation with the private sector, the public sector, and civil society organizations. It is used in a range of sectors, including health care, education, security, and energy. RBF is emerging as a particularly important mechanism in efforts to scale up provision of essential health care services, including child and maternal health care, for example in countries like Cambodia and Rwanda. The OECD has designated

88 U.S. Global Health Initiative, "Burundi Global Health Initiative Strategy: 2011–2015," September 2011, https://www.ghi.gov/wherewework/docs/BurundiStrategy.pdf.

89 Trading Economics, "Burundi GDP Per Capita: 1960–2017," http://www.tradingeconomics.com/burundi/gdp-per-capita.

90 U.S. Global Health Initiative, "Burundi Global Health Initiative Strategy: 2011–2015," September 2011, https://www.ghi.gov/wherewework/docs/BurundiStrategy.pdf.

91 *BBC News*, "Burundi Country Profile," December 14, 2016, http://www.bbc.com/news/world-africa-13085064.

92 Soeters Bonfrer, Presentation, Erasmus University, Rotterdam, 2015, http://rghi.nl/wp-content/uploads/2015/06/5.-Presentation-Igna-Bonfrer-PBF-in-Burundi-Bonfrer-et-al-Symposium-11062015.pdf.

93 U.S. Global Health Initiative, "Burundi Global Health Initiative Strategy: 2011–2015," September 2011, https://www.ghi.gov/wherewework/docs/BurundiStrategy.pdf.

94 RBF is sometimes also referred to as performance based financing (PBF) or output based aid (OPA). In some contexts, PBF refers specifically to RBF in the health care sector. See Jurien Toonen, et al., *Learning Lessons on Implementing Performance Based Financing, from a Multicountry Evaluation*, Royal Tropical Institute, Cordaid and WHO, May 2009, http://www.who.int/contracting/PBF.pdf.

95 Swedish International Development Cooperation Agency, *Results Based Financing Approaches: What are they?* SIDA, 2015, http://www.sida.se/contentassets/1869345299754bddbf58857e2d92c726/110557c1-7b5e-4a0d-97b0-cbeae5258533.pdf.

RBF as a key tool for achieving WHO Universal Health Coverage goals.[96] Studies also show that RBF increases health care provider performance, with important differences identified "before and after" the introduction of RBF. RBF was further shown to strongly influence health system development at the operational level in RBF projects in some countries.[97]

Burundi was one of the first African countries to introduce results based financing (RBF). Second on the African continent only after Rwanda, it began implementing RBF in its health care systems in 2010. In 2015, Burundi also began using RBF in the education sector.[98]

Technology and RBF

The key to a successful RBF program is effective daily management, and information management tools are essential for this. Large amounts of data have to be entered, verified, and validated for RBF programs to function, and that data must then be processed against pre-set criteria to calculate and disperse subsidy payments. Technology plays a vital role in ensuring that this is all done effectively and accurately.

While many RBF programs use Microsoft Excel for this purpose, an increasing number use Open RBF, a customizable financing management tool designed specifically for RBF projects. Because this tool easily makes data open and machine readable, it has the added benefit of making RBF data accessible for public consumption and analysis.

KEY ACTORS

Key Data Providers

The key data providers are Burundian health service providers who participate in RBF programs that use the Open RBF tool. These service providers generate qualitative and quantitative data relating to the services provided, and the Open RBF tool manages and processes that data and the different stages it passes through. These stages include recording, verification, processing, and calculation and dispersal of payments. Outcomes are also shared in the public domain.

---

96 György Bèla Fritsche, Robert Soeters and Bruno Meessen, *Performance-Based Financing Toolkit*, Washington, DC: World Bank, 2014, http://www.oecd.org/dac/peer-reviews/PBF-%20toolkit.pdf.

97 See Jurien Toonen, et al., *Learning Lessons on Implementing Performance Based Financing, from a Multicountry Evaluation*, Royal Tropical Institute, Cordaid and WHO, May 2009, http://www.who.int/contracting/PBF.pdf.

98 "RBF IT system for Education sector in Burundi." OpenRBF, http://www.openrbf.org/project/rbf-it-system-for-education-sector-in-burundi/Ve_9qR8AABUBfdDj.

Key Data Users and Intermediaries

Several entities make use of the data. Primarily, participating RBF programs use it to ensure accurate and timely recording, verification, processing, and publication of data, as well as payments dispersal. Also, funding organizations use the data to oversee program progress and to determine allocations. In addition, Burundi's Ministry of Public Health and the Fight Against AIDS uses the data to coordinate their nation-wide health sector improvement efforts. Medical practitioners and policymakers also use the data. Finally, citizens have access to the data (although, as explained elsewhere in this case study, citizen uptake seems somewhat limited).

The key data intermediaries are Burundi's Ministry of Public Health and the Fight Against AIDS, which together spearhead Burundi's national health system improvement efforts. In addition, Cordaid, a Netherlands-based organization that works to create "opportunities for the world's poorest, most vulnerable and excluded people,"[99] has implemented community health and education sector RBF programs in Burundi using the Open RBF tool.

Key Beneficiaries

Entities working directly and indirectly with RBF programs benefit from the technological functions Open RBF provides. Also, governments, policymakers, funding organizations, students, and citizens benefit from the publicly-available data and data comparisons. Most broadly, all citizens of Burundi benefit from any health and education sector improvements that have been achieved as a result of Open RBF platforms.

Project Description

Initiation

Open RBF's origins are in Belgium, where Nicolas de Borman, the founder and current CEO of BlueSquare, a company that works to harness technology for the public good, sought a way to promote RBF in developing nations. Borman correctly identified high demand for a tool that would help collect, analyze, and disseminate RBF data. As a result, Borman and a team of five partners created such a tool and named it Open RBF.[100] The tool is deployed and administered around the world by BlueSquare.

RBF pilot projects began in Burundi in 2006 across six provinces, with such pilots covering the entire country by 2010. The Open RBF platform was first

---

99   See: https://www.cordaid.org/en/.

100 GovLab interview with Antoine Legrand and Elena Ignatova, Program Managers at BlueSquare, August 9, 2016.

delivered in Burundi in 2010, in response to a request from the Burundian government and coinciding with the national-level embrace of results-based financing.[101] The Burundian Ministry of Health was seeking ways to improve health care functioning at the national level and strengthen accountability mechanisms.[102,103] Early returns were positive and Open RBF then entered into a longer-term partnership with the government. Open RBF has also been applied to both the health and education sectors in Burundi. [104,105]

Open RBF in Burundi operates in a similar way to Open RBF around the world. Its broad aims are to improve the openness of data to enable its access by a range of stakeholders in healthcare, thereby promoting the overall RBF goals of efficiency, transparency, accountability, and good governance.[106] The platform is built as an open-source, web-based solution, using a combination of technologies, including Php, Mysql, Jquery, Bootstrap, Highcharts, and Dompdf. The tool also integrates with Google Maps.[107]

To access the Open RBF tool, users visit a portal that has both a private and a public interface. The private area contains dashboards that display project data from the field—data that has been recorded and verified by different parties, and only then published on the platform. Data in this area includes information relating to project progress, including quality, quantity, and performance indicators.

The public, front-end interface (image shown below) includes slightly more data than the private interface. The public area allows users to view information at a province or national level, for example, information related to vaccination rates, reproductive health, preventative health, and HIV/AIDS. In the representative image included here, the interface shows that 100 percent of children attending participating clinics were verified as having been fully vaccinated in March 2015, while 80.36 percent were fully vaccinated in November of that year. It also shows that, in September 2015, almost 50

---

101 GovLab interview with Elena Ignatova, Program Manager at BlueSquare, January 19, 2017.

102 Christel Jansen and Jurrien Toonen, "Learning from Experiential Performance Based Financing Knowledge in Burundi and Cameroon," KIT Health Blog, June 21, 2016, https://www.rbfhealth.org/blog/learning-experiential-performance-based-financing-knowledge-burundi-and-cameroon.

103 György Bèla Fritsche, Robert Soeters and Bruno Meessen, *Performance-Based Financing Toolkit*, Washington, DC: World Bank, 2014, http://www.oecd.org/dac/peer-reviews/PBF-%20toolkit.pdf.

104 *Aléa Kagoyire, "Inspiring Change in Burundi's Education System with OpenRBF, BlueSquare.org, March 17, 2016,* https://medium.com/@BlueSquare.org/inspiring-change-in-burundi-s-education-system-with-openrbf-by-al%C3%A9a-kagoyire-project-manager-af1fbb6d31d9#.ac8i9w7es.

105 See: http://www.bluesquare.org/technologies.

106 Alice Irakoze, "An OpenRBF portal for the Community PBF in Makamba, Burundi: verified data, transparent management and budget monitoring!" BlueSquare.org, July 17, 2015, https://medium.com/@BlueSquare.org/an-openrbf-portal-for-the-community-pbf-in-makamba-burundi-verified-data-transparent-management-8afc0610fd99#.tyefjelsl.

107 See: http://www.openrbf.org/faq.

percent of patients were screened for TB.[108] Each key indicator is compared with regional and global figures.

All the information contained within the portal (especially the private area) is used to determine the progress of projects, and whether they are eligible for performance-based subsidies. Once subsidies have been calculated and paid, this information is displayed on the public interface, which includes provider performance indicators that allow citizens and policy makers (and anyone else interested) to gauge progress of particular projects or groups and see how public funds are being allocated. One goal of the public interface is to open up data to encourage greater civic ownership and participation.[109]

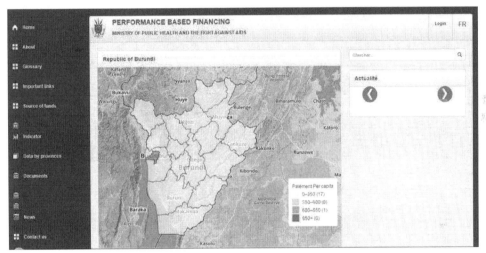

Image from http://www.fbpsanteburundi.bi/ which displays health data for Burundi as generated by Open RBF.

Demand and Data Use

As mentioned above, demand for Open RBF comes primarily from within RBF programs. Such programs could be managed by non-profit organizations, civil society groups, or government departments. In Burundi, additional demand comes from Burundi's Ministry of Public Health and the Fight Against AIDS. All these organizations use the data available on the portal not only to track the progress of their own projects, but also of other projects throughout the country. Civil society actors and journalists also draw on Open RBF data to

---

108 Ministere de la Sante Publique et de la Lutte Contre Le SIDA, Performance Based Financing, 2013, http://www.fbpsanteburundi.bi/data/indicators.html#dataelt11.

109 Cordaid, "Open RBF," https://www.cordaid.org/en/topics/healthcare/result-based-financing/open-rbf/.

inform their work, but neither group represents a prime target audience for the platform.[110]

Impact

Measuring the impact of open data projects is never easy, especially as some projects may have indirect effects that are harder to capture. Nonetheless, a range of indicators suggest that Open RBF has not only had a positive impact Burundi, offering important lessons for the potentially transformative role of data in improving healthcare and more generally solving complex public problems in the developing world.

Improving Health

Overall, as noted, the state of healthcare in Burundi remains poor. But there are encouraging signs of improvement within RBF programs in particular that suggest the positive impact of Open RBF. One example can be found in Cordaid's work with community health workers in Makamba province, which has resulted in a significant reduction in cases of severe malaria.[111] In addition, Cordaid's work in 81 Burundi preschools, which includes 27 local organizations verifying community education indicators and a network of 12 regulatory boards, has been found to correlate with improved educational access for students of all ages, a better gender balance in programs, better teaching methods, and improved academic performance scores among students.[112]

These improvements are of course the result of many factors, but people familiar with the results cite the important role played by Open RBF. For example, Dr. Etienne Nkeshimana, RBF and health system strengthening expert in Burundi who currently coordinates a Cordaid community RBF project, says: "I cannot scientifically say that Open RBF has led to some of the positive results we see in RBF programs. However, I can say that without Open RBF, we would not have achieved these positive results."[113]

---

110 GovLab interview with Elena Ignatova, Program Manager at BlueSquare, January 19, 2017.

111 Republic of Burundi, Ministry of Public Health and the Fight Against AIDS, "Evaluation Final de Projet Pilote FBP Communautaire au Burundi," December 2015.

112 GovLab interview with Simone Soeters, Cordaid Program Manager and Vincent Kamenyero, Cordaid, September 22, 2016.

113 GovLab interview with Dr. Etienne Nkeshimana, Cordaid Community RBF Coordinator, and Simone Soeters, Cordaid Program Manager, September 13, 2016.

Better Project Management and Cost Savings

A significant benefit of Open RBF is its role in improving project management, which in turn enhances the services that use it and introduces greater cost efficiencies. Open RBF achieves better project management by allowing stakeholders to regularly and rigorously follow project results in virtual real-time, including through sophisticated visualizations. Such monitoring not only improves the outcomes of the projects but also leads to financial savings, helping organizations manage scarce development resources more efficiently. As Vincent Kamenyero, Data and Portal Manager at Cordaid, puts it: "The Open RBF portal has allowed for greater transparency in finance management, cost reduction of organizational functioning, and is a considerable time saver for our verifiers."[114] Rigorous project management is particularly important in the early or pilot stages of a program, when donors may be monitoring to determine the effectiveness of a method and whether or not to scale up funding.

Open RBF also helps aid agencies and governments monitor projects remotely, a factor that is of great help to foreign funding groups. The benefits of remote project management were apparent during the recent political upheaval in Burundi, when foreign agencies were more comfortable monitoring their projects from the relative safety of their host countries.[115] Similarly, Cordaid's work with community health workers in the remote Makamba province is significantly facilitated by its ability to follow projects from the national capital of Bujumbara. For instance, if there is a problem with health worker data collection methods on the ground, program experts can quickly identify it and attempt to solve the issue on their dashboards in the capital.[116]

The Inherent Value of Data

Open RBF Burundi is also a good example of the powerful role that data can play in solving public problems in the developing world. Increasingly, it is becoming clear that the data generated by specific RBF programs can be used in other situations as well; the data has *inherent* value. For example, in its current efforts to expand community health efforts (known as the Kira program), the Ministry of Health is making extensive use of publicly available Open RBF

---

114 Cordaid, "Open Development Movement: Co-creation leads to transformation," Position Paper, May 2014, https://www.cordaid.org/en/wp-content/uploads/sites/3/2014/05/OpenDevPaper-MAY2014-LR_5.pdf.

115 GovLab interview with Antoine Legrand and Elena Ignatova, Program Managers at BlueSquare, August 9, 2016.

116 GovLab interview with Dr. Etienne Nkeshimana, Cordaid Community RBF Coordinator, and Simone Soeters, Cordaid Program Manager, September 13, 2016.

data generated by previous programs. The data includes various qualitative and quantitative costing indicators, as well as information pertaining to patient numbers and vaccine rates that had been used to assess earlier interventions.[117] In this way, publicly available Open RBF data can serve as an important reference point and guide for developing future programs.

Several donor organizations and student groups similarly rely on publicly available Open RBF data. For example, the World Bank, which will help fund the above-mentioned Kira project, has relied on earlier existing Open RBF healthcare sector data to determine its funding packages. Likewise, students researching Burundi health or other sector outcomes regularly access Open RBF public-facing pages for their research.[118]

Empowering Citizens

As indicated by the example of students, Open RBF data can play a powerful role beyond the development community, empowering citizens at large with information and insights. The Open RBF tool in Burundi provided the public with its first opportunity to review and potentially comment on healthcare (and other) projects across the country. Through community groups and other advocacy channels, citizens can contribute to healthcare planning, verify performance, track government spending, and generally ensure greater accountability. "It puts communities in the driver's seat," said Dr. Rose Kamariza, Cordaid Program Officer, Burundi.[119]

It is of course important to mention that many citizens lack Internet access and thus direct access to the data generated by Open RBF. But organizations like Cordaid play an important role in overcoming such barriers, suggesting the important role of intermediaries in spreading the benefits of open data. For example, Cordaid organizes bi-annual feedback workshops where it shares data with citizens and allows them to engage with RBF findings and Open RBF results.[120]

---

117 Ibid.

118 Ibid.

119 Cordaid, "Open Development Movement: Co-creation leads to transformation," Position Paper, May 2014, https://www.cordaid.org/en/wp-content/uploads/sites/3/2014/05/OpenDevPaper-MAY2014-LR_5.pdf.

120 GovLab interview with Dr. Etienne Nkeshimana, Cordaid Community RBF Coordinator, and Simone Soeters, Cordaid Program Manager, September 13, 2016.

Risks

Burundi's Open RBF initiative is not intended to make any personally identifiable information accessible to the public. Some level of privacy risk does remain, however, when open data projects are active in sectors like health care. There has been no evidence to date that Open RBF has introduced any privacy issues, but it will be important to maintain vigilance when redacting personal information from data releases or anonymizing datasets going forward.

Lessons Learned

Several important lessons with wider applicability emerge from this particular case study. These can broadly be categorized by considering the key enablers of the project, as well as the most important barriers or challenges to its success.

Enablers

Government support

Burundi's Ministry of Public Health and the Fight Against AIDS were significant enablers in Open RBF's success. They incorporated RBF into the government's national health program, using the Open RBF tool in delivering that program. The ultimate impact and success of that tool has, to a large degree, flowed from the support received by the national government, which helped fund its implementation, adapt it to a range of health sector categories, and generally propagated it throughout the country. In this respect, Open RBF in Burundi is a good example of how strong institutional support and political and administrative buy-in are instrumental to the success of open data projects. Many of the projects discussed in this series lack such support.

It is worth mentioning that the current political climate in Burundi may prove to be a challenge in the months and years ahead. Although this project is both beneficial and useful for the nation, the possibility of further political strife may limit the ability to monitor the efficacy of programs within the health care sector.

International development organizations

International development organizations also played a key enabling role in Open RBF's success. Cordaid, which adopted the tool for its community health, education and security sector programs, was among the most important supporters. The World Bank has helped too, especially by using and thus validating the usefulness of publicly-available Open RBF data.

Barriers

Regional and Sectoral Specificity

Open RBF's use in a variety of countries is testament to technology's cross-border potential. However, it is also true that the first version of the Open RBF software used in Burundi was not entirely adapted to local conditions and the different needs of various RBF programs. Not all such programs are alike. Each has a different set of pre-determined criteria. Some may receive funds from one donor while others from several donors. [121] This first version of the platform was tweaked and a second unveiled in 2014. This second version allows for the possibility of multi-management funding, includes new data visualizations, and also includes an alert system to allow auditors to update the data.[122]

Technical Expertise

According to the International Telecommunication Union (ITU), the percentage of Burundian citizens who use the Internet more than tripled from 2014 to 2015. Nonetheless, fewer than 5 percent of Burundians regularly use the Internet—a low rate even by the typical standards of less developed economies. To an extent, the negative consequences can be mitigated by the use of intermediaries who share information with citizens that are not connected. But overall, the country's poor state of Internet readiness curtails citizens' and users' ability to access Open RBF-generated data.

Even among those who are connected to the Internet and generally technically proficient, a lack of data knowledge and expertise often limits the potential of Open RBF projects. Open RBF teams find that many statisticians they work with are not trained to work with data in a manner that Open RBF requires. This complicates and slows training missions. For example, statisticians at the province level in some countries are not always versed with data management beyond the use of Microsoft Excel.

---

121 Ibid.

122 Alice Irakoze, "Un portail OpenRBF pour le FBP communautaire à Makamba, Burundi : des donnéees verifiées, une gestion et un suivi budgétaire transparents!" BlueSquare.org, https://medium.com/@ BlueSquare.org/un-portail-openrbf-pour-le-fbp-communautaire-%C3%A0-makamba-burundi-des-donn%C3%A9ees-verifi%C3%A9es-une-f419eb6b6ebc#.ptx0n29b4.

Design Flexibility

Building reliable and truly useful software requires adapting it to local conditions and needs. Software is often designed from the top-down, but in order to be useful across a variety of contexts, it must also adapt to new information from the field and from users. Software design is an iterative process. This has proven to be a challenge not only in Burundi, where, as mentioned above, users struggled early on to adapt the software to local conditions, but virtually everywhere where Open RBF has been implemented. For example, program managers Antoine Legrand and Elena Ignatova estimate that up to 80 percent of Open RBF clients come back to the BlueSquare team requesting changes, and as a result the RBF program itself changes over time. Enabling this level of flexibility based on the initial Open RBF design continues to present challenges, but is essential to the success of open data projects—and more generally technical interventions, especially in the developing world.[123]

Replicability

Open RBF has been replicated repeatedly, within and beyond the healthcare sector—suggesting the value of the model and its tool to a wide variety of stakeholders. Since its inception in the health and education sectors within Burundi, Open RBF has also been used in the security sector.[124] And, of course, the dissemination of Open RBF has also extended far beyond Burundi. A total of 15 countries now use Open RBF to facilitate RBF program management, including Benin, Cameroon, DRC, Haiti, Kyrgiztan, Laos, and Nigeria.[125] The cases of DRC and Nigeria are particularly interesting because of their sheer size: 1,000 facilities are included in Nigeria's program and 2,000 in DRC's.[126] So while Open RBF efforts require some level of customization for specific contexts, the platform and general approach rolled out in Burundi has proven flexible enough to scale geographically and across sectors.

---

123 GovLab interview with Antoine Legrand and Elena Ignatova, Program Managers at BlueSquare, August 9, 2016.

124 Cordaid, "Open Development Movement: Co-creation leads to transformation," Position Paper, May 2014, https://www.cordaid.org/en/wp-content/uploads/sites/3/2014/05/OpenDevPaper-MAY2014-LR_5.pdf.

125 GovLab interview with Antoine Legrand and Elena Ignatova, Program Managers at BlueSquare, August 9, 2016.

126 Ibid.

Looking Forward

The organizers of Open RBF are working on several initiatives to improve their software and programs across implementation areas.

Mobile Platform Updates

Expanding functionalities and improving the responsiveness of the mobile elements of Open RBF are clear focus areas going forward. For health care implementations of Open RBF, like in Burundi, BlueSquare is testing a new patient feedback mechanism to collect information directly from those receiving health care. Additionally, a mobile data collection tool was introduced in July 2015 to allow for data to be uploaded onto the Open RBF platform. Developed by BlueSquare specifically for RBF efforts to improve Burundi's education system, the tool was designed to improve data collection and verification. It includes a simple interface and allows for data storage until the tool is connected to the internet and data can be uploaded to the system. The tool saves time for data verifiers and enhances the quality of data collected.[127] Both cell phones and tablets are being tested, keeping cost requirements in mind.

A More Stable, User Friendly Platform

Open RBF working to solve connectivity issues by establishing interoperability between information systems. The goal here is to better correlate collected and validated data analysis which in turn will enable better and more complete reading of the performance of each RBF approach.[128] Teams are working to improve interoperability layers between support tools using DHIS2 systems and integrating them with Open RBF.[129]

Open RBF is also taking steps to improve data visualization on their dashboards. They aim to improve the way that results are displayed to make the platform more user friendly, especially at a glance.

---

127 *Aléa Kagoyire*, "A New Mobile Data Collection Tool Is Out!" BlueSquare.org, July 17, 2015, https://medium.com/@BlueSquare.org/a-new-mobile-data-collection-tool-is-out-c3746ae4233d#.alv6gelpm.

128 Alice Irakoze, "Un portail OpenRBF pour le FBP communautaire à Makamba, Burundi : des donnéees verifiées, une gestion et un suivi budgétaire transparents!" BlueSquare.org, https://medium.com/@BlueSquare.org/un-portail-openrbf-pour-le-fbp-communautaire-%C3%A0-makamba-burundi-des-donn%C3%A9ees-verifi%C3%A9es-une-f419eb6b6ebc#.akspjkv9h.

129 Nicolas de Borman, "How Can New Technologies Enhance Efficiency and Good Governance of Results-based Financing," RBFHealth Blog, July 16, 2014, https://www.rbfhealth.org/blog/how-can-new-technologies-enhance-efficiency-and-good-governance-results-based-financing.

Integrations and Plug-Ins

Finally, the next stage of Open RBF will feature a number of new plug ins and integrations to bring new functionalities to the platform, and to better connect it with other platforms users are likely to frequent. Likely the most important new integration will be improved geolocation capabilities and mapping features. Organizers are also pushing forward more social media integration, with Facebook and Twitter functionalities representing first priorities.[130] Beyond the specific integrations under development, the plug-in and integration focus exhibited by Open RBF makes clear that a key part of the plan for evolving the platform over time involves finding ways to bring existing platform features to bear for Open RBF users.

Conclusion

The results-based financing approach is growing in momentum, especially across developing countries. The rapid expansion and scaling of the Open RBF platform shows how quickly successful open data projects can be replicated across regions and sectors when a clear value proposition can be articulated and early positive impacts can be demonstrated. Perhaps even more importantly, the Open RBF platform itself is helping to make it easier for governments to quickly roll out open data-driven RBF efforts, with the key out-of-the-box features and functionalities ready to implement once a clear problem area is identified and political will and buy-in is present.

---

130 Alfred Antoine U., "Efficient Health Financing: Transparency, accountability and benchmarking in health systems," Open RBF Initiative, October 22, 2013, http://www.health4africa.net/wp-content/uploads/local_health_systems_future_technology_impact_OPENRBF_Data.pdf.

CHAPTER 6

India's ESMI

Civil society complementing government data in an open manner

Michael P. Canares, Anirudh Dinesh, Andrew Young and Stefaan Verhulst

Summary

Across the developing world, roughly 1.2 billion people[131] do not have access to electricity. Of this number, at least 30 percent live in India. In addition, at least 247 million people in India experience irregular access to electricity, with many receiving only around four hours a day. The government of India, under Prime Minister Narendra Modi, has committed to establishing universal access across the country. However, India's electricity problem is not just about insufficient coverage; it is also about poor power quality, especially in the form of voltage fluctuations.

Poor power quality impacts all segments of consumers; it can damage equipment and cause various other problems, including data loss and other forms of loss or inefficiencies for businesses and other entities. Improving power quality is, however, challenging, and requires real-time access to data. In 2007, The Prayas Energy Group (PEG), an Indian NGO, launched the Electricity Supply Monitoring Initiative (ESMI) to complement existing data sources and collect real-time power quality information by installing Electricity Supply Monitors (ESMs) in various locations. ESMI now works in 200 locations[132] in 18 Indian states. The initiative has made power supply

---

131 Energy Access Database, *World Energy Outlook* http://www.worldenergyoutlook.org/resources/ energydevelopment/energyaccessdatabase/.

132 "Using technology for evidence based feedback to ensure quality electricity access", Electricity Supply Monitoring Initiative (ESMI), *Prayas Energy Group*, https://d2oc0ihd6a5bt.cloudfront.net/wp-content/ uploads/sites/837/2016/04/2-Shantanu-Dixit.pdf.

monitoring data available for different users across the country, in the process increasing awareness of the state of electricity supply, helping to advocate for better service provision, and influencing policy at both the state and country level. Despite certain limitations—and the daunting scale of the problem—ESMI represents an important example of how civil society can address public problems, and fill gaps arising from government data failures, when NGOs take an open approach to data collection and use.

Context and Background

Problem Focus / Country Context

According to conservative estimates, at least 300 million[133] of India's 1.25 billion people do not have access to electricity. The problem is aggravated by the fact that, even for those who do have power, approximately 26 percent get only irregular access, sometimes as little as four hours a day. In 2015, the World Energy Outlook[134], considered the world's most authoritative source of energy market analysis, projected that the country would require 110 billion USD a year to meet its energy requirements.

Prime Minister Narendra Modi, elected in 2015, included universal access to electricity as one of his top priorities. The government has devoted considerable resources to a rural electrification program[135] that aims to electrify 121,225 un-electrified villages, improve power supply to 592,979 partially electrified villages, and provide free electricity to all rural households. As of June 30, 2016, it is estimated that between 50 and 80 percent of these targets have been achieved.

Nonetheless, the quality of electricity service provision remains poor, as emblematized by India's infamous 2012 blackout[136], in which 680 million people were affected. The root causes of the problem are manifold. Distribution on India's antiquated and poorly connected grid is one of the main issues; by some estimates, up to 30 percent of the nation's electricity is lost in grid inefficiencies. But the problem isn't only about distribution. The nation simply doesn't generate enough power. According to a 2015 report from the Institute

133 Martin, "India's Energy Crisis", MIT Technology Review, 2015, https://www.technologyreview.com/s/542091/indias-energy-crisis/.

134 "World Energy Outlook 2015 Factsheet", International Energy Agency, 2015.

135 "Rural Electrification: Status of Rural Electrification (RE) under DDUGY, Ministry of Power, Government of India, http://powermin.nic.in/content/rural-electrification.

136 "India's Power Network Breaks Down", The Wall Street Journal", 2012, https://www.wsj.com/articles/SB10000872396390444405804577560413178678898.

for Policy Research[137], an independent policy research institute, the nation's power deficit stands at 3.6 percent. Even this figure probably underestimates the problem, given that energy statistics calculate demand only on the basis of existing connected consumers, meaning that such power deficit figures fail to take into account the millions who do not have power at all.

One of the biggest, though perhaps least acknowledged, problems concerns the *quality* of India's power supply. Power Quality[138] encompasses voltage variations (sags and swells), voltage reductions, power interruptions, voltage surges and harmonic distortions in the supply. Simply put, poor power quality refers to interruptions in power supply (which might last from a few minutes to a few days) or dangerous spikes in supply that could damage household electronic devices.

Such quality problems are widespread in India and they have major implications for domestic as well as industrial consumers. While it is difficult to quantify the consequences, one study conducted in 2009[139] suggested that businesses had to invest 15.5 billion USD in back-up power generation facilities to avoid the various adverse impacts[140] of poor power quality. These adverse effects include frozen computer screens, data loss, flickering lights and equipment damage, among other issues.

Addressing power quality issues represents a considerable challenge—in some ways, more so than addressing the problem of non-existent supply. To address the issue, real-time data is required, and such data is hard to come by. Regulators, electricity producers and consumers need as much information as possible on when electricity is likely to be cut or spike, and on what factors typically trigger voltage fluctuation. Data that can help to predict power fluctuations and provide forewarnings on voltage dips or spikes are also extremely important.

To make progress toward meaningfully addressing the many current problems in the Indian energy sector, a far more sophisticated data setup is needed. According to a recent study[141], there are different regulations on power quality in India, issued by the Central Electricity Authority (CEA) and also by

---

137 "Vital Stats: Overview of issues in the power sector in India", PRS Legislative Research, 2015, http://www.prsindia.org/administrator/uploads/general/1449060077_Vital%20Stats%20-%20power%20sector.pdf.

138 "Power Quality- What is it?", HSB.com, https://www.hsb.com/TheLocomotive/PowerQualityIsImportantHereisWhatYouCanDo.aspx.

139 Wärtsilä, *The Real Cost of Power*, Wärtsilä, 2009, http://www.wartsila.com/docs/default-source/Power-Plants-documents/downloads/White-papers/asia-australia-middle-east/The-Real-Cost-of-Power.pdf?sfvrsn=2.

140 "Impact of Power Quality on Indian Industries", Asia Power Quality Initiative, http://apqi.org/download/delhi/01-dr-bhuvaneswari.pdf.

141 "White Paper: Power Quality Regulations in India", Forum of Regulators (FOR), India, 2015, http://www.forumofregulators.gov.in/Data/Achievements/apqi.pdf.

the State Electricity Regulatory Commissions. There exist several shortcomings and variations in these regulations, notably when it comes to enforcement, but also in the way data is handled or treated. For example, voltage variation limits[142] for some states is 10 percent but for others it is 12.5 percent. Across states, there exists no reliable voltage monitoring program to provide power quality data. The only way to report low voltages or power outages is to call the local power company and lodge a complaint—a time consuming, manual process, which in any case is unlikely to have any meaningful impact.

Such shortcomings affect policymakers and those who seek to improve power quality. Consumers are also directly affected by a lack of data, for example in lodging complaints against distribution companies regarding problems in power supply. Without data, they have no evidence to back their claims. While there do exist clear standards regarding acceptable variations in supply parameters, defined[143] by the Institute of Electrical and Electronic Engineers (IEEE), citizens or even regulators often have no reliable data to show that those standards are not being adhered to.

Open Data in India

The Government of India approved the National Data Sharing and Accessibility Policy (NDSAP) in early 2012. This policy can be considered the first enabling regulation regarding the proactive disclosure of government data and extends the mandate of the Right to Information Act (RTIA). The act established policies and procedures in the publication of government datasets from different agencies in the central government through a single national portal.

The national open data platform[144] was launched in the same year. Since then, the portal has become the main repository of government data sets, covering 102 departments and involving at least 111 chief information officers. To date, the portal houses 44,174 resources in 4,043 catalogs covering essential sectors, such as health, environment, education, agriculture, commerce, mining, legislation, labor, power and energy, tourism, among others. However, the 2015 Open Data Barometer[145] has shown that despite the increasing number of data sets, there is little evidence of impact on government's accountability, effectiveness, and efficiency and in environmental stability or social inclusion.

---

142 Voltage variation limit, simply put, is the maximum allowable value for voltage value to fluctuate.

143 "IEEE Std 1159-2009- IEEE Recommended Practice for Monitoring Electric Power Quality", IEEE, 2009, http://ieeexplore.ieee.org/document/5154067/.

144 "Open Government Data Platform India", https://data.gov.in.

145 "Open Data Barometer", 2015, http://opendatabarometer.org/data-explorer/?_year=2015&indicator=ODB.

The Open Data Index places India at 55 percent open and ranked the country at number 15 in its 2015 edition.[146]

The power and energy sector database in the national portal consists of at least 137 data catalogs, 47 of which are dedicated to electricity and power. The others include information on areas like the functioning of thermal power stations, efforts to expand the use of renewable energy and the supply of and demand for natural gas. None of the datasets includes information on power quality; they are largely focused on power generation. The data catalogs are also difficult to navigate, as several of the datasets are structured by state and are not linked in any way that would permit a national or otherwise aggregate analysis.

KEY ACTORS

Key Data Providers

Ministry of Power, Government of India

The Ministry of Power of the Government of India governs the three major pillars of the country's power sector: generation, transmission, and distribution. On policy and regulation, at least two agencies have a mandate: the Central Electricity Authority (CEA), in charge of overall power development in the country; and the Central Electricity Regulatory Commission[147] (CERC), in charge of tariffs, inter-state transmission, grid standards, and adjudication of power-related disputes. CERC is also mandated to ensure that stakeholders have access to information related to electricity service provision. These agencies collect various datasets related to their mandate.

Generation, Transmission, and Distribution Companies (GTDs)

Power generation in India is divided into three sectors: central, state, and private. As of June 30, 2016[148], the private sector accounts for at least 41.45 percent of installed capacity, with the central and state sectors generating 22.15 percent and 33.59 percent, respectively.

The PowerGrid Corporation of India[149] is responsible for the inter-state transmission of electricity and the development of the national grid. It is the country's Central Transmission Utility (CTU) responsible for transmitting power of central generating utilities and interstate independent power producers. State Transmission Utilities (STUs) are responsible for wheeling power from state generating companies and

---

146 "India," Global Open Data Index, Open Knowledge International, http://index.okfn.org/place/india/.

147 Central Electricity Regulatory Commission, Government of India, http://opendatabarometer.org/data-explorer/?_year=2015&indicator=ODB.

148 "Power Sector at a glance- All India", Ministry of Power, Government of India, http://powermin.nic.in/content/power-sector-glance-all-india.

149 https://www.powergridindia.com/.

state-level independent power producers. The power grid plays an important role in establishing new transmission systems as well as strengthening existing transmission systems at the central level.

Power distribution is the final and the most important link to the consumer in the electricity value chain. Unfortunately, power distribution is highly inefficient, with an average of 20 percent distribution loss on an annual basis. Distribution at the state level is done either by state companies or private firms (averaging a slightly better 13 percent distribution loss).[150] The efficiency of distribution differs from one state to the other.

Power distribution companies hold vast amounts of data, covering generation, transmission, and distribution. The information contained is quite granular, down to household-level consumption data. Data held by the Ministry of Power, in the Central government, is collated from submissions made by these state-level companies.

Key Data Users and Intermediaries

Prayas Energy Group

Prayas Energy Group is part of Prayas, a non-governmental organization based in Pune, India, that protects and promotes the public interest—more particularly of disadvantaged sectors of the society.[151] It has four working groups: energy, health, resources and livelihoods, and learning and parenthood. The energy group has been one of the strongest and longest-acting advocates for better power service delivery in India, especially among the poor.

Prayas Energy Group is a key user of electricity data for its work. However, because of the lack of official government data devoted to power quality (open or otherwise), Prayas launched the Electricity Supply Monitoring Initiative (ESMI), thus becoming a provider of data as well.

The Energy Resources Institute (TERI)

Based in New Delhi, TERI is one of the leading energy think-tanks in India. It focuses its research on clean energy, water management, pollution management, sustainable agriculture, and climate resilience. TERI's projects in the energy sector includes research studies on renewable energy—including biomass, wind, solar, and hydro power—to explore options for India in the energy sector. Over the past few years, TERI has conducted several analysis papers on the state of power generation in India.

Private Companies and Research Groups

Data on electricity in India is widely used by different private companies and consulting firms to predict future scenarios, influence investing opportunities and inform power

---

150 Lori Aniti, "India Aims to Reduce High Electricity Transmission and Distribution System Losses," *Today in Energy*, October 22, 2015, http://www.eia.gov/todayinenergy/detail.php?id=23452.

151 See the Prayas website, http://www.prayaspune.org/peg/index.php.

stakeholders of opportunities and challenges. McKinsey & Company, KPMG, and AT Kearney, for example, regularly use power sector data for their work in the country.

Key Beneficiaries

Consumer Watch Groups or Organizations

Consumer organizations are generally advocacy groups that promote consumer protection from different types of corporate abuse. In India, there are several consumer groups that also work in the energy sector, such as New Delhi's Consumer VOICE, Chennai's Citizen Consumer and Civic Action Group, Kolkata's Federation of Consumer Association, among others. ESMI was designed partly with these groups in mind; they were seen as key users that could help strengthen advocacy for power quality monitoring at local levels by using existing consumer grievance redressal channels.

State regulators

State-level regulatory commissions perform the same functions as the CERC, but they focus on individual states. India has 29 states and seven union territories. These are managed by 27 state-level electricity regulators, and two joint commissions (one of which covers the union territories and the other two states). State regulators can use power quality data to monitor power delivery and enforce standards of quality.

Project Description

Initiation of the Open Data Activity

In 2007, the Prayas Energy Group (PEG), an Indian NGO, launched the Electricity Supply Monitoring Initiative (ESMI)[152] to collect real-time power quality information by installing Electricity Supply Monitors (ESM) in various locations in the city of Pune, India. The initiative was part of an ongoing effort by consumer groups and regulators in the Indian state of Maharashtra to monitor power quality after numerous complaints about frequent interruptions and power outages. Having been involved in evidence-based advocacy in the Indian power sector since the early 1990s, Prayas was aware of these issues and created the ESM initiative in line with its "proactive approach to point out gross inefficiencies"[153] and to bring greater transparency and citizen participation into the power sector. The organization has also carried out numerous regulatory and policy interventions in areas such as capacity

---

152 See the ESMI website, http://www.watchyourpower.org/.

153 "Electricity Generation and Supply", Research Areas, Prayas Energy Group, http://www.prayaspune. org/peg/research-areas/electricity-generation-supply.html.

addition, capital expenditure in electricity transmission and distribution, and service delivery to un-electrified consumers.

Initially, there was some skepticism regarding the viability of a technology-based solution for monitoring electricity supply. Concerns included the possibility of mobile network failures (the ESMs transmitted information via cellular networks), the difficulty of finding field volunteers to host the monitoring devices, and the challenges of developing a low-cost monitoring module. In addition, some questions were posed about the need for such a system in a rapidly developing environment of intelligent hardware (e.g., smart meters) and software tools (e.g., Supervisory Control and Data Acquisition, or SCADA, systems, which provide industrial monitoring and control mechanisms for complicated processes like energy distribution).

Over time, however, it became apparent to all stakeholders that there was indeed a pressing need for a transparent and automated data collection system. As of May 2016, ESMI covered 200 locations in 18 states, with 1.5 million hours of power quality[154] monitoring data available.[155] It has also become apparent that the project can play a powerful developmental role, in particular by helping to address certain inequalities in power distribution and consumption. As Shweta Kulkarni, a Research Associate at Prayas and one of those chairing the ESM project, put it:

Most energy sector policies focus on financial viability and economic growth while good governance and equity remain neglected. This often leads to poor supply quality, especially in marginalized neighborhoods. One of the important avenues to change this situation is to improve the transparency and accountability in the sector by creating a publicly-accessible database on supply quality information to show the variations in supply quality between urban and rural areas, different states, distribution companies and areas of economic importance.[156]

Funding

ESMI was one of six finalists in the 2013 Google Social Impact Challenge awards. Each finalist was awarded ₹15 million (roughly $225,000) in seed funding. With the funding, Prayas was able to install power quality monitors

---

154 "Using technology for evidence based feedback to ensure quality electricity access", Electricity Supply Monitoring Initiative (ESMI), *Prayas Energy Group*, https://d2oc0ihd6a5bt.cloudfront.net/wp-content/uploads/sites/837/2016/04/2-Shantanu-Dixit.pdf.

155 Electricity Supply Monitoring Initiative, "Using Technology for Evidence-based Feedback to Ensure Quality Electricity Access," Presentation at ACEF, June 2016, https://d2oc0ihd6a5bt.cloudfront.net/wp-content/uploads/sites/837/2016/04/2-Shantanu-Dixit.pdf.

156 Interview with Shweta Kulkarni, Research Associate, Prayas Energy Group- Pune.

in 60 locations across eight states, including in at least five megacities.[157] That initial coverage has expanded rapidly in the years following.

Demand and Supply of Data Type(s) and Sources

ESMI has made it clear that good power quality management is impossible without real-time data. This is true not only for consumers, who suffer the most direct impact of poor power quality, but also for electricity producers and distributors, and even for regulators. For producers and distributors, real-time power quality data is important in identifying problems in production, transmission and distribution. Such data helps them identify and potentially address shortcomings in their own processes and management. In addition, regulators can use data to hold private companies to account, potentially assessing fines or other penalties for under-performers; overall, data helps regulators ensure the quality of electricity distribution across the country.

The institutional arrangements, in this case, are complex. Demanding accountability regarding power quality in many ways creates an endless cycle of buck-passing from one stakeholder to the other. While grievance and redress mechanisms are enshrined in India's Electricity Act[158], through a legalistic and layered procedural mechanism, use and impact of this process is hardly visible, and normally ends in frustration and subsequently, consumer apathy. A few organizations, however, focus time and resources into research and advocacy on power issues, among them The Energy and Resources Institute[159], monitoring groups like Andra Pradesh's People's Monitoring Group on Electricity Regulation, and Prayas.

It is important to note that some useful open energy data did exist before the advent of the ESMI project. For example, the Ministry of Power[160] and the Central Electricity Authority[161] (CEA) have released several data sets on the national open data portal (data.gov.in). These are available for free download. However, the bulk of this data relates to power generation, supply and demand, and tariff information. For example, the government publishes the number of electrified villages and other information pertaining to its monthly rural electrification mission on a monthly basis. As of late 2016, there is virtually no

157 Prayas (Energy Group), "Electricity Supply Monitoring Initiative (ESMI)," March 2015, http://www.prayaspune.org/peg/publications/item/61-electricity-supply-monitoring-initiative.html.

158 The Electricity Act, 2003, http://www.cercind.gov.in/Act-with-amendment.pdf.

159 The Energy and Resources Institute (TERI), http://www.teriin.org/about-teri.

160 Ministry of Power datasets, data.gov.in, https://data.gov.in/ministrydepartment/ministry-power.

161 Central Electricity Authority datasets, data.gov.in, https://data.gov.in/ministrydepartment/central-electricity-authority.

data available to gauge the quality of power—hence the vital importance of the data being generated by ESMI.

Open Data Use

All the data being used for this project are generated by the ESMs installed by Prayas. ESMs are "smart, connected energy meters" that can accurately measure voltage fluctuations as low as 90V and as high as 320V. The devices use very little power; they simply need to be plugged into a socket and immediately start measuring and transmitting voltage data over 2G/3G networks using an internal SIM card. Currently, three Indian companies supply Prayas with ESMs, each of which also offers a one-year maintenance contract: Syslabs Automation Pvt. Ltd., HelioKraft Technologies Pvt. Ltd, and Altizon Systems.

The data generated by the ESMs is made available for free at a website set up by Prayas[162]. The data is presented in three different forms: (1) minute-by-minute voltage information of all monitored areas; (2) reports that analyze voltage data for each location; and (3) more general analysis of the aggregated data that considers the voltage situation at a regional as well as the national levels. The analysis is often presented in the form of reports, which typically include information about the number and duration of power disruptions (including fluctuating voltages and frequency of supply). A sample report for March 2016 is shown in Figure 1.

Currently, data cannot be downloaded from the portal in bulk, and instead must be downloaded for a single location at a time. Users can view data for a given 31-day period on the website itself, but data for up to 100 days can be downloaded and viewed offline. Downloading of multiple locations or for longer periods is only possible through a user-request made directly to Prayas. Prayas assesses the request and can choose to grant a one-time username and password to access bulk data. Overall, the system requires very little technical knowledge, and the easy availability of data on a digital platform adds a new, automated level of transparency to the industry.

---

162 http://watchyourpower.org.

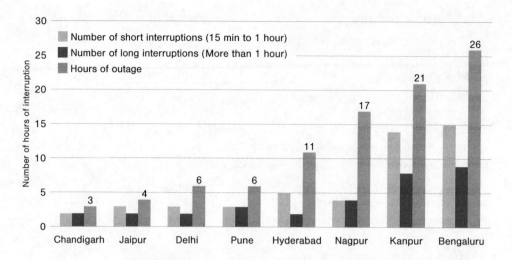

Figure 2. ESMI Sample Analysis of Power Quality

Impact

At the project's inception, Prayas envisioned that several different types of users would be able to use the data and make a positive impact on the power situation in India. Consumer rights groups would be able to implement evidence-based advocacy on power quality. Government regulatory agencies at the country and state levels would be able to use the data to monitor performance of power generation, distribution, and transmission companies, and to identify new policy and legal interventions to improve the power situation. Prayas also expected researchers to use the data to find new mechanisms to improve power quality across the different states, as well as to identify alternative sources and channels for better power service delivery.

While direct evidence of impact is often hard to capture, it is clear that many of these envisioned uses have, to a greater or lesser extent, in fact been borne out. An internal assessment conducted by Shweta Kulkarni, the person within Prayas responsible for the program, claims that ESMI has had an impact in bolstering, consumer satisfaction, improving power quality improvement, and enabling evidence-based advocacy.

However, perhaps no surprise due to the newness of the project and the many stakeholders needed to make meaningful progress action, at this stage we do not yet have documented cases that show the power quality has actually improved as a result of the advocacy mentioned above using ESMI data (outcome-level results) or improved satisfaction of consumers because of improved service (impact level results).

As Dr. Pendse puts it:

"The question is, in the 200 houses that it (ESMs) has been placed in, has the power quality improved? And if it hasn't then at least has someone been made accountable using this evidence? The whole idea is that the use of data should lead to improvement. Otherwise, it isn't working."

Nonetheless, in our assessment of the evidence, through desk research and interviews with key stakeholders, we do identify the following three main areas of impact.

Awareness Raising

ESMI has been used by various individuals and organizations to raise awareness on the serious power quality problem faced by India. One of the most important constituencies for the data are journalists who write on power supply conditions.[163] Several of these journalists have raised the profile of issues related to power quality in India, which are often eclipsed in public discussions by the topic of electricity access.

In addition, Prayas was able to present its project and findings to the CERC's meeting of regulators, also raising their awareness of power quality issues.[164] As a result, some state-level energy regulatory commissions volunteered to use ESMI to monitor the performance levels of utility companies that fell under their jurisdiction. We discuss this issue further below.

Effectiveness of Power Quality Advocacy

There is some clear evidence that data from ESMI has been effective in enhancing the efforts of those advocating for greater power quality. For example, in the Akola Industrial Area, in the state of Maharashtra, data recorded by an ESMI device was presented by a consumer to the local officials of the distribution company. This data proved that the Akola Industrial Area had experienced unplanned interruptions and other power quality problems which caused loss and damage to industrial products and equipment. The local distribution company officials were thus to acknowledge the problem, and to plot out some remedial actions.

---

163 See for example, Manasi Mathkar, "Making Power Supply Data a Tool for Progress," *India Together*, May 6, 2015, http://indiatogether.org/a-easy-to-use-interface-to-view-ones-power-supply-and-consumption-information-via-a-simple-electricity-supply-monitor-esm-environment.

164 "Minutes of the Forty-eighth Meeting of Forum of Regulators (FOR) Held at New Delhi," June 10–11, 2015, http://www.forumofregulators.gov.in/Data/Meetings/Minutes/48.pdf.

The ESM reports available on watchyourpower.org, also helped identify a number of lapses in the system including non-adherence to protocols for load shedding[165] and exposing loopholes in claims of zero power deficit by the government.[166] There has been little evidence that these insights have led to any concrete actions, however. A common challenge across this series of case studies is a lack of institutional responsiveness to act upon insights generated through such data analyses.

Re-emphasizing Power Quality Monitoring at the Regulatory Level

As mentioned, ESMI has helped to raise awareness of power quality problems. While journalists and advocacy groups have been among the most important target groups, ESMI and its data have also succeeded in raising awareness among regulators and more generally putting the issue of power quality back on the regulatory table.

ESMI has been presented at several regulatory meetings, including the Forum of Regulators, the Delhi Electricity Regulatory Commission, and the Joint Electricity Regulatory Commission—each of which plays a different but important role in the national and state-level regulatory framework. In addition, ESMI data has also been presented to private distribution companies and researchers at various forums and seminars. ESMI has also received support from the Joint Electricity Regulatory Commission to install ESMs in the Union Territory of Chandigarh and State of Goa.[167] As of late 2016, Prayas is in dialogue with another regulatory commission and distribution utility which agrees to support deployment of ESMI in their areas of operation.

Risks

As evidenced by the example of ESMI and various other case studies included in this series, open data holds tremendous potential for positive transformation. But as we also see throughout this series, open data also poses certain risks. It is important to understand these risks in order to ensure that open data

---

165 Suggestions and Objections from Prayas regarding the Maharashtra State Electricity Distribution Company Limited's Petition for Multi Year Tariff for FY 2013–14 to FY 201516).

166 Debjoy Sengupta, "Contrary to Government's Claims, Small Towns, Rural Areas Still Suffer from Power Outages," *Economic Times: Energy World*, July 26, 2016, http://energy.economictimes.indiatimes.com/news/power/contrary-to-governments-claims-small-towns-rural-areas-still-suffer-from-power-outages/53393538.

167 "PUNJAB STATE ELECTRICITY REGULATORY COMMISSION SCO NO. 220–221, SECTOR 34-A, CHANDIGARH," Order in Petition No.46 of 2013, http://www.pserc.nic.in/pages/Order%20in%20Petition%20No.46%20of%202013.pdf.

projects are implemented in as safe a manner and in a way that maximizes the potential upside and limits the downside.

The problem of power quality is multifaceted. While power quality data at the consumer level is useful to emphasize a consumer's complaint, as Dr. Priya Jadhav, Associate Professor at the Indian Institute of Technology-Bombay points out, utility companies are often aware that the power they are supplying is low voltage. Data such as ESMI only re-emphasizes what is already known. But because of the poor financial situation that the distribution companies are in, they are in no position to fix the underlying issues that result in poor quality. While identifying the areas where poor quality is persistent is a useful piece of the puzzle, the real solution may lie in understanding why distribution companies suffer losses (electrical as well as financial) and rely repeatedly on government bail-out packages. To cut their losses, distribution companies often do not purchase power from the power generation companies, which explains why many places in power-surplus India suffer so many power outages.

So, the risks of ESMI not succeeding lies at its very strength—that of providing power quality data. Given that there is already a sophisticated way of monitoring power quality and providing the results of this monitoring to the public, the expectation that this will be able to improve power quality supply may not necessarily happen as users will not use the data and advocate for power reform, or that generation, transmission, and distribution companies will not be made to act on the transgressions that the companies committed. Without power supply improvement, ESMI will just become, sadly, a resource useful for researchers and journalists with no real difference to power consumers, especially those at the base of the triangle.

Lessons Learned

The Prayas initiative has brought to the fore why power quality monitoring is important, and it has re-emphasized a problem that has long been ignored by power sector stakeholders. It is now clear that, properly scaled, ESMI has the potential to identify under-performing power companies and regulators, impose a level of accountability in India's power sector, and, most importantly, contribute to better power quality.

This section considers some key lessons learned from the project—lessons that are potentially applicable to other open data projects, in other parts of the world. We split our analysis into a discussion of Enablers (positive lessons) and Barriers (negative lessons); both are equally important to better understanding the impact and implications of a project like ESMI.

91

Enablers

High level vision

The India Smart Grid Task Force,[168] which was set up in 2011, released a "Vision and Roadmap" document in 2013,[169] recognizing that improving reliability and quality of power to consumers was one of the key drivers of the smart grid.[170] Real-time monitoring, automated outage management, and faster restoration are some of the key targets of the Smart Grids in order to improve overall power supply quality across the country. While this was not achieved, ESMI took hold at a time when political and public will to leverage technology to improve power supply was at a peak. Drivers of the effort at Prayas point to this growing priority among the public and institutional stakeholders helped to clear the way for the ESMI initiative. This background also points to the ways in which open data can be used to evaluate performance, but a set of indicators or expressed expectations are important for guiding efforts and evaluating success.

Collaboration between civil society and the private sector

The success of ESMI is in large part attributable to the vision, commitment and hard work of Prayas. It was Prayas' prior work in the field of electricity that led the organization to look for new ways of monitoring power supply quality and enforcing accountability. The existence of a civil society champion such as this one, with experience and contacts in the field, cannot be under-estimated.

Prayas' vision was critical. But its ability to scale ESMI to more than 200 ESM locations was boosted by an external grant from Google. In addition, the existence of private companies able to manufacture the ESMs at low cost, and with a commitment to service the monitors, also helped ensure the success of the project. Overall, it is clear that ESMI was the beneficiary of an existing (if under-exploited) ecosystem of both private sector companies and civil society organizations. This inter-sectoral collaboration offers a powerful model for other similar projects around the world.

---

168 "India Smart Grid Forum Website Launched", Press Information Bureau, Ministry of Power, Government of India, http://pib.nic.in/newsite/PrintRelease.aspx?relid=71397.

169 "Vision Roadmap" National Smart Grid Mission, Ministry of Power, Government of India, http://www.nsgm.gov.in/upload/files/India-Smart-Grid-Vision-and-Roadmap_DSG.pdf.

170 India Smart Grid Forum, *Smart Grid Vision and Roadmap for India*, August 12, 2013, GOI, Ministry of Power, http://www.nsgm.gov.in/upload/files/India-Smart-Grid-Vision-and-Roadmap_DSG.pdf.

Barriers

ESMI has seen some success, but it has not managed to really turn the tide on power quality issues in India. Its lack of wider impact also offers lessons, specifically:

Lack of use of ESMI data from key power stakeholders

Despite enthusiasm among existing users, ESMI's data has not really found a critical mass of users that could help scale the project and hold power sector stakeholders accountable. In particular, while journalists and advocacy groups have shown interest in the data, there has not been equal interest shown by consumers—citizens or corporates. This can be attributed to several factors, like the need for more awareness building efforts. The apathy may also have something do with a general sense of hopelessness and disempowerment among consumers; given the scale and long-standing nature of India's power problems, consumers may not hold out much hope for a solution such as ESMI's. Addressing such shortcomings may require greater coordination with intermediaries to spread awareness and confidence, as well as a concerted effort to introduce consumers to the very real potential of open data—both within the electricity sector in particular, but also more generally.

Lukewarm reception from state regulators

While Prayas has been relatively successful in presenting ESMI to power regulators, it is not clear that the willingness of regulators to listen and learn about the project is accompanied by the actual will to use it. Indeed, to date, only one state regulatory agency has actually developed a concrete plan to implement ESMI. This lack of regulatory will (if not interest) suggests that the inherent value of a project may not be enough to get it adopted and that Prayas needs to find new forms of leverage on regulators—e.g., through enhanced public or political pressure.

Lack of capacity on GTD companies to solve power quality problems

As earlier stated, power quality is a problem with a myriad of causes. ESMI data is only able to systematize the provision of data on already-known symptoms of the problem. But the deeper causes—why power companies are not able to supply quality power and why regulators are not able to provide penalties as well as incentives—remain unaddressed, and are unlikely to be solved through this type of initiative, regardless of the level of uptake.

Looking Forward

For Prayas, the existing 200 monitors deployed in ESMI represent just a starting point. The organization is also in the process of expanding the reach of ESMI through partnerships with the public sector and other stakeholders interested in power supply quality monitoring.

Sustainability

Prayas believes that the sustainability of ESMI will depend in large part on collaboration and partnerships. Initially, Prayas faced significant challenges in developing its technical solution for remote monitoring of supply quality, owing to lack of in-house expertise in hardware and software development. But it initiated a dialogue with other stakeholders and shared information on the type of technology that it wants to develop to the tech community who are also willing to contribute to and support their goal. In this case, India-wide implementation is only possible if state regulators become convinced of ESMI's value. Thus, Prayas is very actively reaching out to regulators and presenting in the regular regulators' forum so that more support in scaling up and adoption can be gathered.

Replicability

India's ESMI has generated considerable global interest. In fact, Prayas is now in discussions with different stakeholders to pilot ESMI in other countries. Discussion with stakeholders from Kenya, Tajikistan and Tanzania are currently ongoing. In addition, the first overseas pilot implementation is already happening in Indonesia, with the Institute for Essential Service Reform based in Jakarta as local partner.

Conclusion

The main goal of ESMI is to make available reliable data on the quality of electricity supply. Consumers, civil society organizations, researchers, regulatory commissions and other concerned actors can use this data to increase the accountability of electric utilities. The actual performance of companies can be compared to the standards of performance prescribed by regulatory commissions. In addition, utilities' capital expenditures on improvements in supply quality can be scrutinized to verify whether supply quality has actually improved as a result of the investments. The openness of the collected data also enables multiple stakeholders to verify the government's many goals for rural electrification, notably whether villages receive their mandated six hours of daily supply. Overall, the data generated and opened by ESMI can create greater pressure on regulators and utilities to become more transparent, more accountable and more efficient. The project offers great social and developmental potential.

In order for ESMI to truly reach its potential, stakeholders need to know that the data exists and is accessible. This remains a challenge, and a work in progress. For all its initially impressive results, scaling up ESMI will require a concerted effort to raise awareness about the possibilities offered by open data among average citizens, corporate consumers, and government regulators. In addition, ESMI could benefit from greater political support and public will to ensure that regulators actually use its data and take advantage of the many benefits it does potentially offer. The opportunity—for India's electricity sector, and more generally for its social and economic development is real; the coming years will tell whether Prayas and other stakeholders can seize that opportunity.

CHAPTER 7

Open Development Cambodia

Opening information on development efforts

Michael P. Canares, Andrew Young and Stefaan Verhulst

Summary

Cambodia has shown impressive improvements in political, economic, and social conditions over the last 10 years. The country has managed to end long years of civil war, grow the economy by at least 7 percent annually, and improve health and education outcomes, especially for children. Despite this, there are underlying weaknesses in Cambodia's political institutions that constrain its economic, social, and cultural development. These include a growing opacity in decision-making and a lack of information regarding different development efforts sweeping across the country. Open Development Cambodia (ODC) was born out of a desire to address these issues. Its goal is to provide "access to current and historical information about Cambodia's development trends in an online 'open data' platform compiling freely available data from a wide range of public sources." Launched in 2011, ODC's online portal (https://opendevelopmentcambodia.net/data/) has been instrumental in providing information to different users from government, civil society, media, and the public sector.

Context and Background

Problem Focus/Country Context

Cambodia has shown impressive improvements in political, economic, and social conditions over the last 10 years. The country has managed to end long years of civil war, grow the economy by at least 7 percent annually, and improve health and education outcomes, especially for children. Despite this, there are underlying weaknesses in Cambodia's political institutions that constrain its economic, social, and cultural development. Entrenched patterns of political patronage limit governance reforms; the government's intent to be more transparent is overshadowed by a growing opacity in decision-making in governmental transactions; civil society's ability to question and hold government officials accountable remains constricted; and corruption is still prevalent.

Many of these issues could be addressed by increased public access to governmental information. However, Cambodia does not have a freedom of information law, and many legal provisions restrict information disclosure. For example, in the exploration of natural resources, where corruption is reported to be rampant, a legal provision treats applications, reports, plans and notices as confidential. In addition, civil society organizations have questioned the government's failure to disclose details about the national budget for outside scrutiny.[171] In general, there is limited availability of governance information in Cambodia. Even when information is available, it is stored in formats that prohibit easy sharing and re-use. In addition, the little information that does exist online is disorganized, not linked, and hard to locate.

Open Data in Cambodia

In 2015, Open Knowledge Index rated Cambodia as 12 percent open[172]—a rating that means there is very little data available online and in open format. Key critical datasets such as company registers, land ownership, national maps, government spending, national statistics, and weather forecasts are not available online.

To date, there exists no central government repository for government information in the country, and the government does not implement any comprehensive open data initiative. For example, there exists no national directive to disclose government data on websites (though a few agencies publish some datasets on their own initiative). Some encouraging signs are evident in the birth of a few civil society organizations now advocating for open data in the country. Cambodia is one of many countries studied as part of this series where civil society and international organizations stepped up to drive the open data movement as a result of governmental failure to provide

---

171 Erin Handley and Bun Sengkong, "Civil Society, Opposition Criticise Budget's Opacity," *Phnom Penh Post*, November 4, 2016, http://www.phnompenhpost.com/national/civil-society-opposition-criticise-budgets-opacity.

172 Open Knowledge, "Global Open Data Index: Cambodia," http://index.okfn.org/place/cambodia/.

easy access to important datasets. Some of the increasingly active civil society actors in Cambodia include Open Data Cambodia (ODC), the founder of the project under study here, and discussed further below; Open Knowledge, a global open data non-profit organization; the local offices of the World Bank; and a few transparency organizations and international non-governmental organizations advocating for more inclusive information disclosure practices.

KEY ACTORS

Key Data Providers

ODC gathers data from at least five major sources—government, non-governmental, private sector, academics, and from internal local newsrooms and major Cambodian newspapers. ODC gathers data from these various sources (e.g. from websites or printed documents), and converts them into open formats to be published in the ODC portal.

Key Data Users and Intermediaries

ODC acts as an aggregator of the different data and information obtained from these various sources. Its portal has a broad range of users, with the largest category coming from the academic community and non-governmental organizations. Professors and students, for example, cite ODC's database in their research papers, journal articles, and books. Some international non-governmental organizations use map layers and other related geo-referenced documents to analyze development projects. In addition, members of the media also use the data to analyze development trends, projects and patterns.

Intended Beneficiaries

ODC's intended beneficiaries, besides the researchers and academics who directly use the data, can be grouped into four categories. First, government agencies or policy makers who may use the data analyzed by media or NGOs in crafting their policies or in conducting development planning. Second, the business sector, which benefits from looking at maps and geo-referenced data on natural assets and resources, as well as demographic data that may be useful in business decision-making. Third, civil society and community-based organizations use the datasets on the portal for their for development work or to advocate for greater transparency. Finally, average citizens who may be able to access the data from ODC or from the outputs of intermediaries mentioned above.

Project Description

Initiation of the Open Data Activity

Open Development Cambodia (ODC) was born out of a need felt by local grassroots land and natural resource activists working in Cambodia. Terry Pernell, a long-time American resident in Cambodia who worked with different grassroots organizations, including the East West Management Institute (EWMI), a civil society organization seeking "to build accountable, capable and transparent institutions," found that getting access to useful data in Cambodia was often difficult if not impossible. Accessing government data, in particular, was a challenge, and meant going from one office to another, dealing with bureaucracy at each step.[173] As noted, Cambodia does not have a central repository of government data that one can physically visit or consult online.

ODC was developed with the goal of aggregating information about the country from different sources—not only government, but also international organizations, civil society groups, private sector, universities, academic institutions, and individual researchers who had been studying the country for decades. The vision was to create a central repository, to be hosted online, that would consist of raw data, independently collected, edited, and aggregated. The group that would manage it needed to be independent and without political bias—its main role would be to provide information and let those who seek data and information use it for their own purposes. The site was officially launched in August 2011. After almost four years of being implemented as a project of EWMI, it became registered as a non-governmental organization in August 2015.[174]

The platform now houses data-driven information on three central topic areas: Environment and Land (e.g., disaster and emergency response and extractive industries); Economy (e.g., industry and labor) and People (e.g., aid and development and law and judiciary). As of early 2017, raw data is directly available for download on laws, policies and agreements, while other topics feature detailed Wikipedia-like write-ups aggregating a diversity primary datasets, charts and graphs, policies and other relevant information. ODC also offers a number of interactive maps that allow users to deploy and combine layers built from, for example, agriculture, demographic and infrastructure data. It also provides a mapping toolkit and guide using the Harvard WorldMap interface.

---

173 Kyle James, "Cambodia sets pace with open data," *DW Akademie*, December 20, 2013, http://onmedia. dw-akademie.com/english/?p=16857.

174 Interview with Thy Try, Executive Director, Open Development Cambodia, and Penhleak Chan, Regional Network and Partnership Support Manager of EWMI, November 17, 2016.

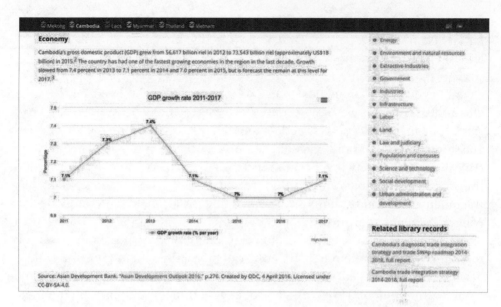

Figure 1. Information on the ODC Economy and Commerce Topic Page

Funding

Initiated by EWMI in 2011 as a part of its USAID-funded Program on Rights and Justice, ODC received its first grant from the Swedish Program for ICT in Developing Regions (SPIDER) in 2012. With a total budget of around 230,000 USD, SPIDER contributed slightly more than 55,000 USD "to develop the existing Proof of Concept site (http://ww.opendevelopmentcambodia.net) into a fully functional open data online platform that will facilitate a network of civil society actors to share, analyze, and publish their data in a coordinated, egalitarian, and secure way."[175] Since then, ODC has received funding support from other USAID-funded projects, American Jewish World Service, Open Society Foundation, and other funders.

Demand and Supply of Data Type(s) and Sources

ODC collects data based on what is already available in the "public domain." By public domain, ODC means data that are generally available for public access and not specifically prohibited by law to be shared widely. Its sources of data include (1) Royal Gazettes, (2) official websites of governmental institutions, (3) published reports from government, (4) Developers/Company websites, (5)

---

175 SPIDER, "Open Development Cambodia: Promoting transparency through open data," http://spidercenter.org/2.31936/project-overview/open-development-cambodia-promoting-transparency-through-open-data-1.149787.

information released to the Media (i.e. news and press releases), (6) published reports from NGOs, and (7) academic research reports and other reports from NGOs. ODC researchers collect the data, submit it to editors for review, and convert this into open formats for publication on its portal.

Open Data Use

While ODC draws information from a variety of sources, open government data is a key driver of the sites offerings. The interactive maps on the site, the raw datasets available for download and the information on topics like the quality of Cambodian governance, environmental policy and construction codes would not be possible without government data being made accessible.

Figure 2. ODC's Open Data Portal

Impact

ODC's mission is to "strengthen public knowledge and analysis of development issues to enable constructive dialogue between public, private, civil society, and international sectors to support development of effective policies and practices bearing on sustainable resource use."[176] The organization has been striving to achieve these goals now for some three years. Although always difficult to clearly measure impact, particularly for relatively young projects, our research

---

176 Interview with Thy Try, Executive Editor, Open Development Cambodia, and Penhleak Chan, Regional Network and Partnership Support Manager of EWMI, November 17, 2016.

indicates at least four ways in which ODC has taken early steps toward having a concrete effect on Cambodian society and development.

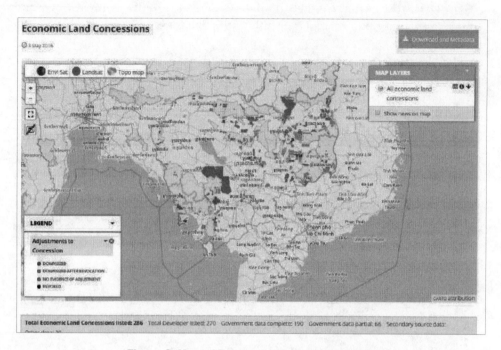

Figure 3. Map of Economic Land Concessions

Seeding Interest Cambodian Open Data

The ODC portal is gaining increasing attention from a number of different kinds of users. As of October 2016, it has an average of 70,000 pageviews per month. Since the launch of the portal, a total of 35,000 users per month, mostly from within Cambodia, have visited the site, with approximately 80 percent being unique visitors. The ODC team based in Phnom Penh has received numerous personal inquiries and interview appointments from journalists and researchers, and the portal has been increasingly quoted as a source in both local and international research publications and media reports.[177]

According to Thy Try, ODC's Executive Director,

"Quite often, maps attract the most attention from media and GIS persons while the database tracking the investment and concessions projects along with references is

---

177 Interview with Thy Try, Executive Director, Open Development Cambodia, and Penhleak Chan, Regional Network and Partnership Support Manager of EWMI, November 17, 2016.

usually used by advocates and workers from NGOs and community-based organization. In this sense, it seems that the tracking database on specific development projects is gradually helping the work of these organizations. However, this requires key persons of the communities to have a better understanding of the development trends and data/ data tools in order to use it with the most impact, either through their own direct work or through their knowledge sharing with their community members."[178]

Journalists from the outlets like *The Guardian*,[179] *Tech President*,[180] and the *New York Times*,[181] among others, have written about ODC's efforts and/or drawn upon the data and information it makes available. They also include agencies such as the United Nations, The Mekong River Commission, and the International Land Coalition. In addition, ODC says that government agencies have also used the site – perhaps not surprising given its focus on bringing together useful datasets from across sectors, not just data already held by the government.

Strengthening Issue Advocacy through Collaboration

ODC has played an important role in strengthening advocacy on issues surrounding open data, a role whose impact has been particularly evident in the way land is granted by the government. Before the emergence of ODC, civil society advocates that monitored the government's grant of land concessions collected their own data and did not coordinate with each other. This fragmentation resulted in inconsistencies in the data presented by these different actors, a weakening of advocacy messages, and a lack of attention from the concerned government agencies. ODC facilitated the process of data sharing, cleaned the data to get rid of inconsistencies, and provided the data on its secure, centralized platform.[182] With a unified basis and voice, coupled with international media coverage and pressure, the government postponed the grant of land concessions to the private sector and hastened the grant of social

---

178 Interview with Thy Try, Executive Director, Open Development Cambodia, November 24, 2016.

179 Naly Pilorge, Virak Yeng, Vuthy Eang, "Think of Cambodia before you add sugar to your coffee," *The Guardian*, July 12, 2013, https://www.theguardian.com/commentisfree/2013/jul/12/cambodia-sugar-eu-policy.

180 Faine Greenwood, "As the Internet Raises Civic Voices in Cambodia, a Struggle Brews Over Net Control," *Tech President*, March 27, 2013, http://techpresident.com/news/wegov/23659/internet-civic-voices-cambodia-struggle-net-control/.

181 Julia Wallace, "Development and Its Discontent," *The New York Times*, April 12, 2013, https://latitude.blogs.nytimes.com/2013/04/12/development-and-its-discontent/?_r=0.

182 Nicolas Mansfield, "Open Development Cambodia: How open data can promote land use transparency," *Devex*, September 20, 2013, https://www.devex.com/news/open-development-cambodia-how-open-data-can-promote-land-use-transparency-81848.

land concessions to the poor. While these results cannot be directly attributed to ODC, it is quite apparent that ODC contributed to the process.

Increasing Access to Important, Previously Inaccessible Data

In Cambodia, Environmental Impact Assessment (EIA) reports are not made publicly available. EIAs are required by law, but several agencies do not seem to place importance on the practice. ODC made available EIA reports on its portal and has made an analysis of currently available EIA data. The resultant increase in public awareness around the topic, particularly among civil society actors, has the potential to push the government to take further action, though there has not been clear evidence that they have done so at this point.

Additionally, natural resource data, including information related to agriculture—one of Cambodia's competitive advantages—is hard to come by. ODC had numerous requests in the past to get data on soil type published on its portal and was able to do so recently. This information was used by the private sector, more particularly by the Cambodian Rice Federation, to determine potential growth areas in crop production. Anecdotal evidence also shows that resource data at the ODC portal has been used by international organizations, such as the World Bank and ANZ.

Risks

Since its inception, ODC has faced numerous challenges, among them lack of support and even resistance from government agencies and certain private sector players. For example, when ODC published forest cover data in 2013, the Forestry Administration, the governmental body under the Ministry of Agriculture, Forestry, and Fisheries, refuted the ODC data that showed a significant decrease in forest cover—from 72 percent in 1973 to 46 percent in 2013—and alleged that the organization did not have a credible applied methodology on forest classification. Attempts to discredit ODC, such as this one, will likely happen again, especially when government is harmed by the narratives that arise from the analysis of sensitive data.

As ODC transitions to a registered civil society organization in Cambodia, it may face several challenges brought about by the adoption of new laws that could potentially impose restrictions on ODC's work. For example, the Law on Association and Non-Governmental Organizations requires all NGOs to report their activities to the government—resulting in additional workloads and restricting freedom of movement via surveillance. Also, the Sub-Decree on Publication of Maps and the use of Produced Maps introduces a new requirement that any organization which produces maps must get a license from the government. Also, a draft law on Cyber Crime can potentially harm some of the activities of ODC. All of these represent commonly seen risks for an organization seeking to introduce greater transparency and work against vested interests. In a sense, the scale of the risks (and opposition) is also indication of the project's success or at least potential.

Lessons Learned

Several important lessons with wider applicability emerge from this particular case study. These can broadly be categorized by considering the key enablers of the project, as well as the most important barriers or challenges to its success.

Enablers

Trust of different actors in ODC's work and capacity

ODC's ability to tap into an existing ecosystem greatly accelerated its move from idea to implementation. The fact that ODC started as a project under EWMI, and with the support of several international donors, strengthened its reputation as an organization that has the capacity to deliver on its commitments—its vision and mission. The "independent" stance of ODC, presenting the data and factual information it aggregates without necessarily attaching itself to any political agenda or ideology, worked both on the part of government and other actors. In general, government stakeholders do not project animosity against ODC and even use its data, despite initial questions on data integrity. Advocacy groups also view ODC as an independent organization, and not necessarily a mechanism of government.

This increased trust from different actors also made possible ODC's ability to get grants to fund its work and operations.

Volunteerism of different actors in the open data space

Like any new technology that relies on the generosity not only of donors but also of volunteers, ODC benefitted from different individuals who participate in ODC's efforts on proactive disclosure without costs, and from organizations and universities which send interns to ODC to assist them in research and editing processes. ODC has a very lean team—nine people dabbling in work on research, editing, infographics, mapping, writing, finance, among others—and

105

in order to increase breadth and depth in its work, it has to advertise volunteer opportunities and take in as many volunteers as necessary.

Collaboration among different actors from within Cambodia

As earlier indicated, ODC relied on different data sources to be able to publish quality and comprehensive information in its portal. Non-governmental organizations, advocacy groups, researchers, universities, and government agencies shared data with ODC for it to clean, edit, and publish. Without the collaboration of these actors, data at the ODC portal would be lesser in scope than its current state, and probably less meaningful to the user.

Lack of information fuels the need for this collaboration. Currently, more and more people are interested in data on land, water, and forest governance and have been asking ODC to make these datasets accessible to the public.

ODC also participated in shorter-term collaborations with Columbia University's School of International and Public Affairs (SIPA) toward developing a greater understanding of international development efforts in Cambodia.[183] A partnership with Save Cambodia's Wildlife produced the 2014 Atlas of Cambodia, which provides detailed information and maps on the "changing spatial structures of Cambodia's geography as well as its economic and social development, especially natural resource and environment management"[184] – the elements found in the Atlas are downloadable on ODC and available as layers on its interactive maps.

Barriers

Format and Data Quality

ODC acknowledges that data and information in the public domain are difficult to obtain as sometimes some data have strong restrictions in terms redistribution, reproduction, and reuse. Several of the government data sources are inconsistent, not up to date, and in closed formats (e.g., PDFs). According to Penhleak Chan, Regional Network and Partnership Support Manager of EWMI's Open Development Initiative:

> *"One challenge is that many of the documents released by the government into the public domain are not machine-readable, and so digitizing and analyzing them is*

---

183 "Columbia SIPA," Open Development Cambodia, https://opendevelopmentcambodia.net/about/partnerships/columbia-sipa/.

184 "Save Cambodia's Wildlife," Open Development Cambodia, https://opendevelopmentcambodia.net/about/partnerships/save-cambodias-wildlife-scw/.

very time-consuming. Another challenge is that data and information are not always consistent so there's a need to have a neutral and independent review team that makes sense of the data. For instance, in a project where we looked at reports on rubber production in Cambodia, the numbers provided by two different ministries on the same indicator greatly differed."[185]

These limitations make the work of ODC more difficult and resource-intensive.

Low data literacy on the part of local users

As earlier indicated, the ones that benefitted largely from information availability are organizations that already have the capacity to access and use data—international media outfits and international non-governmental organizations. This is largely because there is low data literacy on the part of local users. To address this, ODC has been doing several capacity building trainings across the country but, given the lack of resources, the ability to cover different sectors across the country is limited.

Looking Forward

ODC believes that its work likely has impacted indirectly on the Cambodian government's recent policies and reforms in the forestry sector and land concessions. This can be observed in the growing number of established natural protected areas, the development of the protected areas management plan, the introduction of eco-tourism, the downsizing of around 1 million hectares of economic land concessions from inactive investors and granting land ownership to the poor through social land concessions. These recent events have inspired ODC to work even harder to make more data more accessible to the public and to those stakeholders in need.[186]

But ODC acknowledges that there are significant challenges to achieving these results—especially with the increasingly limited space for civil society within Cambodian political processes. As ODC wants to maintain its independent stance, it relies largely on other organizations that will take the data that ODC is able to demystify and proactively disclose into processes that influence the way development in Cambodia unfolds. This can be civil society organizations, advocacy groups, or community-based organizations interested

---

185 "DW Global Media Forum: Open Data in Cambodia," DW Akademie, July 3, 2014, http://www.dw.com/en/dw-global-media-forum-open-data-in-cambodia/a-17755220.

186 Interview with Thy Try, Executive Director, Open Development Cambodia, and Penhleak Chan, Regional Network and Partnership Support Manager of EWMI, November 17, 2016.

in particular issues, such as natural resource governance. It can be transparency watch groups that seek to unravel corruption in the public sector. It can even be champions from within government that want to see a more sustainable development model for the country.[187]

Within these processes, ODC has to play at least two roles—that of an advocate for greater openness in public-interest data, and that of a resource institution that builds the capacity of local actors to use data more effectively in decision-making. ODC is committed to ensuring that data-based decision-making processes are institutionalized not only within the halls of government but also in every community in the country.

Conclusion

While Cambodia's open data ecosystem is still in its infancy, Open Development Cambodia is acting as an important leader in pushing the country toward a more transparent, collaborative and data-driven approach to governance. Beyond demonstrating the importance of making important government data available to the public – from open contracts and other legal information to census and demographic data to insight into shifts in forest cover in the country – ODC makes clear the value of taking a broader view of what types of data could be beneficial if made more open and accessible. Rather than relying strictly on government data for its offerings of data and maps, ODC, from the start, sought to aggregate relevant information from across sectors to provide a more multi-faceted view of topics of concern to Cambodians. As the site and Cambodian open data ecosystem continue to mature, we will gain a better sense of whether ODC's still largely aspirational impact will have a larger positive effect on public life in the country.

---

187 Interview with Thy Try, Executive Director, Open Development Cambodia, and Penhleak Chan, Regional Network and Partnership Support Manager of EWMI, November 17, 2016.

CHAPTER 8

Uganda's iParticipate

Open data for achieving better health outcomes

Michael P. Canares, Andrew Young and Stefaan Verhulst

Summary

Uganda has among the worst systems for providing health care in the world, and, as a result, among the poorest health outcomes for its citizens. Several factors contribute significantly to poor health outcomes—a lack of health workers to attend to the needs of a growing population; pervasive corruption in the health service sector; and a lack of data (e.g., related to disease prevalence, health care service delivery indicators, and health outcomes) that could be used for informed judgment and prioritization.

In 2011, the Collaboration on International ICT Policy for East and Southern Africa (CIPESA) began promoting the use of ICT to monitor governance and service delivery in Uganda. The project was funded by the Swedish Program for ICT in Developing Regions (SPIDER).[188] Building on the experience and networks developed by CIPESA through this earlier project, the iParticipate project seeks to leverage the use of open government data to enable citizen participation and more accountable governance. CIPESA used open data available from government portals and sources to analyze service delivery and public investments, especially but not exclusively in the health sector.

The most tangible outcome of this initiative has been better training for civil society organizations and journalists in using data to advance health care advocacy. This has led to increased public awareness about poor public investments in health. Beyond this, however, there is little evidence of tangible improvements in health care service delivery. The initiative has encountered

---

188 Swedish Program for ICT in Developing Regions website, http://spidercenter.org/.

numerous challenges—including those related to technical infrastructure and low ICT capacity—and the future of iParticipate remains somewhat unclear.

Context and Background

Problem Focus / Country Context

According to the World Health Organization (WHO), Uganda has among the worst health service delivery provisions in the world, resulting in poor health outcomes for its citizens. The country has among the lowest life expectancy (54 years in 2015) and highest mortality rates (344 in 2013) in the world.[189] As of 2015, one in every 300 births ends a mother's life, and one of every 30 children born will not be able to survive beyond one year.[190] Communicable diseases, especially tuberculosis, claim the largest portion of lives in the country. HIV prevalence is high, with at least 1.5 million people affected, and the country is among those with the highest new cases of HIV/AIDS globally.[191]

Several factors contribute to such poor health outcomes. First, there is a serious dearth of health workers who can attend to the needs of a growing population. A recent study pointed, for instance, to the very low ratio of health care providers to population in the country, coupled and aggravated by an insufficient budget.[192] Most medical personnel are concentrated in urban areas, to the disadvantage of patients in rural areas. Another problem is pervasive corruption in the health service sector—manifested in a variety of ways, including paid workers failing to arrive at work on time with no fear of repercussion[193] and the misappropriation of public funds for construction of health service facilities.[194]

---

189 African Health Observatory, "Comprehensive Analytical Profile: Uganda," WHO, http://www.aho.afro. who.int/profiles_information/index.php/Uganda:Index.

190 African Health Observatory, "Uganda: Factsheets of health statistics, 2016," http://www.aho.afro.who. int/profiles_information/images/f/fb/Uganda-Statistical_Factsheet.pdf.

191 AVERT, "HIV and AIDS in Uganda," http://www.avert.org/professionals/hiv-around-world/sub-saharan-africa/uganda.

192 Merlin L. Willcox, et al., "Human Resources for Primary Health Care in sub-Saharan Africa: Progress or Stagnation?" *Human Resources for Health*, 13, 2015, https://human-resources-health.biomedcentral.com/articles/10.1186/s12960-015-0073-8.

193 Simon Peter Ogwang, "Fighting Corruption, Empowering People in Uganda's Health Service," Transparency International Blog, July 11, 2012, http://blog.transparency.org/2012/07/11/community-empowerment-in-uganda-using-icts-for-better-health-service-delivery/.

194 Act!onaid, *Corruption and the Service Delivery Tragedy in Uganda: Stories from the eastern leg of the anti-corruption caravan*, Act!onaid, September 2014, http://www.actionaid.org/sites/files/actionaid/anti-corruption_report.pdf.

A lack of data also hampers the quality of service delivery. Studies point in particular to a shortage of data related to disease prevalence,[195] service delivery indicators, and health outcomes.[196] While some forms of health data are collected, these are largely in paper formats and not shared publicly. The Ugandan Ministry of Health Website,[197] which is supposedly the repository of publicly accessible data on health in the country, publishes all information as PDF files. The data is often insufficiently granular to contribute to useful analysis and access to much information, including health human resource data, is often restricted.

Open Data in Uganda

According to the 2015 Open Data Barometer,[198] Uganda ranked 70th out of 92 countries surveyed. The government has made some efforts to use information technology and e-government practices to improve the delivery of public services. In addition, several of its ministries, especially health, environment, and national statistics, have practiced proactive disclosure of data online, though in separate, unlinked websites, and in incompatible formats that make the data difficult to use.

In 2015, the World Bank report on open data readiness in Uganda[199] emphasized that while the country is well-positioned to implement an open data initiative, its ability to actually do so will depend on several issues related to policy, data capacity, and civic engagement. To date, there is no policy which mandates disclosure of government data and protects privacy. In addition, there is a definite lack of technology skills on the part of government employees. Citizens are also limited in their ability to access data by poor broadband access and low data literacy.

A review[200] funded by the Indigo Trust, a funding organization focused on transparency and accountability in Sub-Saharan Africa, found that there exist more than 10 data disclosure mechanisms within the Ugandan

---

195 Jeremy I. Schwartz, et al., "Toward Reframing Health Service Delivery in Uganda: The Uganda initiative for integrated management of non-communicable diseases,"*Global Health Action*, 8, 2015, http://www.globalhealthaction.net/index.php/gha/article/view/26537.

196 African Health Observatory, "Uganda: Health information, research, evidence and knowledge," WHO, http://www.aho.afro.who.int/profiles_information/index.php/Uganda:Health_information,_research,_evidence_and_knowledge.

197 Ministry of Health, Republic of Uganda website, http://www.health.go.ug/.

198 Open Data Barometer, "Rankings and Data: Uganda," http://opendatabarometer.org/data-explorer/?_year=2015&indicator=ODB&open=UGA.

199 World Bank, *Open Data Readiness Assessment: Uganda*, World Bank, http://opendatatoolkit.worldbank.org/docs/odra/odra_uganda.pdf.

200 Development Research and Training, *Unlocking the Potential of a More Harnessed Partnership among Open Data Actors in Uganda*, Indigo Trust, November 2015, https://indigotrust.files.wordpress.com/2016/02/drt-indigo-trust-uganda-final-report.pdf.

government, but that these cover only a few government agencies, namely public finance, water and environment and national statistics. The absence of a centralized open government data portal prompted several actors to publish data relevant to Ugandan governance and public life in different portals like data.ug (supported by UNICEF), uganda.opendataforafrica.org (supported by the African Development Bank) and several other sector-focused initiatives initiated by civil society organizations, international agencies, and academia. The tendency of actors from non-governmental sectors to step up to fill open data gaps left by governments is a common theme across this series of case studies.

Data Collection and Disclosure in the Ugandan Health Care System

Uganda's Ministry of Health is responsible for one of the important sectors in the country. Its primary mandate is to formulate policies related to health, manage partnerships, resource mobilization, capacity building, and quality control on health service delivery, as well as to monitor and evaluate overall health sector performance across the country and at every level of government.

Health care provision in Uganda is undertaken by both public and private actors. Public health service providers have a decentralized structure which consists of national referral hospitals, semi-autonomous regional referral hospitals, and a well-established District Health System under the leadership of the District Directorate of Health Services in each of the country's 111 districts. The intent behind decentralization was to make services reach even the most remote communities, and health centers in the country are broken up into four categories (ranging from the most rudimentary facilities, Health Center 1, to the more advanced, Health Center 4). Health service delivery is based on a referral system, with cases escalated up the categories depending on their level of complexity and facilities required.

Private sector health service provision is offered by a number of actors. These include facility-based private providers, not for profit (PNFP) providers, non-facility based PNFPs, private health practitioners, and traditional medical service providers. Facility-based PNFPs are those who own or operate their own hospitals and clinics; an example of a non-facility based PNFP would be an NGO offering medical services. Private health practitioners refer to those that provide primary and secondary level health services and include a wide range of actors, such as diagnostic centers, private medical and dental clinics, and pharmacies.

The capacity of Ugandans to seek treatment from private sector health service providers, without having to go through the long process of referral in the government system, is affected by their financial capacity and geographic location. In some areas, especially in rural Uganda, there are no private PNFPs or private health practitioners. For residents of these areas, many of whom also lack the financial capacity to pay for private health care, government health centers are the only option (they may also submit themselves for treatment to traditional herbalists or other "informal" healers without formal training).

The government collects health care data from both the public and private sectors (though it does not collect information from the informal sector). The data collected is largely stored in paper-based formats,[201] based on a set of standardized forms issued by the Ministry of Health (MoH). Aggregation of data is done at the level of MOH, through a Health Management Information System (HMIS[202]) which aims to ensure timely aggregation, storage and retrieval of health information. Data quality is largely (and often negatively) affected by the capacity of lower-level administrative agencies to collect and report data in an effective manner. As a WHO report puts it: "lower administrative levels chronically lack the capacity to capture and report vital events such as community births and deaths."[203] Another study[204] reported that data collected regarding inpatient, outpatient, and health coverage indicators was less than 85 percent complete.

The MOH has made several noteworthy attempts to address these issues. For example, in 2010 the MOH launched the Human Resource for Health Information System (HRHIS),[205] a database platform developed in partnership with USAID that paved the way for comprehensively identifying staffing gaps down to the district level. The MOH has also sought to address data shortcomings by increasing the budget for human resources in public health centers.[206] Despite improvements, however, most of the data collected is not available to the public, and even when available, is difficult for ordinary citizens to understand. HMIS data, for example, requires registration for access and is available only to authorized users through a dashboard. HRHIS data, on the other hand, can be downloaded in spreadsheets format, but needs a trained user for the spreadsheets to be understood.

---

201 African Health Observatory, "Uganda: Health information, research, evidence and knowledge, analytical summary," WHO, http://www.aho.afro.who.int/profiles_information/index.php/Uganda:Health_information,_research,_evidence_and_knowledge#Analytical_summary.

202 Ministry of Health, Republic of Uganda website, http://hmis2.health.go.ug/#/.

203 African Health Observatory, "Uganda: Overview of the Flows of Information," WHO, http://www.aho.afro.who.int/profiles_information/index.php/Uganda:Overview_of_the_flows_of_information.

204 Vincent Michael Kiberu, et al., "Strengthening District-based Health Reporting through the District Health Management Information Software System: The Ugandan experience," *BMC Medical Informatics and Decision Making*, 14, 2014, http://bmcmedinformdecismak.biomedcentral.com/articles/10.1186/1472-6947-14-40.

205 Human Resources for Health Information Systems website, http://hris.health.go.ug/reports/.

206 Jillian Larsen, *Uganda: Winning human resources for health*, International Budget Partnership, December 2015, http://www.internationalbudget.org/wp-content/uploads/case-study-full-uganda-human-resources-for-health-2015.pdf.

KEY ACTORS

Key Data Providers

The Ugandan government, through different portals, makes accessible the majority of data used for iParticipate. In particular, open data provided through the portal by the Ministry of Health plays an important enabling role. The project also leverages some limited data from private sector health providers, demonstrating the potential for more cross-sector data collaborative arrangements.

Key Data Users and Intermediaries

Established under the United Kingdom Department for International Development-funded Catalysing Access to Information and Communications Technologies in Africa (CATIA) initiative, the Collaboration on International ICT Policy in East and Southern Africa (CIPESA) is a civil society organization that "facilitates the use of ICT in support of development and poverty reduction."[207] CIPESA's iParticipate project was established with funding from the Swedish Program for ICT in Developing Regions (SPIDER), a resource center working across sectors to leverage ICTs for development purposes. SPIDER, in particular, seeks to enable "the collaboration and sharing of experience between different actors in the field to reach better development results."[208]

Intended Beneficiaries

The iParticipate initiative aims to catalyze the use of ICT in citizen's engagement and participation in governance.[209] The project intends to build the capacity primarily of journalists and civil society organizations to use ICT tools in increasing public awareness on government issues, especially related to health, as well as potential solutions. iParticipate trains NGOs and journalists to conduct more data-driven analyses of the government information so that they can use these skills to advocate for public service reform, with the view that ordinary Ugandans will enjoy better services in the future.

Project Description

Initiation of the Open Data Activity

In 2011, the Collaboration on International ICT Policy for East and Southern Africa (CIPESA), a technology for development NGO, began promoting the

---

207 Collaboration on International ICT Policy in East and Southern Africa (CIPESA) website, http://cipesa.org/about-us/.

208 Swedish Program for ICT in Developing Regions website, http://spidercenter.org/.

209 "CIPESA," Promoting Human Rights and Democracy Through ICT, http://ict4democracy.org/about/partnerproject-briefs/cipesa/.

use of ICT in monitoring good governance and service delivery in Uganda. The project, called Catalyzing Civic Participation and Democracy Monitoring Using ICTs, was funded by the Swedish Program for ICT in Developing Regions (SPIDER), a development resource center.[210] It established partnerships with three grassroots-based organizations, namely, the Busoga Rural Open Source and Development Initiative (BROSDI) in the Mayuge district (Eastern Uganda); the e-Society Resource Centre (eSRC) in the Kasese district (Western Uganda); and the Northern Uganda Media Club (NUMEC), in Gulu (Northern Uganda). These organizations had been working directly with communities to promote the use of ICTs as tools for citizens to engage with decision-makers and demand accountability. Under their projects, citizens used various tools in engaging with local government officials, including radio (NUMEC), email, blogs, social media (BROSDI), and geo-coded mapping for eSRC.

Informed by the experience and networks developed by CIPESA through these previous efforts, iParticipate, the project under study here, sought to support these existing efforts and to build on them by leveraging open government data (much of it already available in various portals but often in incompatible or inaccessible formats) as an enabler of citizen participation and accountable governance, focusing especially on the health sector. CIPESA's interest in open governance started when it conducted research on open governance network building in Uganda, funded by the International Development Research Center in 2012.[211] Among other results, the research helped identify key datasets that citizen groups would like the government to proactively disclose, as well as the general level of government readiness to implement open governance in the country.

Much of the work undertaken under the iParticipate initiative focused on training intermediaries – particularly media and civil society actors – to enable and promote citizen participation in Ugandan governance. iParticipate also provided support to grassroots citizen-focused ICT centres like eSRC in Kasese. Finally, the project engaged with government officials and policymakers to help communicate the opportunities, tools and tenets of open data and open governance processes to push forward the supply side of open data and ensure that the institutional culture acted as an enabler of greater participation in governance and service delivery.[212] This multi-audience focus helped iParticipate to diversify its offerings, engage relevant stakeholders in a targeted way, and avoid the "if you build it, will they come" question that

---

210 Ibid.

211 "Uganda Open Government Data Readiness Study," CIPESA and Association for Progressive Communications, April 2012, http://cipesa.org/?wpfb_dl=139.

212 "2015 Projects," CIPESA, http://cipesa.org/projects/.

often plagues open data efforts focused solely on citizens with little attention paid to intermediaries or actors on the supply side.

As explained further below, iParticipate provides detailed GIS-maps and visualizations to present mashed up datasets from a number of government data sources, in the process making clear where, how and why health care resources are being used across the country. Much of the project's offerings are real-world rather than digital. iParticipate efforts have included, for example, multi-stakeholder meetings between government officials and educators focused on the challenge of implementing tools to improve community participation.[213] Traditional media outlets are also leveraged – including through the previously mentioned radio broadcasts. The effort also involves the use of a number of training and engagement centers, including the eSRC in Kasese, which "provides ICT training programmes...aimed at enhancing citizens' competence in monitoring government services, promoting accountability, civic participation and good governance."[214]

One specific initiative undertaken in collaboration with NUMEC aimed at making government information more accessible to citizens in the districts of Gulu, Nwoya and Amuru – the regions most affected by Lord's Resistance Army's (LRA) destruction. The project set out to "document service delivery failures as a result of donor aid cuts to the Peace, Recovery and Development Plan (PRDP), and to generate debate by citizens through community debates, radio talk shows and ICT-based engagements on improving service delivery needs of post-conflict communities." The PRDP was launched by the government in 2009 to "revitalise the economy and livelihoods of communities in the post-conflict region" through health service delivery, new infrastructure, clean energy and education initiatives, but widespread allegations of corruption destroyed citizen trust in the effort.[215]

The project's overarching goal was to increase citizen participation in monitoring government service delivery through the use of ICT; advocate for government stakeholders to practice open governance; and document and propagate to the wider public the results of these processes. CIPESA performs the role of an intermediary that gathers government data and translates it into useful, relevant, and meaningful information for citizens. CIPESA's aim is also to increase the capacity and ability of citizen groups and the media to demand

---

213 Caroline Wamala Larsson, "SPIDER Stories 2013–2014," SPIDER Center, 2015, http://spidercenter.org/wp-content/blogs.dir/362/files/2016/11/spider_stories_2013-2014_for_web.pdf.

214 Ashnah Kalemera, "Citizens' Use of ICTs in Social Accountability in Uganda's Kasese District," CIPESA, January 19, 2015, http://cipesa.org/2015/01/citizens-use-of-icts-in-social-accountability-in-ugandas-kasese-district/.

215 Gladys Oroma, Promoting Community Dialogue on Service Delivery Failures in Northern Uganda," Promoting Human Rights and Democracy through ICT, February 28, 2015, http://ict4democracy.org/promoting-community-dialogue-on-service-delivery-failures-in-northern-uganda/.

better data, and to use this data to exact accountability from governments, especially in the health and education sectors.

Funding

The Swedish Program for ICT in Developing Regions (SPIDER) provided CIPESA with 500,000 SEK (approximately 55,480 USD) for a two-year implementation beginning 2013. The project from which this new initiative was built was also supported by SPIDER at the same funding level. In addition, Indigo Trust also provided 12,000 GBP (14,870 USD) for the initiative.

Demand and Supply of Data Type(s) and Sources

iParticipate's health advocacy was focused on health service delivery and how access to health care, especially by the poor and marginalized in rural areas, is affected by government investments in people and facilities. There were a few primary data sets that were used by CIPESA in this process—those related to health clinics, health centers, and general hospitals, including the location and number of beds for each of these facilities. This existing data originated on the Ministry of Health website and was made accessible through Uganda's Open Data for Africa portal.[216]

The Open Data for Africa portal allowed for online search and query, with the capacity to filter and visualize results (see Figure 1). The platform also allows downloading of data as CSV, XLS, or OData files. Similar datasets are also available at the Electronic Health Management Information System (eHMIS),[217] though this portal requires formal log-on procedures to be able to get access to the data.

To see investments in health per jurisdiction, CIPESA used budget data from the Ministry of Finance Planning and Economic Development available at the ministry's budget portal.[218] The portal has an elaborate query facility and also publishes PDF reports of spending performance for each sector. Access to the data, however, is not fully open, as it requires registration with the data providers, and acceptance of registration is not assured.

---

216 Open Data for Africa, "Uganda Regional Health Statistics Database, 2011," http://uganda. opendataforafrica.org/lhcqofd/uganda-regional-health-statistics-database-2011.

217 Ministry of Health, Republic of Uganda website, http://hmis2.health.go.ug/#/.

218 Ministry of Finance Planning and Economic Development, "Uganda Budget Information," http://budget. go.ug/index.php?p=budget_dashboard.

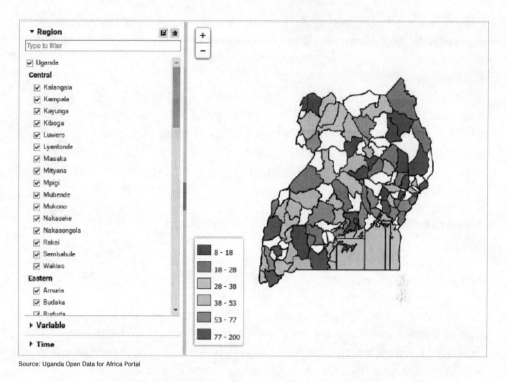

Source: Uganda Open Data for Africa Portal

Figure 1. Location of hospitals, health clinics in Uganda

Open Data Use

CIPESA used the data available in these portals and from other sources to analyze health service delivery and public investments in health projects. Much of iParticipate's training efforts, for example, focused on providing individuals and journalists with the capacity to access and use geocoded maps made possible by open government data.

CIPESA used data to identify a number of features related to health service delivery. For example, iParticipate's maps could help identify populations with limited access to health care, as well those health facilities that had limited or no beds. This information was cross-

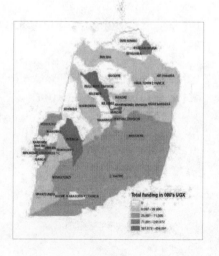

**Figure 2.
Sub-County Health Funding in
Kasese (2012–2013 estimates)**

118

tabulated with funding information. As a result, iParticipate was able to show the need for more data sharing at all levels of the health service delivery infrastructure in Uganda. As Lillian Kisembo, the Assistant Town Clerk in Kasese, put it: "If we can embark upon sharing information at the local level, we can reduce these challenges at District planning."[219]

In addition, CIPESA also made use of open data coming from different sources to build a platform to show how projects implemented through the PRDP, described above, collect reports coming from the field through users with Android phones, and aggregate different reports on health issues and health-related information. Community residents can report information using the Ushahidi[220] crowdsourced mapping application and this, together with different reports and information, are consolidated in a crowd-mapping portal (see Figure 3).[221]

Figure 3. Crowd-mapping Platform developed by CIPESA – PRDP

219 "ICT4Democracy in East Africa: A Year in Review 2015," CIPESA, 2016, http://cipesa.org/?wpfb_dl=221.

220 Ushahidi website, https://www.ushahidi.com/.

221 CIPESA, "Promoting Transparency, Civic Agency and the Right to Information in Northern Uganda's Peace Recovery and Development Programme," https://cipesa.crowdmap.com/main.

Impact

The CIPESA project had three main objectives: (a) increasing citizen participation in monitoring government service delivery through the use of ICT; (b) advocating for government stakeholders to practice open governance; and (c) documenting and propagating to the wider public the learning that resulted from these processes. In our analysis, we find that impact is primarily evident only in the area of advocacy, increased engagement of citizens in health governance and information dissemination. In addition, a certain (though limited) impact is evident in the other areas.

Advocacy

Although impact remains relatively limited and difficult to assess, there is some evidence that iParticipate's data offerings and training efforts with civil society and the media have made some impact. By enabling these intermediaries to better understand the conditions of the health sector, highlight issues associated with poor investments in health and publicize the poor's lack of access to quality health care, iParticipate is playing a key role in pushing for improvements to public- and private-sector providers, and also in empowering citizens to demand better service.

Improved Dissemination of Health Information

This advocacy is coupled with wider dissemination of information on health and other health- related issues to different communities using different media—radio, SMS, printed materials, e-resource center, e-library, e-discussion groups, Facebook pages, and web portals. These increased not only information availability, but also user's access to relevant health governance information.

Increasing Citizen Engagement in Health Governance

The advocacy and dissemination activities were done alongside building the capacity of different stakeholders, more particularly journalists, local government officials, civil society organization leaders, and students, on the use of ICT for governance. These trainings increased their capacity to analyze and make use of government data for advocacy, while at the same time monitoring the quality of public health service delivery by government.

Risks

Central to ICT-enabled information dissemination and open data monitoring initiatives is the capacity of these initiatives to actually make a difference in the lives of citizens. For example, data that highlights health spending and inconsistencies in prioritization, as well as those public reporting mechanisms on health governance, will only be useful for citizens if there are actual improvements in government spending and public health service delivery. If positive results are not obtained, citizens will get disillusioned and will likely discontinue availing themselves of these initiatives.

Also, as is the case with many health-focused open data initiatives, the primary risk involves personally identifiable information. While the focus of the government's data provision and iParticipate's data-driven analysis tools are not at all on sharing personal health information, continued vigilance and targeted data responsibility strategies will be essential to ensure that no potentially damaging personal information slips through the cracks.

Lessons Learned

Enablers

Cross-sector collaboration

Without access to resources and expertise from SPIDER, CIPESA's implementation of iParticipate would have been significantly more challenging. While the funding provided by the Sweden-based international organization obviously played a major enabling role, the ability to plug into SPIDER's international network of businesses, universities, NGOs and governments working to leverage ICT for development also helped to shape the approach and offerings of the initiative.

CIPESA's reputation as a development organization

Additionally, CIPESA continues to be a driving force in Uganda's desire to improve transparency and accountability in governance. Just as it was able to tap into an international network of expertise, CIPESA leveraged its own network of development actors, both at the national and sub-national level, to inform the project. Its reputation with donors, government agencies, civil society organizations and other stakeholders is an important element in

CIPESA's ability to influence policy-making as well as government decision-making despite the limitations mentioned below.

Barriers

Lack of demand-side capacity

CIPESA experienced challenges in achieving desired results. First, driving citizen participation is affected by at least two significant barriers—low connectivity and low levels of awareness of ICT use among citizens. While progress has been made in efforts to train citizens in ICT use, the lack of consistent access (especially outside of resource centers) hampered efforts. Also, especially regarding efforts focused on health and budget information, many technical concepts require sophisticated knowledge to enable meaningful participation—highlighting the need for intermediaries who perform the task of making complex information understandable to citizens.

While journalists could have performed this intermediary or explanatory role, CIPESA seems to have found it a challenge to incentivize journalists to spend time learning and educating themselves on the relevant issues. Journalist participation was also limited by geography, as health service delivery generally remains a big problem outside the urban/semi-urban areas where most journalists are based. Citizen groups in these areas were also limited in their ability to participate, primarily by a lack of connectivity and capacity.

Citizen media habits

While CIPESA made use of ICT as a means to disseminate and collect information, a study[222] it conducted in 2015 revealed that newspapers, radio, and television were in fact the most trusted sources of information by Ugandans. The same study indicated that very few Ugandans use ICT as a means to monitor and report on government services. This suggests that the means used by CIPESA to engage citizens with health governance data did not match with the manner in which citizens habitually acquire and share trusted information.

The survey did find that a growing number of people in the country are starting to use the Internet, and especially social networks like Facebook and Twitter, to discuss issues of national and local concern. However, citizen use of such networks was generally limited to information sharing, and not to actually raising concerns to accountable officials (most of whom do not in any

---

222 CIPESA, *ICT in Civic Participation and Democracy in Uganda: Citizens' knowledge, attitudes and practices,* CIPESA ICT Policy Research Series, No. 4/15, 2015, http://www.cipesa.org/?wpfb_dl=196.

case have social media accounts). The main limits on more widespread use of ICTs were illiteracy, and language and cost barriers.

Availability of resources

The capacity of CIPESA to proactively elevate health service delivery concerns to accountable government officials was also hampered by resource constraints. CIPSA tried to surmount fund shortages by using health service delivery reports received by one of its partners, Transparency International Uganda (TIU). But the organization was nonetheless constrained in its outreach and awareness-raising efforts. For example, while CIPESA succeeded in producing potentially useful health service delivery maps, it was often unable to disseminate these widely enough to reach their intended audiences. Funding constraints also affected CIPESA's ability to follow up on adverse findings reported by citizens using its platform.

Looking Forward

CIPESA main goal is to increase the impact that iParticipate will be able to make in using ICT for health service delivery monitoring. Currently, it is trying to find new ways of addressing the challenges identified above through more creative and well-targeted outreach and communication efforts. For example, the previous SPIDER project that was the basis for iParticipate made extensive use of radio programs to increase debate and reaching out to public officials on key concerns of the communities. The radio program implemented with NUMEC was able to reach approximately 1.6 million listeners.

As mentioned above, and as concluded by CIPESA's own research,[223] a number of factors limit the potential of ICT as a tool in monitoring government performance and enforcing accountability. The most important of these factors include poor technological infrastructure, including slow internet speeds and irregular electricity; low levels of ICT capacity among citizens; higher trust and use of traditional media as sources of data and information; and the high cost of internet access. iParticipate's future, and more generally the future of open data as a tool to achieve better health outcomes in Uganda, will be largely dependent on its ability to address and overcome (or at least mitigate) these challenges.

---

223 . Ibid.

Conclusion

Although iParticipate has had relatively little impact on citizen empowerment to date, it has leveraged a number of strategies that have yielded success in other contexts. The initiative's diverse offerings are implemented with a clear understanding of the intended audience – including notably government officials – and efforts are consistently driven through existing intermediaries, like journalists. This focus on empowering intermediaries to act as enablers for greater citizen participation is one reason for optimism regarding the longer-term impacts of iParticipate – including if and when funding is no longer available. Relatedly, the project often seeks to meet its intended audience where they already are – such as at ICT training centers or on popular radio broadcasts – increasing reach and the likelihood that its message is being absorbed by the public. While iParticipate has not yet had a transformative impact on citizen participation in Ugandan health governance, its continued efforts to increase awareness and train potential users of open data have the potential to gradually improve health outcomes by bringing together government actors, intermediaries and citizens to work toward common ends.

Open Data's Impact on Empowering Citizens

CHAPTER 9

GotToVote! Kenya

Improving voter turnout with open data

Auralice Graft, Andrew Young and Stefaan Verhulst

Summary

In the lead up to Kenya's 2013 general election, the country's Independent Electoral and Boundaries Commission (IEBC) released information about polling center locations on its website. The information, however, was difficult to access, indicating the wide gap that separates making data open and actually making it usable. Seeking to bridge that gap, two members of Code for Kenya, a governance innovation initiative, conducted an experiment that aimed to unlock government data and make it more useful to the public. To that end, they scraped the IEBC data and built a simple website where it could be more easily accessed. The result was the initial version of GotToVote! (gottovote. cc), a site that provided citizens with voter registration center information, and also helped them navigate the sometimes complex world of registration procedures. This first version was developed overnight at zero cost.

Context and Background

Problem Focus/Country Context

The Republic of Kenya is a nation of 42.7 million people situated on Africa's eastern coast. Kenya has a sizeable economy, with the highest GDP in East and Central Africa.[224] Despite this, the country is burdened with high unemployment,

---

224 International Monetary Fund, "Data," http://www.imf.org/en/data.

poverty, and crime.[225] Public sector corruption is also a challenge: Transparency International ranked Kenya 139th out of 168 countries in its 2016 Corruption Perception Index (CPI), an index that measures perceived levels of public sector corruption. This ranking places Kenya below countries like Bangladesh and Iran, and even below other Sub-Saharan African countries like Nigeria, Tanzania and Ethiopia.[226]

In December 2007, Kenya held a hotly contested presidential election that ended in a stalemate and protests. Anger over perceived vote rigging and manipulations of the electoral process rapidly metastasized into a national crisis characterized by conflict and violence, including targeted ethnic violence. As many as 1,400 people were killed and 600,000 displaced from their homes during the crisis. A resolution was reached after a few months, following the intervention of former UN Secretary General Kofi Annan; one of the main elements of the resolution was a roadmap toward a series of reforms designed to overcome political divisions and curb electoral manipulation.[227]

Among the most important of the reforms was a redrafting of Kenya's constitution, including a redrawing of constituency boundaries and a provision for a new national Independent Electoral and Boundaries Commission (IEBC). This commission was established in 2011 with a stated mission "to conduct free and fair elections and to institutionalize a sustainable electoral process."[228] One of the IEBC's first tasks was to register all Kenyan voters afresh, according to the new constituency boundaries as designated in the new constitution. Accordingly, a mass voter registration drive was initiated by the IEBC in November 2012 and 19 million people were registered.[229]

In order to achieve its ambitious registration goals, the IEBC released information about polling center locations on its website in late November 2012, a month ahead of the voter registration deadline. This information was considered critical as constituency boundaries had been redrawn, and voters needed to know where to go to register. Yet while the IEBC's release of data represented an important step, the data was actually quite complicated to access: the website itself was almost never available, and the information was provided in PDF format. Moreover, downloading the information was cumbersome because of the file's large size. As Jay Bhalla, executive director of Open Institute, a Kenyan open governance organization, put it: "The file

225 BBC News, "Kenya Country Profile," BBC, http://www.bbc.com/news/world-africa-13681341.

226 Mathews Muthai, "Kenya Ranked 139 Out of 168 in Global Corruption Perception Index (CPI)," *Citizen Digital*, January 27, 2016, https://citizentv.co.ke/news/kenya-ranked-139-out-of-168-in-global-corruption-perception-index-cpi-112912/.

227 James Brownsvell, "Kenya: What went wrong in 2007?" *Aljazeera*, March 2013, http://www.aljazeera.com/indepth/features/2013/03/201333123153703492.html.

228 Independent Electoral and Boundaries Commission website, http://www.iebc.or.ke/.

229 GovLab interview with David Lemayian, lead technologist, Code for Africa, November 1, 2016.

was so big it would have taken days for ordinary Kenyans to download. And, once they opened the document all they would have found was complex lists and tables of constituency centers."[230]

It was at this point that a Code for Kenya fellow and the lead developer of the software development team decided to step in and unlock the data with the aim of making it more accessible to the public. Their intervention marked the birth of the GotToVote! website.

KEY ACTORS

Key Data Providers

Two datasets were ultimately used for the GotToVote! Project; both were made publicly available by the IEBC on its website. The first dataset consisted of national polling center location information, and the second visualized a map of registered voters.

Key Data Users and Intermediaries

Kenyan citizens wanting to determine the location of their local polling station in order to register to vote are the main users of the data. Other users included the team of Code for Kenya fellows who scraped the data, built the GotToVote! website, and uploaded the scraped data onto the GotToVote! website. Code for Kenya is a "non-profit civic technology lab and data journalism initiative" that uses digital tools to provide ordinary citizens with "actionable information" and a stronger voice around public interest issues. Code for Kenya opens data, builds tools, and supports progress.[231] Code for Kenya began as a pilot program with funding from the World Bank, with the Africa Media Initiative (AMI) acting as a fiduciary sponsor. The pilot program consisted of four data fellows being embedded into major Kenyan newsrooms and civil society organizations for a period of five months in an effort to kickstart experimentation with data-driven civic engagement tools. The Code for Kenya team also included a four software developers. The above-mentioned Open Institute also provided support by incubating the Code for Kenya fellows.[232] After the initial launch of GotToVote!, Code for Kenya became a founding member of Code for Africa, a "federation of civic technology and data journalism labs," which now manages the initiative.[233]

230 Kenya GotToVote! website, https://kenya.gottovote.cc/about.html.

231 Justin Arenstein, "Finding Voter Registration Centre in Kenya Is Now Just a Click Away," Code for Africa, March 7, 2016, https://medium.com/code-for-africa/finding-voter-registration-centre-is-now-just-a-click-away-102d8206b12c#.gzqcxzzek.

232 Al Kags, "GotToVote! A Way to Bring Open Data to the Ground," Open Institute, November 22, 2012, http://www.openinstitute.com/gotovote/.

233 Justin Arenstein, "Finding Voter Registration Centre in Kenya Is Now Just a Click Away," Code for Africa, March 7, 2016, https://medium.com/code-for-africa/finding-voter-registration-centre-is-now-just-a-click-away-102d8206b12c#.gzqcxzzek.

Key Data Beneficiaries

Kenyan citizens looking to register to vote, to locate their local polling center, or to get answers relating to the registration process benefited from the project. The IEBC, whose voter registration drive was facilitated by the data, was another beneficiary.

Project Description

Initiation

(https://www.iebc.or.ke/)

Figure 1. Independent Electoral and Boundaries Commission website

In late November 2012, Code for Kenya fellow Simeon Oriko logged on to his Twitter account and saw that the IEBC had shared voter polling center information on its website (https://www.iebc.or.ke/). He also saw that the information was difficult to access. He quickly contacted a colleague, David Lemayian, about the information release and the problems with accessibility. According to a third Code for Kenya fellow, Muchiri Nyaggah, who managed the GotToVote! project early on, "they decided to turn the information into a spreadsheet. They had not planned for this; the idea was purely opportunistic."[234]

---

234 GovLab interview with Muchiri Nyaggah, Executive Director, Local Development Research Institute, Kenya, October 20, 2016.

Mr. Oriko and Mr. Lemayian downloaded the polling center data, scraped it, and built a simple website. They spent some time trying to decide on a name, feeling a certain amount of pressure as they needed to purchase a domain name. Finally, they settled on GotToVote! and quickly built an initial version of the site, which made the IEBC data far easier for citizens to access and use. For instance, rather than downloading and scrolling through a cumbersome PDF file, users could select their county or constituency from a drop-down list and find out immediately where to register.

The first version of the site was developed overnight, at no additional cost.[235] "I stayed up all night to build it," says co-creator David Lemayian.[236] The next morning, Mr. Oriko and Mr. Lemayian Tweeted the site out and it immediately got traction. "It did really well during those first days," says Mr. Nyaggah, pointing both to site usage and shares on social media. "People such as Dr. Evans Kidero, the now-Governor, were using and sharing the site," says Mr. Lemayian. "Celebrities were using and talking about it." Overall, GotToVote! received about 6,000 hits during that first week.[237] After this early success, GotToVote! partnered with United States-based Mercy Corps to incorporate a feature that allowed users to spread messages of peace through the GotToVote! website. Users could send free SMS messages that urged constraint at the ballot box. This feature was intended to promote peaceful election and post-election environments, a sorely felt need after the violence of the 2007 elections.

In addition to the peace SMS tool, GotToVote! added a feature to help users find the voter registration center nearest them by mapping data in conjunction with IEBC-released data. Another new feature provided an overview of the registration process, with an explanation of who was eligible to register, and what documents and other material were required.[238,239]

Not all of these efforts were successful. For example, an IEBC map indicating newly changed boundaries could not be incorporated into GotToVote! as was hoped. The map had proprietary issues as a result of a IBEC-Google deal that meant other users were locked out.[240]

While this first GotToVote! iteration focused on helping citizens register, a second iteration, developed after the IEBC's mass registration ended on

235 GotToVote! Kenya website, https://kenya.gottovote.cc/about.html.

236 GovLab interview with David Lemayian, lead technologist, Code for Africa, November 1, 2016.

237 GovLab interview with Muchiri Nyaggah, Executive Director, Local Development Research Institute, Kenya, October 20, 2016.

238 GovLab interview with Muchiri Nyaggah, Executive Director, Local Development Research Institute, Kenya, November 22, 2016.

239 Eric Mugendi, "This Website Is Using Publicly Available Data to Help Kenyans Register to Vote," *TechCabal*, March 8, 2016, http://techcabal.com/2016/03/08/got-to-vote-kenya/.

240 GovLab interview with Muchiri Nyaggah, Executive Director, Local Development Research Institute, Kenya, November 22, 2016.

December 19, 2012, aimed to mobilize people to vote in the upcoming March, 2013 elections, and then analyze results after the elections. Here, GotToVote! partnered with Dutch human rights organization Hivos and arranged to access data from the Kenya-based Ushahidi, a non-profit software company that develops free, open-source software. While these partnerships encountered a series of setbacks (see section on barriers below), they did produce a second GotToVote! iteration included a new post-election feature that provided access to official election results in local counties and constituencies, contextualization of those local level results by overlaying them with local level trends and official reports of fraud or irregularities. This feature was implemented to counter some of the hype that tended to prevail over post-election periods when the media focus was almost uniquely on presidential contest outcomes but ordinary citizens also wanted news about local level outcomes.

Figure 2. Image from the GotToVote! homepage

Demand and Data Use

The GotToVote! Kenya database contains a list of all Kenya's 47 counties, 290 constituencies, and 1450 wards, arranged by administrative area, with polling stations in each ward listed alphabetically. All the data used by GotToVote! Kenya is available for free reuse on the openAFRICA portal, another open data initiative from Code for Africa.[241] Demand for this data comes from would-be voters wanting to register and/or searching for the polling station closest to them. Demand also comes from users looking for basic voter education information.

Impact

As often is the case with relatively recent open data projects, very little data exists to indicate GotToVote!'s impact. The very newness of these projects contributes to the difficulty. As Mr. Nyaggah put it: "It is difficult to assess the impact because we didn't have baseline or anecdotal data to compare outcomes with." Nonetheless, certain forms of impact were evident.

Solving Public Problems through Data-driven Engagement

Given its popularity, GotToVote! appears to have helped many Kenyans register to vote by providing them with accessible information on voter center location. As mentioned, the site received approximately 6,000 hits during the first week after going live. Although neither baseline nor anecdotal data exists to contextualize this information or indicate actual impact on solving public problems, it suggests that the site was perceived as useful and was in fact used.

The apparent success of GotToVote! in helping voters register is indication that open data can be used—rapidly and with minimal cost—to provide citizens with tools that help them solve real public problems. One of the most powerful testimonies to the site's usefulness came from the IEBC itself, which built an almost identical platform soon after the GotToVote! site was unveiled, in the process clearly indicating that policymakers and government leaders recognized the project's tremendous potential. [242] As Code for Africa Director Justin Arenstein puts it: "[GotToVote!] proved that the real power of civic technologies is their ability to quickly and cheaply translate complex data into 'actionable' information, and to then calibrate the information to a citizen's exact location or other circumstances."[243]

---

241 "Voter Registration 2016," openAFRICA, https://africaopendata.org/dataset/voter-registration-2016.

242 GovLab interview with David Lemayian, lead technologist, Code for Africa, November 1, 2016.

243 GotToVote Kenya website, https://kenya.gottovote.cc/about.html.

Cross-Border Dissemination

According to co-founder David Lemayian, many sub-Saharan countries share similar problems (and opportunities for resolution) when it comes to the need for enabling more peaceful and inclusive elections. He believes that a tool like GotToVote! could be useful beyond the Kenyan context. "If we look at ways we can take tools that work in one country and apply them to other countries GotToVote! is clearly one of them," he says.[244]

Since its launch GotToVote! has, in fact, been replicated in several other African countries—a phenomenon that has been made possible by the open source nature of the original site. For example, Hivos, the Dutch organization that partnered with Code for Kenya to launch the original site, also showcased GotToVote! in Zimbabwe ahead of that country's 2013 general elections. "That was really heart-warming," says David Lemayian. "That's when we had a sort of light bulb reaction, realizing this is wanted in different countries in Africa."[245]

The site has also been replicated in Malawi, where a similar platform (http://gottovote.malawivote2014.org/) was implemented by the Malawi Election Information Center, a local NGO, and the Malawi Electoral Commission. The project was adopted by the government as its official voter registration solution and was used to register 7 million citizens. One distinctive trait of the Malawi project distinct was an SMS-to-SMS feature that allowed users to send messages containing their voter identification number, and then to receive a message in reply confirming whether they were registered to vote. Overall, 400,000 people in Malawi accessed registration information by SMS and online. "It was a fantastic roll-out," says David Lemayian.[246]

GotToVote! was also replicated in Ghana, where local organization Odekro and civic technologists Emmanuel Okyere and Nehemiah reached out to Code for Kenya expressing interest in the technology. While Odekro chased down polling station data, Code for Kenya providing technical assistance in this project. Ghana's case offered a particular challenge (and opportunity) because polling station information was maintained separately in each province, with no centralized list. A first step was therefore to create Ghana's first ever national consolidated voters roll, which was handed over to the government electoral commission. This list provided the basis for GotToVote! Ghana, which was built in two days for just $500 and unveiled for the 2016 elections.[247]

---

244 GovLab interview with David Lemayian, lead technologist, Code for Africa, November 1, 2016.
245 Ibid.
246 Ibid.
247 GotToVote! Ghana website, https://ghana.gottovote.cc/about.html.

Risks

Given that the project is primarily built around information provision and peace messaging, risks appear to be somewhat limited. That said, data quality is of paramount importance, due to the potential of providing citizens with incorrect – or biased – information regarding their voting process. Additionally, the two-way nature of the SMS functionality could create risks around the security of any personally identifiable information held by GotToVote!, but such risks appear to be minimal.

Lessons Learned

Several important lessons with wider applicability emerge from this particular case study. These can broadly be categorized by considering the key enablers of the project, as well as the most important barriers or challenges to its success.

Enablers

Engagement

The importance of local partner engagement was clear from the outset. "You can't just fly into a country and solve problems," says David Lemayian. "You have to work with local partners." He adds, however, that national, regional or international partners are important as well. Over the years, the trio of Code for Africa, Code for Kenya and the Open Institute have been able to pull together their diverse yet complimentary areas of expertise, incubating and mobilizing skills among their various fellows. Lemayian also notes that, "Governments and international partners add leverage and credibility, as well as funds." Hivos and Mercy Corps, in particular, helped amplify and expand the site's offerings and visibility.

Agility and MVPs

A further key lesson of this project—one seen in other examples in this series of case studies—is that successful open data projects can be built quickly and without considerable expense. The initial development of GotToVote! incurred no additional cost, and the size of the founding team was very small, basically just two people (Simeon Oriko and David Lemayian), though they were later joined and helped by other colleagues.

Finally, the process of building an open data project does not need to be complicated or cumbersome. As noted, for example, GotToVote! was built in just one night. The data contained on the site was relatively simple, and did not require complicated algorithms to make useful. All told, GotToVote! is a good example of how much can be achieved with very little—at least in the early stages of an open data project (see the discussion of Sustainability in Barriers, below).

Barriers

Sustainability of event-based initiatives

The impact of GotToVote! is clear, but the site's focus on a single, time-bound event (e.g., a given presidential election) does raise questions about long-term sustainability. Questions remain about what to do with the project between elections, and whether the user base can be re-engaged during the next election. This lack of certainty also raises questions about access to further funding, a key consideration for the sustainability of open data initiatives. The site's current status, discussed below, only increases this uncertainty.

Unhelpful partnerships

According to Muchiri Nyaggah, it was assumed that relationships with big media companies would translate into those companies utilizing GotToVote! to disseminate election results. However, as it turned out, these companies had actually invested money creating their own results-dissemination platforms. They ultimately had no use for GotToVote! This was a big blow to GotToVote!'s success, with significantly less dissemination and ultimate use than initially assumed and worked toward.[248]

Data access failures

Another barrier came in the form of failed access to data. In one instance, the IEBC's system crashed while results were being tallied after the March 2013 elections. This was a major failure that ultimately led to a crisis in Kenya that had to be resolved by the national Supreme Court. For GotToVote!, the system crash meant it did not have access to election results data that it hoped to incorporate into the project. In an unrelated challenge, GotToVote!'s

---

248 Skype interview with Muchiri Nyaggah, Executive Director, Local Development Research Institute, Kenya, November 22, 2016.

attempted data access arrangement with Ushahidi did not come to fruition as a result of backend technical issues. GotToVote! and Ushahidi had planned to work to tell a political story of what happened post-2013 elections by merging election results with a diversity of other datasets held by Ushahidi (including geospatial data).[249]

Looking Forward

Current Status

Kenya's GotToVote! website was updated ahead of the 2017 general elections, but no concrete plans are in place for rolling it out. "We are definitely looking for people who can pick it up and run with it," says David Lemayian. "We [at Code for Africa] have been approached by three different organizations to run GotToVote! in Kenya ahead of elections planned for August 2017. But we are hoping civil society will take it up. We've also actively reached out to IEBC and election observation groups on the same." With the next election fast approaching, the identification of an organization with the human capital and funding resources needed to maintain the platform capable of taking it up is becoming urgent.

Replicability

As described above, the potential for replicating GotToVote! has been realized across a number of countries in Sub-Saharan Africa. The simplicity and open source basis of the platform, the general availability of the data required and the clearly defined problem it seeks to solve are key drivers of this replicability.

Early project manager Muchiri Nyaggah believes that GotToVote! needs to be established as a more formalized, cross-border civil society program or mission going forward. "Tech-heavy organizations are not very good at old school NGO language," he says. "This needs to be turned into a program with people thinking about how to capture data on impact and other indicators." Mr. Nyaggah also stated that GotToVote! needs to collaborate with the IEBC if it is to have any value in upcoming elections.[250]

---

249 Skype interview with Muchiri Nyaggah, Executive Director, Local Development Research Institute, Kenya, November 22, 2016.

250 GovLab interview with Muchiri Nyaggah, Executive Director, Local Development Research Institute, Kenya, October 20, 2016.

Conclusion

GotToVote's impact is clear in the way it has improved public awareness of election information, the fact that it has been replicated throughout the continent, and in the messages of harmony and inclusiveness it has helped foster in more recent elections. The project's birth and experience are in several ways indicative of many open data projects created across developing economies. It was created on a non-existent budget on a short timeline; it expanded in scope and usefulness as a result of partnerships across civil society and international organizations. These are all markers of success. At the same time, the lack of a longer-term sustainability strategy has raised questions about whether the initiative will survive going forward. This, too, is characteristic of many projects examined in this series of case studies on open data. The opportunities and obstacles are clear for advocates of open data in developing economies: they need to seize the immediate potential of data while also finding ways to address the longer-term questions and challenges.

137

CHAPTER 10

Tanzania's Open Education Dashboards

Improving education with open data[251]

Juliet McMurren, Andrew Young and Stefaan Verhulst

Summary

Low national examination pass rates in 2012 caused a public outcry in Tanzania, but the public's understanding of the broader context and ability to demand accountability was limited by a lack of information about the country's education sector. Two portals tried to remedy that situation, providing the public with more data on examination pass rates and other information related to school quality. The first, the Education Open Data Dashboard (educationdashboard.org), was a project established by the Tanzania Open Data Initiative, a government program supported by the World Bank and the United Kingdom Department for International Development (DFID) to support open data publication, accessibility and use. The second, Shule (shule.info), was spearheaded by Arnold Minde, a programmer, entrepreneur, and open data enthusiast who has developed a number of technologies and businesses to catalyze social change in Tanzania. Although both portals show considerable promise – especially as it relates to visualization open data to make it more comprehensible to a wide audience –they have, to date, had limited success in actually changing citizen decision-making about education or generating greater institutional accountability. This is due in part to the challenges posed by Tanzania's low Internet penetration rates and unfamiliarity with open data.

---

251 This case study builds on and updates a previous piece drafted as part of the GovLab and Omidyar Network Open Data's Impact initiative.

Context and Background

Problem Focus / Country Context

In 2012, education in Tanzania became the subject of significant public discontent and controversy. That year, six out of every ten Tanzanian students failed the standardized national secondary-level examination, resulting in a media outcry and demand for reforms.[252] The poor results were the product of recent changes to the Tanzanian education system, in which tuition fees for government primary schools were eliminated in an effort to raise the country's school enrollment and literacy rates. The move triggered a rapid increase in net primary enrollment, from 66 percent in 2001 to 90 percent in 2004.[253] This increase, however, was not matched by a proportional increase in school funding.

As the Tanzanian school system strained under the burden of the additional enrollments, examination pass rates among the 30 percent of secondary-aged children enrolled in school[254] began to decline. After the particularly bad set of results in 2012, the government introduced changes to the grading system[255] that appeared to raise the pass rate in 2013 and 2014.[256] However, the root causes of the nation's education problems remained unaddressed: inadequately funded and supplied schools, a shortage of trained teachers,[257] limited teacher training and professional development, discontent regarding teachers' pay,[258] and stubborn regional, economic, and social inequalities.

At the same time, information about public education was not easy to come by, making it hard for citizens to understand the true state of the education sector and demand accountability from government officials. Although several Access to Information bills have gone before the Tanzanian Parliament, none has yet been enacted, while other legislation, including the country's defamation law, constrains the media's capacity to function critically and

---

252 Frank Kimboy, "High Pass Rate Greeted as Good as Well as Bad News," *The Citizen*, July 23, 2014, http://www.thecitizen.co.tz/magazine/politicalreforms/High-pass-rate-greeted-as-good/1843776-2394162-14jmnxhz/index.html.

253 UNESCO, "World Data on Education,United Republic of Tanzania," 2010, http://www.ibe.unesco.org/fileadmin/user_upload/Publications/WDE/2010/pdf-versions/United_Republic_of_Tanzania.pdf.

254 World Bank, World DataBank, "Tanzania," http://databank.worldbank.org/data//reports.aspx?source=2&country=TZA&series=&period=.

255 Elisha Mangolanga, "No More Div. Zero as Government Guts National Grading System," *The Citizen*, November 1, 2013, http://www.thecitizen.co.tz/News/Govt-in-major-change-of-national-exam-grading/1840340-2055404-n8mhil/index.html.

256 Frank Kimboy, "High Pass Rate Greeted as Good as Well as Bad News," *The Citizen*, July 23, 2014, http://www.thecitizen.co.tz/magazine/political-reforms/High- pass-rate- greeted-as- good/-/1843776/2394162/-/umh9xl/-/index.html.

257 The Citizen Reporter, "Teacher Shortage Hurtiing Tanzania," The Citizen, October 14, 2014, http:/ http://www.thecitizen.co.tz/News/Teachers-shortage-hurting-Tanzania/1840340-2485582-3ktjd2z/index.html.

258 Jacob Kushner, "Tanzanian teachers learning that education doesn't pay," *PRI*, December 20, 2013, https://www.pri.org/stories/2013-12-20/tanzanian-teachers-learning-education-doesnt-pay.

independently. The Tanzanian media is considered only partly free by Freedom House,[259] and the country was ranked 75th out of 180 countries in the 2015 World Press Freedom Index.[260]

In addition, there is a noticeable lack of independent voices in the Tanzanian media. While media ownership is transparent, it remains concentrated among a few proprietors. All four radio stations with national reach are regarded as favoring the ruling party, although the African Media Barometer did report in 2010 that the state-run Radio Tanzania had demonstrated more balanced views. Media outlets favorable to the opposition reportedly have government advertising contracts withheld.[261] Consequently, when stories about the state of education do make it to press, they tend to favor the official version of events, and often lack balance or context.

Citizens were for the most part unable to turn to the Internet or open data as substitutes for the information they needed. Open data use in Tanzania remains in its infancy. The Open Data Barometer places Tanzania in the "capacity constrained" cluster of countries whose open data initiatives are challenged by limits in government, civil society or private sector capacity, Internet penetration, and data collection and management.[262] Tanzania joined the Open Government Partnership Initiative in September 2011. The second phase of its OGP action plan, currently under development, commits the government to establishing an open data portal (opendata.go.tz) that would release key datasets in the education, health, and water sectors in machine-readable form.[263] As of October 2016, the portal has 100 datasets available for download, 65 of which are supplied by the Ministry of Education.

KEY ACTORS

Key Data Providers

Education Open Data Dashboard (educationdashboard.org)

Data was supplied by the National Examinations Council of Tanzania (NECTA), with additional resources from the World Bank integrated to improve the comprehensiveness of datasets.

---

259 Freedom House, "Tanzania," https://freedomhouse.org/country/tanzania#.VaQZFvlViko.

260 Reporters sans Frontieres, "Tanzanie," http://index.rsf.org/#!/index-details/TZA.

261 Freedom House, "Freedom of the Press: Tanzania," 2011, https://freedomhouse.org/report/freedom-press/2011/tanzania#.VaARQ_lVikp.

262 Open Data Barometer, "Data and Analysis: Clusters," Web Foundation, http://www.opendatabarometer.org/report/analysis/index.html.

263 Open Government Partnership, "Tanzania, 2014–15 Action Plan Documents," 2015, http://www.opengovpartnership.org/country/tanzania/action-plan.

Shule.info

Shule.info was built on similar data sources, but they were often manually scraped and collected by project organizers.

Key Data Users and Intermediaries

Education Open Data Dashboard

The project was developed as part of the Tanzania Open Data Initiative, a government program supported by the World Bank and the United Kingdom Department for International Development (DFID).

Shule.info

Shule.info was developed by Arnold Minde, a Tanzanian programmer, with some practical support and assistance from Twaweza.

Key Beneficiaries

Both portals aimed to improve parents' decision-making regarding their children's schools. In addition, they sought to improve journalism, especially regarding education-related issues, and to inform public debate regarding education.

Project Description

Initiation of the Open Data Activity

In 2013, the National Examinations Council of Tanzania (NECTA), a government body, rolled out a pilot education dashboard[264] offering data downloads, searches, and visualizations of primary and secondary examination results by district and school. The dashboard also included statistics on pupil-teacher ratios, annual and average pass rates, national rankings of school performance, and changes in pass rates since 2011. With the help of the World Bank, an updated version of the pilot was launched in 2015 as Education Open Data Dashboard (educationdashboard.org).[265] Despite some challenges and gaps described in more detail below, the data contained on the site represents a significant advance in the context of Tanzania's previous information drought.

---

264 Available at: http://www.necta.go.tz/opendata/, and subsequently updated at: http://www.necta.go.tz/opendata/brn/.

265 Available at: http://educationdashboard.org/#/.

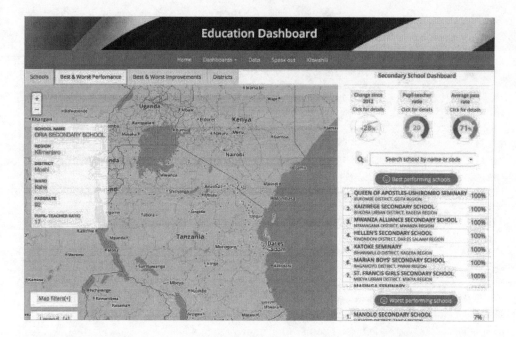

Figure 1. Mapping of school performance on the educationdashboard.org

Shule.info was the brainchild of the Tanzanian programmer Arnold Minde. It was released shortly after NECTA's original dashboard, and was conceived when Minde became aware that NECTA had been publishing individual exam results online since 2004. It wasn't until 2012, however, when poor examination pass rates prompted nationwide soul-searching, that Minde began working on the project in earnest. At that point, he realized the potential value of a single, readily usable, online source of national examination data.[266] Such data needed to be online and presented in a comprehensible format, he concluded, so that citizens could see that the poor results in 2012 were not a new phenomenon, but part of a downward trend over the past six to seven years. Minde had previously been involved in data visualization through his work for the Tanzanian development policy think tank REPOA (formerly Research on Poverty Alleviation); that work convinced him of the power of data visualization to communicate data trends and linkages, and helped shape the development of Shule.[267]

---

266 See: http://www.shule.info/about.
267 GovLab Interview with Arnold Minde, July 9, 2015.

142

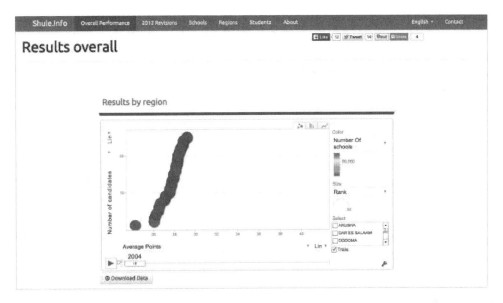

Figure 2. Education results by region on Shule.info

Demand and Supply of Data Type(s) and Sources

Both sites made the data on which they were built open for download by users. In addition, charts and visualizations were available directly on the platforms.

Although the data used to create Shule.info was available in isolated reports and websites, intended for individual students, it had never been made fully open in searchable and machine-readable format for citizens at large. Minde scraped, cleaned, and consolidated the data from the examination results as they were released each year.[268]

Education Open Data Dashboard used the government's own data, much of which is available through the official government open data portal. While there is much useful data available, some gaps do exist, including a dearth of individual examination results, pass rates before 2012, average pass rates over time, and pass rates by gender and region.

Funding

Shule.info was created on Minde's own time and at his expense. Education Open Data Dashboard was funded by the Tanzanian government, with some support from the World Bank.

---

268 Ibid.

143

Open Data Use

Both dashboards rely on government data. The data used to create Shule. info were publicly available but not open, requiring scraping, cleaning and standardization. The data on Education Open Data Dashboard were fully open, having been released on the Tanzanian government's open data portal.

Shule.info presents data for Form 4 examination results from 2004 to 2013 at candidate, school, regional and national levels. It also offers data visualizations of results (broken up by region and gender), which permits users, for example, to track average performance over time, the number of candidates in each grading division over time, and the impact of the government's controversial revision of the 2012 results. All data used to build the site is available for download. Shule therefore offers considerably more, and more granular, data than Education Open Data Dashboard. In addition (and in contrast to NECTA's dashboard), Shule offers commentary on its data visualizations, making it easier for users to understand the significance of the data they are accessing.

Impact

Tanzania is a country with low Internet penetration rates (5.3 percent in 2016, according to ITU, the United Nations specialized agency for information and communication technologies),[269] and is marked by a general lack of technical skills and expertise among the population. As noted, there is very little familiarity with the concept and potential of open data, or data in general. As such, although these projects represent notable advances within the current open data ecology, uptake and usage have generally been limited, making it hard to assess impact.

Nonetheless, a few metrics can be considered to measure the effects—limited though they are–of Shule and Education Open Data Dashboard. Impact can be gauged in three broad ways: engagement and use by both citizens and intermediaries; data quality and diversity; and spillover effects on other open data projects.

---

269 International Telecommunication Union, "ICT Facts and Figures," http://www.itu.int/en/ITU-D/ Statistics/Pages/stat/default.aspx.

Engagement and Use

After Shule went live in June 2013, the site averaged around 1,500 visits per month, according to Arnold Minde.[270] Feedback directly on the site and through Twaweza suggests that visitors fell into two categories. The first consists of data sophisticates, typically programmers or employees of civil society organizations, who were already aware of the potential of open data to inform decision-making, and visited the site to research education in Tanzania and better understand the overall educational context. These visitors may have become aware of the site through Twaweza and its civil society partners, or the emerging open data community in Dar-es-Salaam.

The second category of site visitors consisted of former students making use of the site's archive of examination results to look up their scores.[271] These students may not initially have been interested in or even aware of open data, but they are nonetheless exposed to Shule's visualizations on, for example, school performance by region, and other tools when they access the site. Engaging the ordinary Tanzanian families Minde had originally hoped to reach has been more challenging. Low rates of Internet penetration and a lack of experience using the Internet have restricted the amount of casual traffic received through search engines.

Minde says he fears that average Tanzanians don't have much interest yet in looking at data visualizations, preferring to get their information predigested by the media. "I don't see people asking the real questions," says Minde. "I don't see discussions around the issues, even among people I know."[272] Aidan Eyakuze, Executive Director of Twaweza, believes both the public and policymakers are looking for the insight contained in the data, not the data itself. "Data is frightening for many people, so raw data is going to appeal to a vanishing few," he says. "Open data needs to be open plus curated plus chewed plus digested to appeal to most people, including policymakers."[273] Few in the media, however, have the knowledge and skills to digest Shule's data offerings, despite initiatives like the Data Bootcamp, which was designed to introduce members of the Tanzanian media to open data.[274]

Education Open Data Dashboard's use was similarly constrained by Tanzania's low rate of Internet use. Nonetheless, the site's developers point out that Tanzanians don't necessarily need Internet access to benefit from

---

270 GovLab Interview with Arnold Minde, July 9, 2015.

271 Ibid.

272 Ibid.

273 Ibid.

274 Michael Bauer, "The Data Bootcamp in Tanzania," October 25, 2012, Open Knowledge International Blog, http://blog.okfn.org/2012/10/25/the-data-bootcamp-in-tanzania/.

the information stored on the site. Members of civil society organizations, for example, including Tanzania's active parent-teacher organizations, can act as intermediaries, printing out information about school performance to share on a community notice board or at meetings, for example.[275]

Data Quality and Diversity

The combination of Education Open Data Dashboard and Shule increased the diversity and thus the usefulness of available data on education in Tanzania. Taken together, the information they provided is richer and more interesting than either site would have been on its own (or, of course, than the pre-existing lack of data). Education Open Data Dashboard offered indicators such as pupil-teacher ratios, regional and district rankings, and improvement rankings over time, all of which are navigated via a clickable map and drop-down menu of schools. Shule captured a much longer span of data, with examination results going back to 2004. In addition to results by gender, Shule offered average performance over time, instead of Education Open Data Dashboard's simple pass rate, and looked at the breakdown of candidate numbers per grading division over time. It also modeled the effect of the 2012 grading revision to examine how it changed candidate pass rates.

Although based on government data, the dataset used to build Shule is not completely identical to that used for the government dashboard; this is due to differences in methods of data collection. Perhaps as a result, Shule's figures can depart in significant ways from the government version. For example, NECTA traditionally published an annual list of the ten government and secondary schools with the highest examination results. In 2012, Minde reports that NECTA's official list contained a number of government schools, but Shule's analysis showed that all ten of the top performing schools were private.

For the developers of Education Open Data Dashboard, one of the more surprising discoveries was that feeding a dashboard was a potent incentive to compliance with data reporting. Regional officials and head teachers were excited by finding their school or region in the dashboard, and by seeing what the data they submitted was creating, and this excitement appeared to translate to improved reporting, at least in the short term.[276] This suggests that the novelty of open data use and data visualization can be a useful tool in improving data quality.

---

275 GovLab interview with Samhir Vasdev and Verena Luise Knippel, June 30, 2015.
276 Ibid.

Spillover Effects on Other Open Data Projects

As the developers of the latest version of Educationdashboard have indicated, Shule forms part of a nascent data ecosystem of which they were very much aware during the development and refinement of their own site. For government officials involved in creating the dashboard, the existence of such independent projects validated both the demand for the kinds of open data portal they were building, and provided evidence that the local technical and other capacity existed to build it.[277] Their own dashboard was, in turn, a powerful tool in demonstrating the potential and uses of open data to a non-technical audience, particularly among policymakers. In addition, the data visualizations and linkages it made possible ignited interest in, and impetus for, the development of dashboards in other sectors, such as moves by the Department of Justice to map courthouses across the country.[278]

Lessons Learned

Shule and Education Open Data Dashboard were both experimental projects, launched into a society that was just beginning to grasp the potential of open data. If projects like these are to succeed, they will need to overcome significant societal challenges. This section examines some of the most important enablers of and challenges to these projects. Although these enablers and barriers are particular to this project, they offer hints of what may face other open data projects in other developing countries.

Enablers

Leveraging intermediaries

As Internet penetration slowly expands in Tanzania, civil society organizations like parent- teacher organizations or NGOs have an important role to play as intermediaries that can disseminate insights gleaned from open data among citizens who would otherwise not have access to the data. The developers of Educationdashboard note that ultra-low-tech solutions like posting printouts of information drawn from open data dashboards on school or community notice boards can be effective in getting information to the people who can use

---

277 Ibid.

278 Open Data for Africa, "Tanzania Data Portal," November 22, 2013, http://tanzania.opendataforafrica.org/igcpumb/social-justice.

it.[279] The focus on easily comprehensible data visualizations also made such low-tech solutions possible.

Engaging civil society

Even among such intermediary groups, however, awareness of the potential of open data remains nascent at best. Like the public at large, civil society groups also need to be trained to analyze and visualize data. Some efforts have taken place in Tanzania to involve civil society: in 2012, in an effort to encourage interest and build skills among coders and the media, the World Bank Institute and the Africa Media Initiative combined to offer the Data Bootcamp in Dar-es-Salaam.[280] A similar initiative was offered by Twaweza in 2013, and community groups such as the Open Knowledge Foundation Network TZ have attempted to promote open data meetups in Dar-es-Salaam. Thus far the work has been mostly carried forward by local civil society organizations like Twaweza and REPOA, but international development organizations already operating in Tanzania would be well placed to assist them. As is the case across many of the case studies in this series, the existence of a strong ICT4D and D4D ecosystem cleared the way for these new and innovative open data uses.

Barriers

Internet penetration

Perhaps the most important challenge stems from Tanzania's low Internet penetration and usage rates. The two dashboards begin from the premise that providing information to target audiences will improve conditions on the ground. However, given Tanzania's low Internet penetration rates, particularly in rural areas, where Internet penetration is estimated to be about a quarter of that in urban areas,[281] getting information to those target audiences remains a challenge. This clearly limits the reach of education-related data, and open data more broadly. Furthermore, of the 4.7 percent of Tanzanians who used the Internet in 2014, the great majority did so only by mobile phone; only 0.17 percent of Tanzanians had a fixed broadband subscription.[282] In order to appeal

---

279 GovLab Interview with Samhir Vasdev and Verena Luise Knippel, June 30, 2015.

280 Michael Bauer, "The Data Bootcamp in Tanzania," October 25, 2012, Open Knowledge International Blog, http://blog.okfn.org/2012/10/25/the-data-bootcamp-in-tanzania/.

281 Africa Focus, "Tanzania: Old media, new media," *AfricaFocus Bulletin*, April 5, 2011, http://www.africafocus.org/docs11/tan1104.php.

282 International Telecommunication Union, "ICT Facts and Figures," http://www.itu.int/en/ITU-D/Statistics/Pages/stat/default.aspx.

more widely, any open data site clearly needs to consider launching a mobile application to appeal to "the retail user of data sitting in a bus shelter with a mobile phone."[283]

This is a challenge faced by data projects throughout the developing world, and some have dealt with it by developing low-cost, low-bandwidth solutions more accessible to users on slow mobile connections.[284] In some cases, too, sharing information over SMS has proven effective.[285]

Public interest and trust in technology

Although technology remains inherently a challenge in the developing world, the barriers may be even higher when it comes to using technology (and data) as instruments of social change. Minde notes that, in general, the Tanzanian public is deeply unfamiliar with the potential of the Internet, and perhaps not yet inclined to trust it. He adds that Tanzanians have yet to embrace or commit to digital solutions for the problems of everyday life, whether complex or mundane. As an example, he cites the difficulty he experienced in convincing bus operators to adopt an earlier application he developed that allowed passengers to purchase tickets by phone. "It will only take one [company], and then people will see the benefit," he says. "But first you have to convince the one."[286]

Looking Forward

Current Status

Education Open Data Dashboard displays data visualizations for data only from 2012 to 2014. Given that education data for 2016 is now available on the Tanzanian government open data portal, opendata.go.tz, it appears that the site is no longer being actively updated and may have reached the end of its lifespan.

Similarly, Shule.info has not had any results added since 2013. Although Minde says he contemplated further refinements to his project (including

---

283 GovLab Interview with Aidan Eyakuze, July 14, 2015.

284 See, for example: http://www.aptivate.org/webguidelines/Why.html.

285 See, for example: Participedia, "Enabling Youth Participation through Technology: U-report Uganda, June 21, 2016, http://participedia.net/en/cases/enabling-youth-participation-through-technology-u-report-uganda.

286 GovLab Interview with Arnold Minde, July 9, 2015.

adding Form 4 examination results[287] and an increased range of information about schools),[288] the dashboard should probably now be considered dormant.

Although the short lifespans of these projects make clear the difficulty in sustaining open data projects over the long term absent a clear business model or operational strategy for engaging target audiences, their impact has nonetheless been undeniable and both projects offer valuable insights for open data projects across the developing world.

Sustainability

Projects by sole developers, such as Shule.info, are inherently vulnerable as the developer's available time, energy, and interest in the project change. Minde has indicated that the biggest constraint on Shule's growth was his own time.[289] As a government site, Education Open Data Dashboard should have had greater longevity, but even it was unable to sustain itself. The fact that neither was driven by end-user demand could also have made them more vulnerable to abandonment. Indeed, this appears to have been the case: although Minde says that he is still convinced of the usefulness of and need for the data, there were no demands for updates to it, and he was unable to obtain the necessary investment to build Shule into a commercial product to ensure its long-term sustainability.[290]

Moreover, given low Internet penetration rates, the existence of two separate dashboards for education information could also prove confusing to parents, and limit the effectiveness of both platforms. Greater impact could perhaps have come from integrating the two platforms and cooperatively advancing a single project, rather than providing a limited user base with two separate entry points for accessing essentially the same information. It is worth noting that moves toward greater coordination were in fact made, notably including Minde's involvement in development strategy meetings for Education Open Data Dashboard.[291] However, these efforts at coordination do not appear to have yielded the desired results.

Replicability

These dashboards illustrate the power of a deceptively simple tool, that can be built locally in a matter of a few weeks by a single developer (Shule.info) or a

---

287 See: http://www.shule.info/about.
288 GovLab Interview with Arnold Minde, July 9, 2015.
289 GovLab Interview with Arnold Minde, September 20, 2016.
290 Ibid.
291 GovLab Interview with Samhir Vasdev and Verena Luise Knippel, June 30, 2015.

small team (Education Open Data Dashboard), with little or no outside support or funding, then refined through user feedback. As one of the developers of the Education Open Data Dashboard put it: "Get a minimum viable product [MVP] out there. Make some assumptions about the data, get it out there, and provoke a response."[292] So whether or not the specific tools or methods used by the developers of the platforms are replicated, their general approach—drawing on open data to quickly create platforms aimed at bettering the public good—can be seen as inspiration for similarly community-minded innovators across developing countries.

Conclusion

While neither Shule nor Education Open Dashboard was able to achieve longer-term sustainability or the types of transformative impact on education and parent decision-making that they set out to accomplish, they can be seen as clear indications of how dedicated, data-driven efforts to enhance citizen decision-making and benefit the public good can quickly become tangible. Indeed, the projects also make clear the need for a longer-term business model to ensure that initial MVPs grow into "sticky," widely used platforms—a key lesson for the field of open data practice.

---

292 Ibid.

CHAPTER 11

South Africa's Medicine Price Registry
Cheaper medicines for consumers

François van Schalkwyk, Andrew Young and Stefaan Verhulst

Summary

In 2014, Code for South Africa, a South Africa-based non-profit organization active in the open data space, took a little-known dataset from the national Department of Health website and created the Medicine Price Registry Application (MPRApp, https://mpr.code4sa.org/), an online tool that allows patients to compare medicine prices. MPRApp allows patients to compare the costs of doctor-prescribed medicines with those of other (e.g., generic) medicines containing the same ingredients. It also helps patients verify that they aren't being overcharged by their pharmacies, and ensures cost-savings for both patients and society without compromising on efficacy.

It was initially expected that middle- to upper-class patients with better online access would be the primary beneficiaries of MPRApp. However, there is evidence that doctors also use the information provided by MPRApp to save their patients money. Because MPRApp currently relies on the time and skills of its developer to ensure regular updates its continued use and impact remains uncertain unless sustainable funding can be secured. With no marketing or promotions to speak of, MPRApp has had an impact on the lives of a few South Africans; with a sustainable model and increased awareness of MPRApp, particularly among trusted intermediaries in the health sector, it could provide many more patients access to cheaper medicines.

Context and Background

Problem Focus/Country Context

Healthcare in South Africa is provided by public hospitals and clinics, and by private hospitals and doctors. Private general practitioners (GPs), with surgeries across the country, are the first port of call for many middle-class South Africans seeking medical advice and who can afford private consultation fees that range from USD 20 to USD 50. For those who cannot afford private GPs, state medical facilities such as clinics and hospitals provide the only alternative. Many middle to upper class South Africans take out medical insurance (or "medical aid" as it is known in South Africa) to cover the cost of private hospitalization and/or day-to-day medical expenses.

Medical doctors prescribe medicines, and pharmacies dispense medicines. In the case of private doctors, the doctor will prescribe a specific medicine and the patient will purchase the medicine from a private pharmacy. The patient has access to a choice of medicines, and there are likely to be both branded and generic alternatives to medicine prescribed by a doctor. In some cases, if doctors are unfamiliar with the alternatives available for a particular medicine, they may leave it up to the pharmacist to provide the patient with an equivalent alternative (and may request this on the prescription note). However, the possibility of alternatives will depend on the availability of the medicine from the pharmaceutical company or distributor, and on whether the alternative medicines are stocked by the pharmacist. In the case of the public system, there is no or very limited choice available to the patient if the patient elects to obtain their medication from the dispensary at a public hospital. Public hospitals stock only those medicines made available to them through the public procurement system, and will typically only stock one brand for each type of medicine.

Medicine prices in South Africa are regulated by the government,[293] and generic medicines that are cheaper than their brand-name equivalents are approved by the government to provide patients[294] with access to more

---

293 The restructuring of the South African public health sector resulted in the development and implementation of the National Drug Policy in 1996. The primary objective of the Policy was to decrease the cost of medicines in both the private and public sectors. In 1997, the Medicines and Related Substances Control Amendment Act 90 was gazetted. It allowed government to reduce the cost of medicines.

294 Patients in the public healthcare system access prescribed medication via hospital dispensaries. These dispensaries are stocked with publicly procured medicines. Patients do not have a choice as to which medicine they receive and they do not pay for the medicines as they are charged a single fee (determined by their income level) for both the consultation and the medicines prescribed.

affordable alternatives.[295] Moreover, legislation introduced in 2004 prohibits drug firms from giving customers in the private sector discounts or rebates; they are required to sell their products at what is known as the "single exit price" (SEP) to all buyers. The national government's Department of Health is required by law to publish an annual notice of the maximum price hike allowed. In order to make medicine prices transparent, and in keeping with the Regulations Relating to a Transparent Pricing System for Medicines and Scheduled Substances,[296] the Department of Health publishes a publicly-accessible SEP database on the Medicine Price Registry website (http://www.mpr.gov.za/).

Medicine challenges

The problem in the regulated market for pharmaceuticals in South Africa is that doctors do not always prescribe generic medicines, and although pharmacists are obliged by law to offer private patients lower-priced generic medicines, this does not always happen.[297] According to an article in *Health24*, a South African consumer health site, only 56 percent of patients in the South African private health sector use generic medicines while the global norm is closer to 80 percent.[298] Price differentials between branded and generic medicines can be significant, and this affords private patients with greater opportunity to choose cheaper alternatives than those seeking care in the public sector. According to a study conducted by Bangalee and Suleman, of the 346 branded drugs in the study's sample, the median cost differential was 50.4 percent; 75 percent of the generic drugs considered were more than 40 percent cheaper than the branded version.[299] Although public patients encounter the biggest problems (since they are not given a choice of medicines), private patients also suffer from this price differential as they lack access to information allowing them to identify and purchase more affordable alternative to those prescribed.

As noted in the text box, medicine price data is actually published by the Department of Health (DoH) and available online. However, the information

---

295 V. Bangalee and F. Suleman, "Has the Increase in the Availability of Generic Drugs Lowered the Price of Cardiovascular Drugs in South Africa? *Health SA Gesondheid*, 21, No. 1 (2016), pp. 60–66.

296 *Medicines and Related Substances Act, 1965*, Department of Health, South Africa, 2004, http://www.hst.org.za/uploads/files/pricing_system_for_medicines.pdf.

297 M. Deroukakis, "Mandatory Substitution Successful," *South African Medical Journal*, 97, No. 1 (2007), pp. 63–64.

298 Health24, "Cost of Medicine in South Africa Set to Skyrocket," March 30, 2016, http://www.health24.com/Lifestyle/Health-and-your-money/News/the-high-cost-of-medicines-in-south-africa-20160323.

299 Ibid.

is difficult to find, and requires technical skills and some expert knowledge to use.[300]

KEY ACTORS

Key data provider(s)

The South African national government, through its Department of Health (DoH), has regulated medicine prices for the past decade, and is required by law to make medicine pricing transparent. The DoH does so by publishing medicine price data on its Medicine Price Registry site. The DoH is therefore the primary supplier of medicine price data. Mention should also be made of the Minister of Health, Aaron Motsoaledi, who has championed affordable medicines and has gone so far as to clash with multinational pharmaceutical companies operating in South Africa in his efforts to improve access to medicines through the use of affordable generics.[301]

The primary sources for the data are the privately owned and licensed pharmaceutical companies, which are required by law to submit their medicine prices on an annual basis to the DoH.

Key Data Users and Intermediaries

The central actor in the reuse of open government data is Code for South Africa (Code4SA, http://code4sa.org). Code4SA is a non-profit organization based in Cape Town, South Africa. Code4SA works with governments (national, regional and metropolitan), civil society organizations, the media and the tech community to promote the release, use and impact of open government data in South Africa. Adi Eyal, Director of Code4SA, was the prime driver behind the development of the MRPApp.

Other data intermediaries include private doctors who may rely on the MRPApp to advise private patients on alternative and potentially better priced medicines. Additionally, privately owned pharmacies act as both data users and intermediaries, as they may wish to familiarize themselves with the generic equivalents of prescribed branded medicines in order to provide the generic alternatives that they are legally obliged to offer patients. It is also conceivable that journalists, civil society organizations or consumer watchdog organizations may be interested in using the MRPApp to keep tabs on medicine prices and to call government to account if discrepancies appear in the prices listed online and those actually made available to patients.

---

300 The issue of the prices of medicines in South Africa and their affordability relative to international prices is not addressed here partly because there is limited research available on the issue (see, for example, A. Makholwa, "Medicine Pricing: New prescriptions needed," *Financial Mail*, January 30, 2014, http://www.financialmail.co.za/features/2014/01/30/medicine-pricing-new-prescriptions-needed.), partly because there is unevenness in the affordability of medicines across different medicines types in the South African market, and partly because the specific problem here is the lack of information available to support informed medicine purchasing decision-making.

301 A. Makholwa, "Medicine Pricing: New prescriptions needed," *Financial Mail*, January 30, 2014, http://www.financialmail.co.za/features/2014/01/30/medicine-pricing-new-prescriptions-needed.

Private companies that offer free medical advice services (such as websites), may also embed the MRPApp as a useful tool to attract patients to their services. Similarly, private medical aid providers may incorporate the MRPApp as a value added service into their product offerings.

Key Beneficiaries

Patients in the South African private healthcare sector are the primary beneficiaries of the available information on medicine prices. They are able to alter their decisions on which medicines to purchase based on the information provided by MRPApp. Such price-sensitive decisions may also lead to general efficiencies in the healthcare sector, which would benefit the South African economy as a whole.

Project Description and Inception

Initiation of the Open Data Activity

In 2014, Adi Eyal, the director of Code for South Africa, one of Africa's largest data journalism and civic technology initiatives, began wondering if there was a better way to make the information on medicine prices in South Africa available. He believed that if the information on medicine prices was more accessible and easier to understand, it could save private patients money. He soon realized that he could develop a simple application using a little known dataset from the Department of Health website that would help solve the problem confronting him and millions of South African patients. The dataset was the Medicine Price Registry (described further below) and it contained the single price exit data—the government-regulated price of all available medicines in the South African private health sector. Eyal's goal was to use this dataset to present information to patients in an easy-to-use format that would allow them to identify and request equivalent generics, and to make sure they weren't being overcharged by their pharmacies.

Eyal himself takes a number of medications for his own chronic conditions. In a blog post, he describes how the application he developed has benefited him personally, and how a search for a personal, individual solution led to a potential solution for society at large:

> Here's a real life example of how this app has benefited me. I take chronic medication A and B. The branded version of A costs R741.27 and B costs R947.78. A generic of A is available at R420.22. Not only that but my medical aid pay for it in full whereas

156

they only cover around R420.00 for the branded medicine. I only learnt about this by using the app.[302]

Demand and Supply of Data type(s) and Sources

The primary data source used for the Medicine Price Registry application (MPRApp, https://mpr.code4sa.org/) is the database on medicine prices (the Medicine Price Registry), published by the national Department of Health of the Government of South Africa. The database contains prices, product details (e.g. schedule and form), ingredients and available dosages of all government-approved medicines in South Africa. The database is published annually following the publication of single exit price for medicines as required by law. Occasional updates are made by the Department during the course of the year to correct errors or make unforeseen adjustments. An RSS feed is available to notify interested parties of updates and changes made to the database. The database is also available for download in Microsoft Excel format from the Medicine Price Registry website.

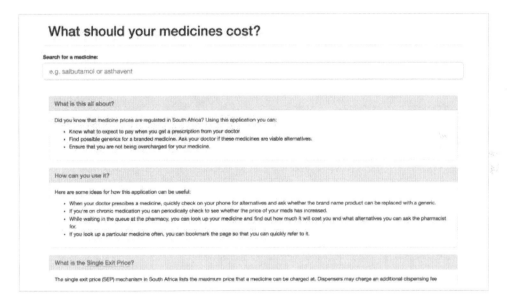

Figure 1. MPRApp Main Page

---

302 Adi Eyal, "Open data FTW!" Code for South Africa, April 2014, http://code4sa.org/2014/04/25/generic-medicines-ftw.html.

Although the data contained on the site is in theory "open," users have to jump through a number of hoops to use it. Here are some of the steps a typical user would have to take in order to compare medicine prices:[303]

1. Know about and locate the Medicine Price Registry website.
2. Locate the page http://www.mpr.gov.za/PublishedDocuments. aspx#DocCatId=21 from the landing page by clicking on "SEP Databases" in the "Frequently Used Links" menu.
3. Download the latest single exit price database, a 40 megabyte Microsoft Excel spreadsheet.
4. Open a large spreadsheet which contains the 14,728 rows of medicines and 22 columns of descriptive data for each medicine listed.
5. Search for the relevant medicine.
6. To find generics, search by ingredient and discard all those alternatives that have a different strength (e.g. 200mg or 400mg) and dosage form (e.g. tablet or suspension).
7. To calculate the over the counter price, add the pharmacist dispensing fees (not provided in the spreadsheet) to the single exit price (provided in the spreadsheet).[304]

Needless to say, this process is complex, cumbersome and well beyond the abilities of most patients. Code4SA's innovation was to simplify the process for the end user to determine the cheapest alternative to a prescribed medicine.

Code4SA's application consists of a single page providing some contextual and instructional information, and a search bar allowing users to search for specific medicines or active ingredients. The results returned contain matching products and/or ingredients. An icon is also displayed, indicating the medicine form (tablet, suspension, etc.). For each matching product, the following information is provided: maximum price, schedule, dosage form, tablets/ml/ doses, number of packs, generic/innovator, and a list of active ingredients (name and amount). Users are able to click on a link labelled "Find Generics" for each result.

The application data is updated on an asynchronous basis. The process involves the director of Code4SA downloading any data updates, cleaning

---

303 These steps are based on the Medicine Price Registry website as of September 14, 2016, and on the Database of Medicine Prices of August 8, 2016.

304 According to the Code for South Africa website, the Medicines and Related Substances Act allows for the following charges (excl. VAT):
- Where the SEP is less than R85.69, the maximum dispensing fee is R7.04 + 46% of the SEP.
- Where the SEP is less than R228.56, the maximum dispensing fee is R18.80 + 33% of the SEP.
- Where the SEP is less than R799.99, the maximum dispensing fee is R59.83 + 15% of the SEP.
- Where the SEP is greater than or equal to R799.99, the maximum dispensing fee is R140.00 + 5% of the SEP.

the data and importing the updated and cleaned data into the application database.[305]

Funding

No external funding was available for this open data initiative, nor is there any intention to generate any income from the MPRApp in order to cover its development or operation. The development of the application was primarily made possible by non-material inputs—in particular, the developers' entrepreneurial spirit, time, energy, and technical skills. Code4SA's existing organizational infrastructure to house and support the application also contributed to its development.

Open Data Use

Initially, the developers of the MPRApp anticipated that it would be used primarily by patients, and possibly to a limited extent by other developers who might feed the data into other personal health applications or platforms.[306] Neither Eyal nor Code4SA did much to promote or market the application, and initial uptake and monitoring appeared to be slow, as evidenced by the fact that the developers were unaware that the website hosting the application went down in mid-2014.[307] As it turned out, the unavailability of the application unintentionally provided evidence of the application's use. This evidence took the form of an email sent to Code4SA, enquiring when the website would be back up, and indicating the application's usefulness to the sender:

It is with sadness that I not [sic] that your medicine price registry website is no longer working. The site was a powerful tool in my medical practice, it really helped me to work out treatments that my patients could afford. I'd like to know if the website will be coming back online anytime soon. Thank you very much for your efforts in general.[308]

Once the online application was restored, the sender followed up with this message:

---

305 At the time of writing, the last update of the MPRApp was on July 19, 2016 while the latest government data available was dated 8 August 2016.

306 Adi Eyal, "How Much Should You Be Paying for Your Medicines?" Code for South Africa, October 2013 http://code4sa.org/2013/10/15/comparing-medicine-prices.html.

307 Adi Eyal, "Open data FTW!" Code for South Africa, April 2014, http://code4sa.org/2014/04/25/generic-medicines-ftw.html.

308 Adi Eyal, "Open data FTW!" Code for South Africa, April 2014, http://code4sa.org/2014/04/25/generic-medicines-ftw.html.

I work in a mixed-income neighbourhood and being able to figure out what works for my patients' budgets is extremely helpful—there's is no point in prescribing medicine that the patient cannot afford to buy. Please keep up the good work.[309]

The emails revealed an unexpected use case for MPRApp. While the application had been created primarily with patients in mind as end-users, and while the MPRApp's creator himself was able to benefit from the application as a patient, in many cases it wasn't patients who accessed the application directly, but rather medical practitioners. These practitioners served as trusted and expert intermediaries for patients, who were unable to understand and benefit from the information contained in the application without guidance. In fact, the situation was even somewhat more complex: it turned out that the medical practitioner who emailed Eyal had not discovered the application directly, but rather through one of his patients. All of this suggests not just the important role of intermediaries (e.g., physicians or pharmacists) in propagating and using such applications, but the symbiotic role intermediaries play with end-users (e.g., patients). Together, intermediaries and end-users are able to maximize the potential of open data.

Impact

Impact is often difficult to measure, especially as many projects included in this series of case studies have been initiated relatively recently. The larger, systemic impact of open data can take many years to be evident, and in most countries is very much a work in progress. Nonetheless, a couple initial forms of impact from the MPRApp project can be identified.

Use Indicators

The above analysis relies heavily on blogs written by Eyal and on the email exchange between Eyal and the appreciative doctor as evidence of use. The reality is that many small-scale open data initiatives simply do not have the time or resources to evaluate the use and impact of their products. In fact, if the MPRApp website had not gone down, Code for South Africa might never even have known that their product was in fact being used.

Eyal confirmed the lack of resources to establish who is using the MPRApp and what they may be using it for. What he could provide were website analytics that show that approximately 2,000 unique visitors per month access

---

309 Ibid.

the application. Most of these visitors are repeat visitors. In addition, Code for South Africa also receives regular requests for the application data to be updated when it is no longer in sync with the latest available government data. All of this suggests that the application is being used, and that users are deriving benefit from it. See Figures 2 and 3 for further web analytics for 2016 providing evidence of frequent and increasing use of the MPRApp to query the prices of medicines (Figure 2) and generic alternatives (Figure 3).

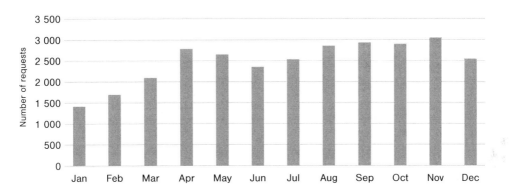

Figure 2. MPRApp Request for Product Details in 2016

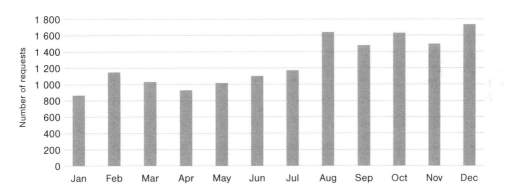

Figure 3. MPRApp Requests for Generic Medicines in 2016

There is also evidence that the MPRApp API is being used by other intermediaries to access medicine price data in their efforts to reach and engage patients (see, for example, HEALTH-E News, a popular South African health news website).[310]

Changed Outcomes

The immediate problem being addressed is a lack of access to usable information on medicine prices, which results in private patients not being able to make informed purchasing decisions in relation to prescribed medicines. There are various ways to measure impact. Key indicators would be those that provide evidence of change directly attributable to the creation of the MPRApp. Measuring change at a macro level and ascribing a causal connection between the introduction of a new piece of technology and the change observed is, however, tenuous. Ascribing causal connections at the micro level is more feasible (though not without challenges). Evidence of impact at the micro level in this case could, for instance, take the form of private patients or other citizens changing their behavior in relation to the prescription and/or purchasing of medicines in South Africa.

Outcomes and Impacts

Demonstrated Use

From the anecdotal evidence available, it is clear that the availability of new information on medicine pricing, extracted from open government data, has changed how certain patients make decisions (in this case, by proxy) related to the purchasing of medicines.

It is not possible to claim that patients are healthier, and even if additional evidence came to light that showed that a particular community or a group of patients linked to a doctor using the application are in fact healthier, it would still be problematic to draw a causal relationship between better decision-making and healthier citizens.

There is also evidence in the form of web analytics of the same people making repeated use of the MPRApp. While it is not possible to say with certainty what the value or benefits accrued from using MPRApp are, it can be said with some degree of certainty that repeated use and the need for up-to-date data are indicative of some form of positive impact being experienced by users.

---

310 "[Updated] Health-e News, Code4SA launch new medicines pricing app," *Health-E News*, March 2, 2015, https://www.health-e.org.za/2015/03/02/health-e-news-code4sa-launch-new-medicines-pricing-app/.

It is acknowledged that impact is claimed based on an extremely limited number of cases and on shallow web analytics data. It is beyond the scope of this study to conduct a large-scale survey on the awareness, use and impact of the MPRApp. Interviews were conducted with two medical doctors who work in both the public and private sectors to get a better understanding of the medicines market and the prescriptions process. Both did, however, reveal that neither of them knew about the MPRApp although both confirmed its value for private patients. While a lack of numerous sources supporting claims of use and/or impact are frustrating, this should not be seen as overly limiting. Breadth of evidence is less of an issue than firm evidence. Moreover, assuming that a particular number of users is indicative of actual use or impact can be highly problematic. As is evidenced in this case study, a single intermediary user may be reaching tens or hundreds of beneficiaries who will not show up in usage analytics. This may be particularly relevant in environments where low technical skills or limited Internet access prevail.

Nevertheless, further research is clearly required to provide additional supportive evidence of the use and impact of MPRApp.

Risks

As evidenced by the example of MPRApp and various other case studies included in this series, open data holds tremendous potential for positive transformation. But, as we also see throughout this series, open data also poses certain risks. It is important to understand these risks in order to ensure that open data projects are implemented in as safe a manner and in a way that maximizes the potential upsides and limits the downsides.

Two doctors were interviewed for this case study in order to assess the risks inherent in the MPRApp. They raised two broad issues. The first concerned the accuracy of the information contained within the application. One doctor suggested, for instance, that the MPRApp needs to make it clearer to users when alternative medications suggested in the search results do not in fact contain *exactly* the same active ingredients as the queried medication. For example, a search for "Sandoz Atenolol 50" (of which the only active ingredient is adenol) provides a list of 12 alternative medicines, two of which contain additional active ingredients (one contains hydrochlorothiazide while the other contains chlortalidone). Such imperfect matches pose several potential risks, including the possibility of adverse reactions or medical inefficacy. Similar examples were found when Code4SA conducted live testing of the application with doctors prior to its full-scale launch.

In addition, the doctors interviewed queried the comprehensiveness of the data provided. They stated, for instance, that they were aware of alternative (and sometimes cheaper) medicines that were not in fact listed in the MPRApp. The reasons for these gaps in information are unclear, but a number of factors could be at play: errors in the source data provided by the government, outdated data, or confusion introduced due to different procurement mechanisms across different aspects of the South African health sector. Regardless of the reasons, if the database does not correspond with existing knowledge and the actual availability of medications, it could result in less-than-optimal cost savings and, more generally, jeopardize the trust that doctors place in the application.

Lessons Learned

While impact, beyond anecdotal stories of use, remains difficult to define in the case of MPRApp, the project did surface some key lessons regarding enabling conditions and barriers for establishing successful open data initiatives in developing economies.

Enablers

Policy and legislative framework

A key enabler for the MPRApp open data initiative was South Africa's legislative framework that promotes and enacts transparency in medicine pricing. The existence of such a framework compels the Department of Health to collect and publish data on medicine prices in South Africa.

The right policy or legislative framework is not, however, on its own sufficient to enable an application such as this one.[311] For example, government departments may collect data in compliance with existing laws, but fail to publish the data in a manner or format that enables access or reuse (despite such an approach being required in the policy framework). In this particular case, the department in question complies with the regulations and publishes timely, complete data on medicines pricing in machine-readable format, allowing a developer to repackage the data into useful information.

---

311 See for example, F. Van Schalkwyk, M. Willmers and T. Schonwetter, "Embedding Open Data Practice: Developing indicators on the institutionalisation of open data practice in two South African countries," UCT IP Unit, University of Cape Town, 2015, http://webfoundation.org/docs/2015/08/ODDC-2-Embedding-Open-Data-Practice-FINAL.pdf, on the disjuncture between policy and practice in the case of Kenya and South Africa.

Committed and skilled technical community

MPRapp also very much owes its existence to the presence of a skilled and committed developer, who was backed by a wider technical ecology. This personal and institutional commitment was especially important given the lack of available funding, which means that the application depended almost exclusively on personal drive and vision.

Trusted and expert intermediaries

As we have seen, MPRapp's usefulness to patients was often mediated through the expertise and knowledge of doctors, pharmacists and other medical practitioners. Such trusted intermediaries often play a vital role in spreading the benefits of open data and, more generally, technology. They serve as vital go-betweens that allow the benefits of technology to manifest, and that ensure its potential is apparent and seized by even those average citizens who may lack the required technical skills to use applications and platforms on their own.

Barriers

Funding

The lack of funding posed a significant barrier in extending the impact of the MPRApp, even though it was apparent that doctors (and not only patients) were using the application. Shortage of funds for expansion and awareness building limited the uptake and possible impact of the MPRApp. According to Eyal, there was interest from government in taking over the management of the MPRApp but the apparent lack of capacity at the government level to do so means that the application's sustainability remains at risk.

Limited reach

Another barrier stems from the fact that the MPRapp has limited reach—it only benefits patients purchasing medicines from private pharmacies, while those in the public healthcare area are not similarly presented with alternative medicines to purchase. The divide between the private and the public health sector, both of which are regulated by government, is a barrier to the broader application, use and impact of the MPRApp to patients outside of the private health sector. More generally, since those in the private sector tend generally to be better off, the limited reach of the application—especially if it were to be used more broadly—could reinforce existing socioeconomic inequalities and lead to an all-too-familiar digital divide.

Data problems

The data published by the Department of Health is not interoperable, meaning that it cannot be easily combined with other data sources or processed with existing tools. This places limits on the usefulness of the MRPApp and could jeopardize the trust that users place in the application. Currently, the application data is updated only when the developer has time to do so or when persistent requests from users for updated data are received. Automatic updates of the application data made possible by the government data being interoperable would help mitigate this barrier.

Looking Forward

Current Status

The application is still active, and the director of Code4SA updates the data as and when time permits. These updates are often prompted by users of the MPRApp, and not conducted according to a regular schedule.

Sustainability

The flow of data and information from the government is likely to continue, but the sustainability of the application itself remains in question. There are at least two reasons for this: (1) the application relies on the infrastructure of an organization that itself depends on donor funding for its functioning; and (2) the application depends on the generosity of one individual—i.e., Adi Eyal —to allocate time and energy to the application and maintaining its data. However, according to Eyal, the Department of Health is supportive, and there has been some indication that it may be interested in taking over the management of the MPRApp. To date, this interest has not translated into concrete action.

Replicability

The open data initiative is replicable in other countries, states or provinces where national or subnational governments make data on medicine pricing available, where there is differential pricing for similar medicines, and where patients have a choice in relation to the brand of medicine. Where government does not collect medicine price data, it is conceivable that data could be collected via crowdsourcing or perhaps even directly from pharmaceutical companies, although a clear incentive (most probably financial) would need to be in place to initiate and sustain data collection.

The open data initiative may also be replicable in other sectors when governments regulate the prices of commodities and consumables. There is not any direct evidence, however, that MPRApp has been replicated in any way to date.

Conclusion

The following points are worth making in terms of how this particular case study could inform a more universal theory of change on the impact of open data in developing countries:

1. It takes a combination of factors and conditions for an open data initiative to have impact. In this case, it was a cocktail of the following: a clear real-world problem; a curious and committed individual with technical skills and a social conscience; a relevant, regular and reliable open data source; an element of luck that allowed the application to be discovered despite no marketing efforts; and, last but not least, genuine usefulness to users who found value in the data (and, in this case, contacted the organizers when the application went down).

2. Relevant, regular and reliable open government data requires effort and resources. The existence of regulations mandating transparency are critical in ensuring that government departments publish open data. It should also be noted that regulations in the absence of compliance is an insufficient condition. What is required is the right regulatory framework combined with a culture of compliance (or tools to ensure compliance).

3. The ultimate beneficiaries of an open data initiative may not necessarily be the best target group in terms of marketing and promoting the use of the application. Trusted intermediaries who possess additional expertise and who have access to beneficiaries may be a better place to start. This is particularly true of data that may require a certain expertise to use and make sense of.

4. Not all open data projects require funding to be initiated. However, external funding does help in spreading the benefits of open data applications, and in particular making them sustainable and enabling them to grow over time.

Open Data's Impact on Creating Opportunity

CHAPTER 12

Aclímate Colombia
Open data to improve agricultural resiliency

Andrew Young and Stefaan Verhulst

Summary

In Colombia, as in many other countries, the effects of climate change are increasingly evident. One sector that has been particularly hard hit is agriculture. In this sector, unanticipated weather shifts and extended drought periods have created major challenges for the country's farms, perhaps especially for small, independently owned farms. The Aclímate Colombia project is a cross-sector partnership led by the International Center for Tropical Agriculture (CIAT), a civil society organization, with private-sector industry groups and government actors. The platform (available at aclimatecolombia.org) leverages a diversity of data sources, including many open government datasets, to help farmers understand how to better navigate shifting weather patterns. Although still relatively young, Aclímate Colombia has already had a tangible impact and received widespread recognition. It is a powerful example of how data-sharing across sectors—along with the use of sector-relevant intermediaries—can take high-level data science insights and translate them into concrete, actionable information, in the process helping farmers increase their livelihoods.

Context and Background

Problem Focus / Country Context

Agriculture is a very important sector in Colombia and in the tropics in general. As Ruben G. Echeverría, Director General of the International Center for Tropical Agriculture (CIAT) put it: "Parts of the humid tropics have the potential to become future breadbaskets for the world. They are where some 70 percent of the world's poor people now live, and they contain most of the world's biodiversity."[312] Colombia, in particular, holds tremendous possibilities as a provider of crops such as coffee, bananas and rice.

However, in order for countries like Colombia to achieve their potential, they must be able to adapt to the effects of climate change. As traditional growing processes are thrown into upheaval as a result of new weather patterns, global warming presents many challenges to the food-growing potential of Colombia. It represents a particularly serious challenge for small farmers, who constitute a large proportion of the crop growers in the country. As Echeverría notes: "Climate change poses a serious threat for these smallholder farmers, who already face significant challenges from poor soils, volatile rainfall patterns, lack of knowledge on best cultivation practices, and lack of investment in new technologies that can help them."[313]

The example of rice is illustrative. Rice is of particular importance to the agriculture sector in Colombia, representing the primary source of income for small farms and a staple food for much of the population, in particular lower-income communities.[314] The country's agriculture sector produced around 1.7 million tons of paddy rice in 2014 – around 65 percent of which was produced by lowland irrigated rice and 35 percent rainfed rice.[315] Recent years, however, have been hard for the country's rice sector. A decade of increases in irrigated rice yields was wiped out between 2007 and 2012 when yields dropped from 6 to 5 tons per hectare.[316] Though explanations vary, climate change is seen as the likely cause of the decrease. As the global research partnership, Consultative Group on International Agricultural Research (CGIAR) puts it, "subtle shifts in rainfall as well as more extreme weather are forcing rice growers to toss aside old assumptions about when, where and what to plant."[317]

---

312 CIAT Communicaciones, "A Powerful Voice for Climate-smart Agriculture in the Tropics," December 6, 2014, CIAT, https://ciat.cgiar.org/news-2-2/a-powerful-voice-for-climate-smart-agriculture-in-the-tropics.

313 Ibid.

314 Elizabeth Stuart, Emma Samman, William Avis and Tom Berliner, *The Data Revolution: Finding the Missing Millions, Research Report 03*, Development Progress, 2015, https://www.odi.org/sites/odi.org.uk/files/odi-assets/publications-opinion-files/9604.pdf.

315 S. Delerce, et al., Assessing Weather-Yield Relationships in Rice at Local Scale Using Data Mining Approaches," *PLoS ONE*, August 25, 2016, http://journals.plos.org/plosone/article?id=10.1371%2Fjournal.pone.0161620.

316 CTIAR and CCAFS, "Big Data for Climate-smart Agriculture," *Change for the Better: The CCAFS 2015 Annual Report*, https://ccafs.cgiar.org/bigdata#.V6jLT5ODGko.

317 Ibid.

Open Data in Colombia

In some ways, the state of open data in Colombia is quite encouraging. For example, in the 2015 Open Data Index, an assessment of data availability across a number of sectors put together by Open Knowledge International, the country ranked number four, up from 12 in 2014. This ranking is probably a reflection of the general openness of data relating to national statistics, procurement tenders, location datasets, and election results. However, despite the country's good performance on such measurements, our research and interviews with key players suggest several remaining shortcomings. While these shortcomings exist in many (perhaps most) countries that have experimented with open data, they are nonetheless important to understand for assessing the overall open data ecosystem.

One notable problem stems from the fact that Colombia's open data supply is fragmented, with little clarity on where and how to access the most useful datasets. As of August 2016, the government's official open data portal, Datos Abiertos Colombia (datos.gov.co), houses around 2,460 datasets and 70 visualizations. An additional data portal, Ciudatos (ciudatos.com), was established by the Corona Foundation in 2015, in collaboration with other civil society actors and funders across the region. The portal contains city-focused public datasets and data drawn from perception surveys conducted by Red Colombiana de Ciudades Cómo Vamos—"the network of city-level networks in Colombia dedicated to improving urban life."[318]

The existence of these two portals, while signs of a strong open data movement, also leads to a certain fragmentation. For example, users may be unsure where to search for data, and may have trouble combining information stored at the two locations for further analysis. Further complicating matters is the World Bank's Climate Change Knowledge Portal, which also hosts a number of Colombian open datasets, mostly on temperature and rainfall.[319]

Colombia originally expressed interest in joining the Open Government Partnership (OGP) in 2011.[320] Many of its OGP commitments—and, perhaps as a result, much of the country's government innovation and data work more generally—is focused on fighting corruption. This points to a further weakness in the open data space—for all its availability, data has had relatively little impact on issues like economic development or catalyzing entrepreneurship and

---

318 Social Progress Imperative, "Contributing to Novel Open Data Platform in Columbia," March 27, 2016, http://www.socialprogressimperative.org/contributing-to-novel-open-data-platform-in-colombia/.

319 The World Bank Group, "Climate Change Knowledge Portal," 2016, http://sdwebx.worldbank.org/climateportal/index.cfm?page=country_historical_climate&ThisCCode=COL.

320 Open Government Partnership, "Columbia," 2015, http://www.opengovpartnership.org/country/colombia.

business.[321] Overall, the lack of incentives for users in the business community to access and use open data has resulted in minimal demand for open data.[322]

KEY ACTORS

Key Data Providers

Government of Colombia

The primary government actor pushing forward Aclímate Colombia is the Ministry of Agriculture and Rural Development (MARD). MARD's mission is to "formulate, coordinate and evaluate policies that promote competitive, equitable and sustainable development of forestry, fisheries and rural development agricultural processes, criteria of decentralization, consultation and participation, to help improve the level and quality of life of the Colombian population."[323]

CIAT project lead Daniel Jimenez notes that the Colombian government, and MARD in particular, were the central funders for the project, and helped to facilitate communication between CIAT and important actors in the agriculture sector, enabling CIAT to access and analyze datasets held by stakeholders in other sectors.[324]

While MARD is the most important government collaborator on the project, the primary government data provider is the National Institute of Hydrology, Meteorology and Environmental Studies (IDEAM), which collects and—as a result of recent legislation[325]—opens climate data for the country.[326]

Key Data Users and Intermediaries

CIAT

The central actor in the development of Aclímate Colombia is the International Center for Tropical Agriculture (CIAT), "an agricultural research institution, nonprofit, focused on generating scientific solutions to combat hunger in the tropics." Originally established in 1970 as part of the Consultative Group on International Agricultural Research (CGIAR), CIAT plays the central data science and project management role in the initiative as part of its research program on Climate Change, Agriculture and Food Security (CCAFS). CCAFS seeks to "address the challenge of increased global warming and declining food security, agricultural practices, policies and measures.[327]

---

321 GovLab interview with Oscar Montiel, Open Knowledge International, September 8, 2016.

322 GovLab interview with Daniel Uribe, Fundacion Corona, September 13, 2016.

323 Aclímate Colombia, "Quiénes Somos," http://www.aclimatecolombia.org/quienes-somos-2/.

324 GovLab interview with Daniel Jimenez, International Center for Tropical Agriculture (CIAT), August 23, 2016.

325 "Information Request," IDEAM, http://www.ideam.gov.co/solicitud-de-informacion.

326 . GovLab interview with Daniel Jimenez, International Center for Tropical Agriculture (CIAT), August 23, 2016.

327 Aclímate Colombia, "Quiénes Somos," http://www.aclimatecolombia.org/quienes-somos-2/

CIAT not only conceptualized and developed the data analytics capabilities that enabled the project but also worked closely with growers associations and other stakeholders to gain access to and analyze relevant historical datasets.[328]

Fedearroaz and Crop Growers Associations

Demonstrating the potential of cross-sector collaboration on open data projects, the other key piece of the Aclímate Colombia puzzle is the stable of crop grower associations in the country. The associations, which represent and advocate for farmers, exist in both the private and semi-public sectors. The crop grower associations in many ways act as the intermediary translating the insights and tools provided by CIAT to the individual-level farmers they represent. CIAT armed these associations with the know-how to "analyze information from big data tools and determine the most limiting factors in production for the crops in specific regions."[329]

Given the focus on spurring growth in the rice sector, Fedearroz (i.e., the Rice Growers Association) was CIAT's central collaborator. According to Miryam Patricia Guzmán García, the deputy director of technology for Fedearroz, the organization has three central missions. First, it represents rice farmers at the ministerial level to ensure that their interests are known to government decision-makers. Second, Fedearroz works to transfer technological capabilities with the ability "to better the productivity and cost effectiveness" of farming in Colombia. Finally, the association seeks to provide farmers with the services they need—from identifying sellers of needed supplies to establishing partnerships with relevant industry players to finding (or providing) new funding streams.[330]

Fedearroz was eager to collaborate on the project to help ensure that, as Guzmán García puts it, "the research that normally takes place in the research centers gets down to the level where it is really needed: to the farmers."[331] This involved both providing access to relevant data and insights on the country's rice growers to CIAT, and also transferring the end results and tools provided by Aclímate Colombia to those who can use it in practice.

Key Beneficiaries

Associated Farmers in Colombia

While there are potentially massive public benefits of increased yields and sustainability in the agriculture sector, the most direct beneficiaries targeted by Aclímate Colombia are farmers affiliated with growing associations in the country. The project seeks to provide such farmers with the decision-making capability to consistently make the right planting choices and better react to the shifting impacts of climate change. As

---

328 GovLab interview with Daniel Jimenez, International Center for Tropical Agriculture (CIAT), August 23, 2016.
329 Ibid.
330 GovLab interview with Miryam Patricia Guzmán García, Deputy Director of Technology, Fedearroz, September 5, 2016.
331 Ibid.

described in more detail in the Risks and Challenges sections, unaffiliated farmers, while theoretically an intended beneficiary of the initiative, are largely disengaged from its current iteration.

Project Description

Initiation of the Open Data Activity

The summer of 2013 was a particularly dry season in Colombia. An extended drought in many regions of the country had a major impact on agriculture and crops. In the northwestern department of La Guajira, for instance, the drought led to food and water scarcity, and the death of around 20,000 cattle.[332] Farmers in the southern Casanare region also faced consistently high temperatures, ravaged plantations and exhausted water supplies.[333] In response to these struggles, the Colombian government began exploring options for strengthening growers' associations. With this goal in mind, the Minister of Agriculture signed an agreement with CIAT aimed at "strengthening the capacity of Colombia's agricultural sector to adapt to climate vulnerability action." This agreement includes evaluations of seasonal forecasting and providing specific recommendations for increasing productivity.[334] The result of these recommendations is evident in many ways on the Aclímate Colombia website, for example through regular, targeted newsletters, context-specific information analysis tools, data-driven agriculture strategy reports, and a searchable data portal.

As a first step, CIAT developed a methodology for leveraging data to develop productivity-bolstering recommendations for farmers (i.e., which crops to grow, and when, depending on region). In this effort, CIAT was inspired by a number of previous data-driven agriculture projects initiated by other NGOs around the world; these included "the use of both supervised and unsupervised artificial neural networks to model Andean Blackberry (*Rubus glaucus*) yields, and the use of mixed models to determine optimum growing conditions of Lulo (*Solanum quitoense*)" in the Andes.[335] CIAT representatives

---

332 "Colombia: The Effects of Drought in La Guajira," World Food Programme, August 27, 2014, https://www.wfp.org/stories/colombia-effects-drought-la-guajira.

333 "Drought threat to Colombia's southern farming belt," *World Bulletin*, April 3, 2014, http://www.worldbulletin.net/news/132752/drought-threat-to-colombias-southern-farming-belt.

334 GovLab interview with Daniel Jimenez, International Center for Tropical Agriculture (CIAT), August 23, 2016.

335 Silvain Delerce, et al., "Assessing Weather-Yield Relationships in Rice at Local Scale Using Data Mining Approaches," PLOS One, August 25, 2016, http://journals.plos.org/plosone/article?id=10.1371%2Fjournal.pone.0161620.

then approached Fedearroz, the rice growers association, with the idea of using the association's data as well as existing open government datasets to improve farmers' decision-making capabilities.

Fedearroz readily agreed to share data gathered over the course of over twenty-five years, including an annual rice survey, harvest monitoring records and results from agronomic experiments.[336] As Guzmán García puts it, "we decided to be part of the project to enable better analysis of all the information we had and to improve practices and recommendations for farmers to reduce the risks they face."[337] Fedearroz was in part eager to collaborate on the project to help ensure that, as Guzmán García puts it, "the research that normally takes place in the research centers gets down to the level where it is really needed: to the farmers."[338] This involved both providing access to relevant data and insights on the country's rice growers to CIAT, and also transferring the end results and tools provided by Aclímate Colombia to those who could really use it in practice: small farmers who lack the type of R&D capacity enjoyed by larger corporate farms. At a most fundamental level, Aclímate Colombia uses these diverse open data sources to "identify the most productive rice varieties and planting times for specific sites and seasonal forecasts."[339]

The CIAT effort is just one manifestation of a growing global effort to leverage open data to benefit the agriculture sector. The Global Open Data for Agriculture and Nutrition (GODAN) network brings together nearly 500 cross-sector entities around the concept, and we examine the Esoko agriculture platform in Ghana in another case study from this series.[340]

Funding

As Latin America continues to grow as a hotbed for open data activity and experimentation, international funding sources abound. Colombia, in particular, is seen by those in the field as receiving a notable amount of international funding for its data-driven projects, along with Mexico and Argentina.[341] Yet despite the apparent availability of grants from international organizations like the Inter-American Development Bank and others, the primary funding source

---

336 CTIAR and CCAFS, "Big Data for Climate-smart Agriculture," *Change for the Better: The CCAFS 2015 Annual Report*, https://ccafs.cgiar.org/bigdata#.V6jLT5ODGko.

337 GovLab interview with Miryam Patricia Guzmán García, Deputy Director of Technology, Fedearroz, September 5, 2016.

338 Ibid.

339 . CTIAR and CCAFS, "Big Data for Climate-smart Agriculture," *Change for the Better: The CCAFS 2015 Annual Report*, https://ccafs.cgiar.org/bigdata#.V6jLT5ODGko.

340 François van Schalkwyk, Andrew Young and Stefaan Verhulst, "Esoko – Leveling the Information Playing Field for Smallholder Farmers," Open Data for Developing Economies Case Studies, July 2017, http://odimpact.org/case-ghana-empowering-smallholder-farmers.html.

341 GovLab interview with Mor Rubinstein, Open Knowledge International, September 8, 2016.

for Aclímate Colombia is in fact the Colombian government. These funds are primarily targeted at supporting the continued technical development of tools and communications and training efforts to increase the uptake of data-driven insights. As the project continues to grow and mature, it is likely that more diverse funding options will be tapped.

Demand and Supply of Data Type(s) and Sources

Three types of data are primarily available on the Aclímate Colombia platform. The first is commercial crop data collected by Fedearroz, for example the previously mentioned annual rice surveys and harvest monitoring records. Much of this data was already accessible in anonymized form, but had to be centralized and digitized to be usable for Aclímate Colombia.[342] As Guzman Garcia put it: the data was previously "public at a general level for each farm, without naming the saint" – i.e., free of personally identifiable information.[343]

Second, the platform contains station-level daily weather data from the National Institute of Hydrology, Meteorology and Environmental Studies (IDEAM), as well as from a Fedearroz-led agro-meteorological network. This data helps provide insight on what CIAT considers the five most important climatic variables determining rice growth: minimum temperature, maximum temperature, precipitation, relative humidity and solar radiation.[344]

Finally, perhaps the most important datasets on the platform actually contain a combination of data, and in particular a yield record for specific fields along with a record of "cropping events"—essentially, everything that happened to a yield's crop between being planted and being harvested. Important elements feeding into cropping events include soil conditions and "management practices implemented by the farmer."[345]

All this data can be downloaded in raw form by users of the platform. In addition, the platform itself subjects the data to a range of analytic methods that provide users with region- and crop-specific insights. The platform also subjects the data to more sophisticated, machine-learning driven analyses that, according to Daniel Jimenez, "explore non-linear functional relationships between various factors – temperature, radiation, rainfall and productivity,"

---

342 Silvain Delerce, et al., "Assessing Weather-Yield Relationships in Rice at Local Scale Using Data Mining Approaches," PLOS One, August 25, 2016, http://journals.plos.org/plosone/article?id=10.1371%2Fjournal.pone.0161620.

343 GovLab interview with Miryam Patricia Guzmán García, Deputy Director of Technology, Fedearroz, September 5, 2016.

344 Silvain Delerce, et al., "Assessing Weather-Yield Relationships in Rice at Local Scale Using Data Mining Approaches," PLOS One, August 25, 2016, http://journals.plos.org/plosone/article?id=10.1371%2Fjournal.pone.0161620.

345 Ibid.

to the end of teasing out the most factors most directly influential to a given farming strategy.[346] The machine-learning algorithms used by CIAT were influenced by similar efforts in biology, robotics and neuroscience.[347]

Open Data Use

Open data feeds into all analyses conducted as part of the Aclímate Colombia suite of tools. So while open data is only one piece of the puzzle for the initiative—along with the industry- and NGO-provided data described above—distinguishing between the use of open data for the initiative and the initiative itself is impossible. In the simplest of terms, Aclímate Colombia could not exist without access to open data.

Aclímate Colombia uses its diversity of datasets to create a number of tools and information products, including newsletters related to farming (Figure 1) that are both informative and easily-digestible (Figure 2). The site also provides research topics, modeling, and information about the Convention agreement that launched the site in the first place. Most helpfully, though, the site offers a searchable data portal (Figure 3) and points visitors toward additional data-driven resources and datasets. The end result is that the project is able to communicate its methods, research, and findings in a clear and accessible manner to those who seek it out and have a positive impact.

Impact

Impact is often difficult to measure, especially as many projects included in this series of case studies have been initiated relatively recently. The larger, systemic impact of open data can take many years to manifest, and in most countries open data is very much a work in progress. Nonetheless, several initial forms of impact from the Aclímate Colombia project can be identified.

---

346 Elizabeth Stuart, "The Data Revolution: Finding the Missing Millions," *Development Progress, Research Report 03*, 2015, https://www.odi.org/sites/odi.org.uk/files/odi-assets/publications-opinion-files/9604.pdf.

347 CTIAR and CCAFS, "Big Data for Climate-smart Agriculture," *Change for the Better: The CCAFS 2015 Annual Report*, https://ccafs.cgiar.org/bigdata#.V6jLT5ODGko.

Figure 1. Aclímate Colombia Newsletter Sign Up

Figure 2. Aclímate Colombia Newsletter

One illustrative example of how Aclímate Colombia can work occurred about a year into the initiative. After the site's analysis predicted that a major dry period would disrupt the growing season and necessitate a delay in planting, Fedearroz broadcast a "simple, site-specific message," providing detailed, granular information to 170 farmers in Cordoba on the "ideal windows for planting or the best variety to grow."[348] The combination of highly specific and actionable information broadcast by a trusted and reliable source (i.e., the farmers' growing association) meant that uptake of the recommendation was significant. Many farmers avoided making premature, doomed-to-failure planting decisions, thus escaping significant losses.

Other initial markers of impact are explored in the section below.

New Knowledge and Insights

One of the most impressive aspects of Aclímate Colombia is how quickly it has enabled the transfer of knowledge and research findings from the lab into the field. As CIAT representatives put it in a journal article about the project: "Whilst previous global and continental scale studies have successfully characterized the impact of climate variability on yields, they have limited direct relevance to farm-level decisions."[349] The highly particular and localized nature of the project, as well as its use of intermediaries—i.e., growers associations—and user-friendly tools, helped Aclímate Colombia break that trend and advance new agricultural practice with real-world impact.

According to the previously mentioned article, these are some of the specific ways in which new forms of knowledge and data have changed agriculture in Colombia:[350]

- The type of analysis found on the platform showed that, in the Espinal region, rice yields are primarily influenced by "the average minimum temperature during the ripening stage." Armed with this knowledge, farmers can ensure that crop plantings are sequenced to ensure that ripening occurs when average minimum temperatures are high enough to positively benefit yields.

---

348 Elizabeth Stuart, "The Data Revolution: Finding the Missing Millions," *Development Progress, Research Report 03*, 2015, https://www.odi.org/sites/odi.org.uk/files/odi-assets/publications-opinion-files/9604.pdf.

349 Silvain Delerce, et al., "Assessing Weather-Yield Relationships in Rice at Local Scale Using Data Mining Approaches," PLOS One, August 25, 2016, http://journals.plos.org/plosone/article?id=10.1371%2Fjournal.pone.0161620.

350 Ibid.

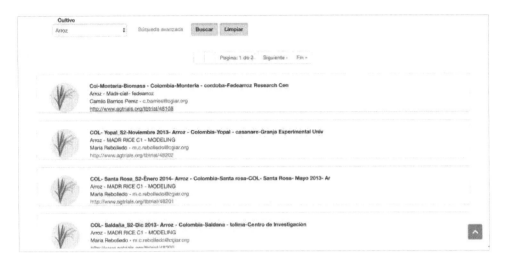

Figure 3. Aclímate Colombia Data Portal

- Analysis has also indicated that hotter regions of the country are not well-suited for planting the Cimarron Barinas rice variety; according to data included on the website, that crop variety is not suitable for growth in regions with temperatures typically exceeding 22°C.
- Farmers in the Saldaña region have also learned that (and why) the level of accumulated solar energy in irrigated rice has probably the largest impact on yield. In particular, the CIAT effort uncovered that the impact of solar radiation is most significant during the ripening stage. As a result, during the El Niño phenomenon, Saldaña faced significant risks because of the dry season. But, as Guzmán García recalls: "Fortunately, the district listened to us, and started rationing water, which, granted, caused less crops to be planted, but minimized the effects compared to another district next door that did not listen to us and had more losses."[351]
- In Villavicencio, the frequency of rainfall of over 10mm during the vegetative stage has the largest impact on yield. The team's findings in this area are particularly important because they show that the *frequency* rather than *total* rainfall is the key to growth. This insight "may foster the development of water harvesting and complementary irrigation infrastructure in that area to adapt to unevenly distributed rainfall."[352]

---

351 GovLab interview with Miryam Patricia Guzmán García, Deputy Director of Technology, Fedearroz, September 5, 2016.

352 Silvain Delerce, et al., "Assessing Weather-Yield Relationships in Rice at Local Scale Using Data Mining Approaches," PLOS One, August 25, 2016, http://journals.plos.org/plosone/article?id=10.1371%2Fjournal.pone.0161620.

181

One further piece of actionable insight (not included in the article) was indicated by Guzman Garcia. In Montería, an area with an irrigation district, Fedearroz and CIAT encouraged farmers to avoid year-round planting—despite farmers' desire to maximize potential yields surrounding stretches of time when many irrigation pumps were broken. Despite some pushback from farmers, Guzmán García recalls, "I really think we got through to them and people did not plant."[353] Follow on evaluations estimate that losses of around 8 billion Pesos, over USD 300 million, were avoided among 179 farmers.[354]

Considered more broadly, the project points to the potential of open data projects—perhaps especially those combining datasets from across sectors—to uncover highly granular insights. Far from just a tool for large-scale trends analyses and predictions, open data can provide truly useful and entirely different information to two individuals a mere town apart.

Benefits to the Agriculture Research Community

Although practitioners of agriculture have been the most direct beneficiaries of the project, it has also had a considerable impact on the wider agricultural research community. Indeed, the project has shown all those involved in agriculture how new forms of information and knowledge can spur progress in the field. This represents a potentially significant theoretical insight. As the scientists behind Aclímate Colombia put it in an article: "The added value of this effort is that it demonstrates how observational data can be used to efficiently generate actionable and contextualized information for on-farm decision making."[355]

More broadly, one of the aims of the project is to make progress by "accelerating agricultural research, in terms of time taken and money spent."[356] The founders of the project hope that it can serve as a catalyst for the wider community to consider new forms of knowledge, and to think through more carefully the link between research and practice.

---

353 GovLab interview with Miryam Patricia Guzmán García, Deputy Director of Technology, Fedearroz, September 5, 2016.

354 Andrés Bermúdez Liévano, "Los arroceros aprenden a vivir en un mundo con menos agua," *La Silla Nacional,* January 17, 2016, http://lasillavacia.com/historia/los-arroceros-aprenden-vivir-en-un-mundo-con-menos-agua-52478.

355 Silvain Delerce, et al., "Assessing Weather-Yield Relationships in Rice at Local Scale Using Data Mining Approaches," PLOS One, August 25, 2016, http://journals.plos.org/plosone/article?id=10.1371%2Fjournal.pone.0161620.

356 Oluwabunmi Ajilore "Big Data, Big Prospects: Crunching data for farmers' climate adaptation," *Change for the Better: The CCAFS 2015 Annual Report,* September 12, 2014, https://ccafs.cgiar.org/blog/big-data-big-prospects-crunching-data-farmers-climate-adaptation#.V6jLZpODGkp.

Financial Impact

The economic benefits of Aclímate Colombia are already becoming clear, and bear testimony to the success of the project. According to an Open Data Institute study conducted in partnership with CIAT, in the year following the launch of the initiative, improvements to farmers' decision-making led to estimated savings of $3.6m.[357] In addition to these broad, aggregate savings, the various insights described above have of course led to a number of localized cost efficiencies in specific areas of the country, and for specific farmers.

UN Big Data Challenge and the Value of a Model

While not a direct, on-the-ground impact of Aclímate Colombia, it is worth mentioning that the project was recognized as one of the 2014 winners of the United Nations Big Data Challenge.[358] This award represents a validation and recognition of the ingenuity and promise of the platform. In addition, the award and its attendant publicity could also help spur other, similar projects in Latin America and beyond. This is a pattern we see repeatedly in the case studies in this series: success leads to more success, and a single, successful project can open up pathways for many more similar projects that, together, have a much wider regional impact.

As noted, impact is often hard to measure. There have been some regional-level impact assessments and estimates of the types of economic losses avoided as a result of Aclímate Colombia performed. On the whole, though, Jimenez believes that, "we've been very clumsy in measuring impact."[359] An understanding of impact is not only important for iterating on the tools and approach for the initiative, but also, as Jimenez highlights, essential for accessing new and sustained sources of funding. Going forward, CIAT and Fedearroz are looking to build an impact assessment component into the project, gaining better visibility into the number of farmers reached and the number of farmers who increased their productivity.[360]

---

357 Global Open Data for Agriculture and Nutrition, *How Can We Improve Agriculture, Food and Nutrition with Open Data?* Open Data Institute, 2015, http://www.godan.info/sites/default/files/old/2015/04/ODI-GODAN-paper-27-05-20152.pdf.

358 United Nations Global Pulse, "Big Data Climate Challenge," Press Release, September 2, 2014, https://www3.wider.unu.edu/sites/default/files/News/Documents/Big-Data-Climate-Challenge-press-release-5633.pdf.

359 GovLab interview with Daniel Jimenez, International Center for Tropical Agriculture (CIAT), August 23, 2016.

360 Ibid.

Risks

As evidenced by the example of Aclímate Colombia and various other case studies included in this series, open data holds tremendous potential for positive transformation. But, as we also see throughout this series, open data also poses certain risks. It is important to understand these risks in order to ensure that open data projects are implemented in a way that maximizes the potential upside and limits the downside.

Empowering Only Farmers Connected with Powerful Growers Associations

CIAT is well-positioned to engage farmers affiliated with growers' associations like Fedearroz. It has little capacity, however, to engage those farmers that are not similarly organized. As Jimenez notes, "this approach is totally feasible as long as farmers are well organized and associated."[361] But, of course, the farmers with no affiliations and support from growers' associations likely face the greatest risks as a result of climate change and stand to see the most benefit from gaining access to new tools for improving their decision-making. A move toward more technological and data-driven efforts to benefit the agriculture sector risks leaving behind those who need the most support.

This particular risk is representative of a larger struggle within the Colombian open data and civic technology sectors, and indeed within a number of open data and data projects around the world. While often aimed at eradicating or narrowing the digital divide, technical and governance innovation projects such as this one in fact often graft themselves on to (and can even exacerbate) existing divides. As Daniel Uribe of the Corona Foundation puts it: "We see there is a big gap in citizen engagement, taking into account the population pyramid where the poor are the largest group of population, but we believe that there is the potential in the population and access to ICT platforms to promote and achieve citizen engagement through civic tech in all the population, closing the digital divide."[362]

CIAT is currently exploring pathways for engaging these unaffiliated farmers through, as Jimenez puts it, "some hybrid between development and research."[363] Developing concrete, implementable strategies for such engagement will likely be a key determinant of longer-term sustainability and success for the initiative.

---

361 Ibid.

362 GovLab interview with Daniel Uribe, Fundacion Corona, September 13, 2016.

363 GovLab interview with Daniel Jimenez, International Center for Tropical Agriculture (CIAT), August 23, 2016.

Encouraging Farmers with Little Room for Error to Fundamentally Change Practices

Given the project's focus on arming small-scale farms with recommendations aimed at changing their traditional growing practices, the accuracy and reliability of those recommendations is highly important. If recommendations are not accurate, there is a risk not only of lower crop yields, but also that farmers who already operate near subsistence level may suffer great economic hardship. The organizers recognize this risk, noting that "farmers have different profiles in terms of risk management" and that some are "able to take risks to bet on good weather and outstanding harvest while others need to guarantee a minimum level of productivity to ensure adequate income."[364] Initial signs do point to Aclímate Colombia improving outcomes for farmers, but vigilance in this area is essential.

Lessons Learned

Several important lessons with wider applicability emerge from this particular case study. These can broadly be categorized by considering the key enablers of the project, as well as the most important barriers or challenges to its success.

Enablers

For Jimenez and his team, perhaps the central lesson learned from the project was the realization that "information that is not shared is not information anymore."[365] The data used to create Aclímate Colombia had existed for years, sitting in databases held by different cross-sector stakeholders. Once that data was unlocked in service of a specific objective, it stopped being a series of numbers but instead became actionable information.

Establish credibility, a theory of change and proof of concept

In order to move forward with the data analysis and dissemination of tools and insights that define Aclímate Colombia, CIAT first had to get grower associations like Fedearroz on board—both to gain access to their data and in order to enable them to act as intermediaries between CIAT and the individual farmers.

---

364 Silvain Delerce, et al., "Assessing Weather-Yield Relationships in Rice at Local Scale Using Data Mining Approaches," PLOS One, August 25, 2016, http://journals.plos.org/plosone/article?id=10.1371%2Fjournal.pone.0161620.

365 GovLab interview with Daniel Jimenez, International Center for Tropical Agriculture (CIAT), August 23, 2016.

To make those partnerships a reality, Jimenez argues, "you have to think about the theory of change."[366] The project's theory of change was clear from the start: that data analysis can help farmers make better planting decisions as a result of an improved understanding of how crops react to different weather patterns in different regions. Establishing and articulating this theory of change helped engage data providers and data intermediaries in an effective manner. Pushing for data access without a clear articulation of how that data will be used—and to what ends—can be a losing proposition.

In addition to a clear theory of change, a proof of concept can also help instill confidence in data providers and/or intermediaries. As much as a theory of change can lend conceptual clarity to a project, true confidence and credibility arise when tangible signs of impact and success emerge. Jimenez notes that, at the early stages, growers' associations tended to only share "a small piece of the database," and then as CIAT used the data available to draw meaningful insights, more and more information was made accessible. He adds, "they are skeptical in the beginning, but they start to believe as you demonstrate what you can do to support more informed decision-making."[367]

Know your audience, engage intermediaries and build a common language

As the story of Aclímate Colombia's genesis and implementation makes clear, growers' associations played an essential role in enabling the creation of the initiative. In particular, they played a role through data provision and its use by acting as intermediaries between CIAT and individual farms. As Jimenez describes their role: "We work through them, we empower them and then through them we bridge this gap between scientists and farmers."[368]

Even when working through a data-driven intermediary like Federarroz, CIAT quickly learned that to encourage engagement and use among the intended audience (i.e., individual farmers), it needed to gain a better understanding of that audience and build a common language. Rather than simply running one-off workshops with growers associations and farmers aimed at increasing data literacy, which have questionable impact, CIAT embedded sector-area experts from growers' associations within the organization. During these three-to-four-month engagements, CIAT was able to "empower them properly"—i.e., give them a grounding in how to put into practice the findings of different regional data analyses on optimal planting practices—and plant the notion that data-driven training and tools are truly worth the investment of

---

366 Ibid.
367 Ibid.
368 Ibid.

time and resources.[369] These engagements not only helped to increase buy-in among the intended audience, but also helped increase the skills present in the growers' association, minimizing the resource and time burdens on CIAT and improving the project's potential for sustainability. Jimenez notes that a big driver of success was the identification of the data use and translation processes that CIAT "just needs to supervise because [the associations] can do it by themselves."[370]

Similarly, Jimenez found that demonstrating that Aclímate Colombia's organizers were working toward common goals and willing to build a common language with the user community (i.e., individual farmers) helped encourage greater uptake of their tools and research findings. In an interview with the Overseas Development Institute, he recalled that, "One farmer said to me that they acted on the research because it was based on their own data."[371] As such, Fabrizio Scrollini, chairman of Data Uruguay, labels Aclímate Colombia a clear example of "inclusive innovation."[372]

Barriers

Initial inaccessibility of important datasets

Much of the value and utility of Aclímate Colombia arises from the aggregation and analysis of diverse datasets drawn from diverse sectors and institutions. Given the fact that "open access and data sharing is still in its infancy in many places," gaining access was a relatively slow and difficult process.[373] As described above, the establishment of credibility, proof of concept and a willingness to build a common language with growers' associations and those they represent helped to—gradually—mitigate that challenge.

Immature ecosystem

By working directly with growers' associations that could act as data providers and intermediaries passing its tools and insights onto individual farmers, Aclímate Colombia was able to avoid one of the major challenges faced by open data efforts around the world: the lack of a mature technology and innovation ecosystem.

---

369 Ibid.

370 Ibid.

371 Elizabeth Stuart, "The Data Revolution: Finding the Missing Millions," *Development Progress, Research Report 03*, 2015, https://www.odi.org/sites/odi.org.uk/files/odi-assets/publications-opinion-files/9604.pdf.

372 GovLab interview with Fabrizio Scrollini, September 13, 2016.

373 Oluwabunmi Ajilore "Big Data, Big Prospects: Crunching data for farmers' climate adaptation," *Change for the Better: The CCAFS 2015 Annual Report*, September 12, 2014, https://ccafs.cgiar.org/blog/big-data-big-prospects-crunching-data-farmers-climate-adaptation#.V6jLZpODGkp.

Actors in the civic technology and open source communities in Colombia are, as Oscar Montiel of Open Knowledge International (OKI) puts it, "really small and really disconnected from one another."[374] Esteban Peláez Gómez of Fundación Corona agrees, arguing that while there are some tech start ups and innovators in the country, "they are not part of a community that has the objective of having a social impact."[375]

But while Aclímate Colombia does not require private sector civic tech actors to leverage its tools, Montiel argues that without such an ecosystem, there can be negative impacts on the types of data released by the government. He argues that the immature open data demand and use ecosystem feeds into issues like unwieldy data licensing frameworks that make the reuse of government data more difficult.[376]

A lack of civil society collaborators in the Colombian open data ecosystem

OKI's Montiel and Mor Rubinstein, both of whom worked with Colombia as part of the Open Data Index effort, note that, especially in comparison to other countries in the region, civil society in Colombia is fragmented and not playing a major role in pushing forward open data. As Rubinstein notes, Colombian civil society's role in advancing open data is "a big question mark in a way."[377] So while there are notable exceptions, like CIAT and Fundación Corona, Montiel argues that there is not widespread collaboration between government and civil society, and rather, government "just does what they can the way they know how."[378]

Replicability

The potential for replication of Aclímate Colombia's analytical tools and algorithms appears promising as the algorithms and processes that inform the project's tools are not context-specific, and can be used wherever relevant data is available.[379] As a result, steps are already being taken to scale the project

---

374 GovLab interview with Oscar Montiel, Open Knowledge International, September 8, 2016.

375 GovLab interview with Esteban Peláez Gómez, Coordinator of Social Projects, Fundación Corona, September 13, 2016.

376 GovLab interview with Oscar Montiel, Open Knowledge International, September 8, 2016.

377 GovLab interview with Mor Rubinstein, Open Knowledge International, September 8, 2016.

378 GovLab interview with Oscar Montiel, Open Knowledge International, September 8, 2016.

379 Silvain Delerce, et al., "Assessing Weather-Yield Relationships in Rice at Local Scale Using Data Mining Approaches," PLOS One, August 25, 2016, http://journals.plos.org/plosone/article?id=10.1371%2Fjournal.pone.0161620.

across Colombia, as well as in Argentina, Nicaragua, Peru and Uruguay, in partnership with the Latin American Fund for Irrigated Rice (FLAR).[380]

Looking Forward

Improving the Tools and Expanding the Data Being Used

Beyond strategizing ways to engage unaffiliated farmers, as described above, the CIAT team is working to improve the functionality and expand the use of Aclímate Colombia through the integration of new datasets. Future research for the platform will explore how to leverage data on "soils, pests, diseases, costs and other factors to increase explanatory power."[381] The team is also exploring the "emergent field of remote sensing and satellite energy," which Jimenez feels "could be a more efficient way to collect information in the field."[382]

Scaling to Other Countries in the Region

As described above, CIAT is partnering with the Fund for Irrigated Rice in Latin America. In addition, CIAT researchers plan also to partner with the Fund for Irrigated Rice in Latin America (FLAR), with the support of CCAFS and the World Bank, to introduce new approaches to rice growers' associations in other countries, especially Nicaragua, Peru, Argentina and Uruguay. CIAT is also partnering with the CGIAR-affiliated International Maize and Wheat Improvement Center (CIMMYT) to bring data-driven insight into maize production in Mexico. These new projects in Latin America will serve as additional case studies, potentially laying the groundwork for further replication and scaling.[383]

Fostering the Open Data Ecosystem in Colombia

Looking beyond Aclímate Colombia, CIAT and the other data-driven actors involved in the project are well-positioned to help push forward the nascent open data ecosystem in Colombia. As Fabrizio Scrollini argues: "there is a niche for new organizations to emerge or for some organizations that are a part of

380 CTIAR and CCAFS, "Big Data for Climate-smart Agriculture," *Change for the Better: The CCAFS 2015 Annual Report*, https://ccafs.cgiar.org/bigdata#.V6jLT5ODGko.

381 Ibid.

382 GovLab interview with Daniel Jimenez, August 23, 2016.

383 CTIAR and CCAFS, "Big Data for Climate-smart Agriculture," *Change for the Better: The CCAFS 2015 Annual Report*, https://ccafs.cgiar.org/bigdata#.V6jLT5ODGko.

the politics side, or from the more social side to jump into data on the market side. The niche is there."[384] Indeed, Scrollini argues that while the value of data-driven work is gaining a foothold in areas focused on wealth generation, there has not been a similar uptake in the use of data toward social ends. Aclímate Colombia could actually represent a powerful example of how open data can have positive impacts on both the public good and the pocketbooks of those leveraging the data (in this case, farmers).

As Scrollini puts it: "I guess it is time to get these people organized and get some more traditional NGOs that are more well behaved and engage the government and some punks as well so they can shake things up and get the party going. I know there are people in government willing to take that challenge, it's a matter of getting the dance started. That's what data hopefully will contribute."[385]

Conclusion

With regard to open data's provision, use and impact, Colombia represents a fascinating case study in the developing world. Based on a number of international assessments, the country can be considered a leader among Latin American countries in the field of open data. A number of open data projects either already exist or may soon, although it is worth noting that the bulk of these are founded by international organizations, with relatively little activity in Colombia's private sector and among start-ups.

In this atmosphere of open data innovation, CIAT's Aclímate Colombia could act as a standard-bearer and catalyst. The platform is aimed at addressing a clearly defined problem, leverages partnerships across sectors to access data and push for its use, and provides benefits to a wide variety of private sector actors in the agriculture sector, regardless of their size. USAID notably selected Colombia as one of three initial countries to participate in the Climate Services for Resilient Development initiative, likely thanks in part to the innovative capacity demonstrated by the government and civil society actors that made Aclímate Colombia a possibility.[386] While many questions and barriers remain—not the least of which is the challenge of engaging those farmers currently not involved with key intermediaries—if Aclímate Colombia continues to grow and evolve along its current trajectory, it could establish itself as a bright light in the emerging open data space in Colombia, and indeed throughout Latin America.

---

384 GovLab interview with Fabrizio Scrollini, September 13, 2016.
385 Ibid.
386 Climate Services for Resilient Development, http://www.cs4rd.org/.

CHAPTER 13

Ghana's Esoko

Leveling the information playing field for smallholder farmers

François van Schalkwyk, Andrew Young and Stefaan Verhulst

Summary

Smallholder farmers generate much of Ghana's agricultural production. However, they have only limited access to important information that underlies increasingly complex global food chains, and this prevents them from fully maximizing the value of their crops. Esoko, a company operating in Ghana, sought to address this problem by using multiple data sources, including open government data, to permit farmers to secure better prices for their produce and level the playing field in price negotiations between farmers and buyers. The provision of information to smallholder farmers is being replicated by Esoko in other developing countries, and new organizations are entering the market to provide similar services to smallholder farmers.

Context and Background

Problem Focus/Country Context

As global agricultural value chain continues to grow in importance. This is especially true for many developing countries, where a larger proportion of the workforce and economy are reliant on the agriculture sector.

Africa loses billions of dollars due to its inability to produce enough and process its agricultural commodities. In its 2014 report, the Africa Progress Panel, an NGO advocated for sustainable development chaired by Kofi

Annan, estimates that Africa spends US$35 billion per year on food imports. Connecting farm production, processing and distribution could introduce various efficiencies into the value chain, in the process creating numerous jobs and lifting millions of Africans out of poverty.[387]

The importance of agriculture is only likely to increase in coming decades. According to the World Bank, global food demand is set to double by 2050, and Africa's agriculture and agribusiness markets could reach US$1 trillion in 2030 (World Bank 2013).[388] Ghana could potentially be one of the key beneficiaries of this process, given that, according to the Food and Agriculture Organization of the UN, over 53 percent of the Ghanaian workforce is in the agriculture sector.[389] The country had made some progress in recent years: Ghana is one of a few African countries to have achieved its Millennium Development Goal (MDG) hunger reduction target as well as the World Food Summit goal of halving the absolute number of hungry in the country by 2015. The Government of Ghana is currently elaborating a long-term national development plan to steer the country through the next 40 years.[390]

Yet if Ghana—and Africa more generally—is to build on this success, the agriculture sector will have to undergo certain changes. As global food and agriculture chains become increasingly complex and information-driven, there is a need for new, innovative approaches that can adapt to the complexity. Agricultural methods will need to become more information-driven, more adaptable to new trends in technology, and more resilient to withstand climate change. Small landholders, in particular, will need support as they move toward a new agriculture paradigm. According to the International Fund for Agricultural Development (IFAD), there are more than 500 million smallholder farms globally that produce about 80 percent of the food consumed in Asia and sub-Saharan Africa (IFAD 2013).[391] This suggests the vital importance of programs and tools—such as the one under study here—that help smallholder farmers adapt. Their viability is particularly important in Ghana, where the production of key crops like coffee and cocoa is dominated by smallholders.

---

387 Africa Progress Panel, *Grain Fish Money: Financing Africa's green and blue revolutions*. Africa Progress Panel, 2014, http://app-cdn.acwupload.co.uk/wp-content/uploads/2014/05/APP_APR2014_24june.pdf.

388 World Bank, *Growing Africa: Unlocking the Potential of Agribusiness*. Washington DC: World Bank, 2013, http://siteresources.worldbank.org/INTAFRICA/Resources/africa-agribusiness-report-2013.pdf.

389 Food and Agriculture Organization, "Ghana: Country Fact Sheet on Food and Agriculture Policy Trends," FAO, March 2015, http://www.fao.org/3/a-i4490e.pdf.

390 Food and Agriculture Organization, *Ghana and FAO: Partnering for agricultural development and resilient livelihoods*, 2016, http://www.fao.org/3/a-az484e.pdf.

391 International Fund for Agricultural Development (IFAD), *Smallholders, Food Security, and the Environment*, IFAD/UNEP, https://www.ifad.org/documents/10180/666cac24-14b6-43c2-876d-9c2d1f01d5dd.

Technology, open data and agriculture

Technology is already being used in several instances to help African farmers make better decisions and make meaningful forays into national and/or global value chains. For example, in Kenya, the SMS information provision app mFARM gives farmers important evidence to inform decision-making. In Nigeria, the Hello Tractor service is an Uber-like tractor-on-demand service. In Ghana, the USAID Feed the Future Program is working to implement technology-driven efforts to improve competitiveness, sustainability and the transfer of research insights into practice.[392]

But while such applications and services can create new value, they could also lead to the creation of data monopolies and information asymmetries that may ultimately hurt or otherwise limit the potential of African agriculture. The economic concept of asymmetric information is that there is an imbalance of power in a transaction when one party has access to more information than the other.[393] This results in buyers not being able to bid as much or in sellers not knowing how to price a commodity. Open data can play an important role in breaking down such asymmetries of information. It can do so, for example, by introducing greater transparency in agricultural value chains, in the process making actors in those value chains more accountable to attentive citizens, civil society organizations, and to others, including farmers.

Open data also makes possible the entry into agricultural ecosystems of a larger number of intermediaries, adding both complexity and new value propositions to value chains. Research has shown that open data "intermediaries are vital to both the supply and the use of open data ... Intermediaries can create data, articulate demands for data, and help translate open data visions from political leaders into effective implementations."[394] Research that delved deeper into how open data intermediaries are able to link actors in data supply chains found that "intermediation does not only consist of a single agent facilitating the flow of data in an open data supply chain; multiple intermediaries may operate in an open data supply chain, and the presence of multiple intermediaries may increase the probability of use (and impact) because no single intermediary is

392 Feed the Future, "Fact Sheet: Feed the future USAID agriculture technology transfer project," IFDC, 2014, https://ifdcorg.files.wordpress.com/2014/12/att-factsheet.pdf.

393 D. Kleine, A. Light and M.J. Montero, "Signifiers of the Life We Value? Considering human development, technologies and fair trade from the perspective of the capabilities approach," Information Technology for Development, 18, no.1, pp. 42–60.

394 T. Davies, *Open Data in Developing Countries: Emerging insights from phase 1*, Washington DC: World Wide Web Foundation, 2014, http://www.opendataresearch.org/sites/default/files/publications/Phase%20 1%20-%20Synthesis%20-%20Full%20Report-print.pdf.

likely to possess all the types of capital required to unlock the full value of the transaction between the provider and the user."[395]

A growing international consensus regarding the potential of open data in agriculture is evidenced by the Global Open Data for Agriculture & Nutrition (GODAN) initiative, which brings together nearly 500 governments, NGOs and businesses seeking "to harness the growing volume of data generated by new technologies to solve long-standing problems and to benefit farmers and the health of consumers."[396] Also, in this series of case studies, we examine the use of open data to benefit smallholder farmers in Colombia through the Aclímate Colombia initiative.[397]

Open Data in Ghana

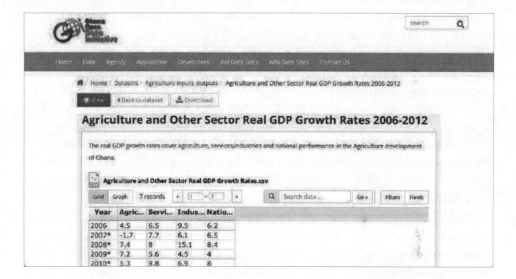

Figure 1. Ghana's National Open Data Portal (data.gov.gh)

Ghana, along with Kenya, was one of the early pioneers of open data on the African continent. The Ghana Open Data Portal was launched in November 2012, as a result of a partnership between the Web Foundation, National Information and Technology Agency (NITA), and a number of civil society

---

395 F. Van Schalkwyk, et al., "Open Data Intermediaries in Developing Countries," *Journal of Community Informatics*, 12, no. 2, 2016, http://ci-journal.net/index.php/ciej/article/view/1146.

396 http://www.godan.info/about.

397 Andrew Young and Stefaan Verhulst, "Aclímate Colombia–Open Data to Improve Agricultural Resiliency," Open Data's Impact, July 2017 http://odimpact.org/case-aclimate-colombia.html.

organizations within the country.[398] The portal launched with 100 datasets available, and a mobile version was released the next year.

Unfortunately, this early success has dampened in some ways. The most recent Open Data Barometer Survey shows a deterioration in the implementation of government open data initiatives relative to Kenya and other African countries such as Mauritius, Nigeria and Rwanda. However, this is mainly attributable to the government open data portal being inaccessible for an extended period of time.[399]

Neither the Open Data Barometer nor the Global Open Data Index has published data on the availability of open data related specifically to agriculture (e.g., weather data or market price data). Currently, the Ghana Open Data portal[400] makes available six datasets in the "Agriculture" category. These relate mainly to financial or economic data from the agricultural sector. The Ghana Statistical Office, CountrySTAT,[401] an initiative to aggregate and increase the interoperability of datasets, also publishes statistical data and metadata on food and agriculture from different sources. In addition, the Ministry of Food and Agriculture publishes data on average crop yields for major crops, production estimates and weekly market prices.[402]

KEY ACTORS

Key Data Providers

Overall, data sourcing by Esoko is structurally complex: open and proprietary data, some self-generated and some from third-parties, are curated and combined to provide information to customers.

Government of Ghana

The Ministry of Food and Agriculture (MOFA) is the primary government source of data. MOFA publishes data on crop yields, production estimates and market prices. Even though agricultural data are obtained from government, the data are extensively

---

398 World Wide Web Foundation, "Ghana Open Data Initiative," http://webfoundation.org/our-work/projects/ghana-open-data-initiative-godi/.

399 The portal might have been done as a result of extended maintenance in preparation for a revamped new offering, but when the Barometer assessment was being conducted no explanation was made available for the outage – so even if the outage was the result of ultimately beneficial work, trust in the platform and Ghanaian open data more generally likely suffered. World Wide Web Foundation, *Open Data Barometer 3rd Edition: Africa Regional Report*, 2016, http://opendatabarometer.org/3rdedition/regional-report/africa/.

400 Website of Uganda Open Data Initiative, http://data.gov.gh/.

401 CountrySTAT, "Ghana," http://www.countrystat.org/home.aspx?c=GHA.

402 Website of the Ministry of Food and Agriculture, Republic of Ghana, http://mofa.gov.gh/site/; and for data on weekly market prices, see http://mofa.gov.gh/site/?page_id=13613.

curated by Esoko. Curation activities include the structuring of the data, its packaging, and its translation into local languages.

Center for Agriculture and BioSciences International (CABI)

An additional source of data is CABI, an international not-for-profit organization. CABI has an extensive repository of information on agricultural issues like invasive species, food security and trade.

aWhere

Esoko is a client of aWhere, an agricultural intelligence firm. It accesses aWhere's weather data via an API service. Esoko translates daily data as well as an eight-day forecast into relevant and accessible weather updates for farmers. Farmers receive information on precipitation, temperature, wind speed, humidity and growing degree days.

Markets and Farmers

Although a portion of the data sourced by Esoko is open, the company also collects its own data. Esoko actively collects data from farmers that may be of interest to agencies and businesses in the agri-sector. In addition, Esoko deploys its own agents in the field to collect price data in about 50 markets in Ghana (some of these agents are in fact employees of the Ministry of Food and Agriculture).[403]

Key Data Users and Intermediaries

Esoko

Esoko is a for-profit private company with private investors, although it should be noted that the company maintains close ties to the public and foreign donor sectors. Managed from its head office in the capital city of Accra, Ghana, Esoko's principal market is agri-business, while individual farmers constitute a secondary market.

Key Beneficiaries

Farmers in Ghana

The principal objective of Esoko has always been to empower smallholder farmers to make farming more profitable. As the company's website states: "Though we'll geek out any day about supply chain efficiencies and organizational cost savings, we live for the human part of this work."[404]

Esoko's clients

In fact, however, smallholder farmers constitute a secondary market for Esoko. In order to develop a more sustainable business model, and because the acquisition of individual farmers is expensive, Esoko principally targets larger agri-business, NGOs, governments and mobile operators with its data collection and communication

---

403 These data are validated by the Council for Scientific and Industrial Research (CSIR).
404 Website of Esoko, https://esoko.com/about-us/our-story/.

products. This allows the company to generate additional revenues, and its mixed business model (targeting both large and small customers) is in many ways critical to its survival and success.

Project Description

Initiation of the Open Data Activity

The origins of Esoko may be traced to TradeNet, a company that was created in 2004 in Uganda, in partnership with FoodNet and with support from the Food and Agriculture Organization of the United Nations (FAO). In 2005, TradeNet entered into the network of regional Market Information Systems and Traders Organizations of West Africa (MISTOWA) project, which seeks to better coordinate regional efforts around the creation, dissemination and use of agriculture and food-security information.

In 2009, Esoko emerged from TradeNet, with the aim of providing a richer and more comprehensive product. One of the key motivating factors in the creation of the company was an identified gap or market failure in the Ugandan agrarian ecosystem. Esoko's founders realized that while information concerning market prices did exist in Uganda, farmers were often unable to access to the information. TradeNet originally tried to bridge this gap by connecting farmers to the available data by means of mobile-phone technology.

Esoko has sought to address similar shortcomings in Ghana. On the one hand, Ghanaian farmers were actively seeking information concerning market prices and weather (in particular, data on rainfall); unable to retrieve such information, they often traded their produce at low prices and were vulnerable to climate variations. On the other hand, the information did in fact exist at a governmental level and from other sources. However, the government 'extension agents' tasked with conveying this type of information to farmers were inefficient and costly. Consequently, Esoko emerged to bridge the gap by connecting farmers to the available information they required.

Currently, there are two main branches of Esoko in Africa, one located in Ghana and one in Kenya. Even though the offices in Ghana and Kenya function under the name Esoko and provide similar products, they constitute two distinct operations managing the two respective markets. In addition, there are resellers and offices in Mauritius, Malawi, Uganda, Mozambique and Benin.

Esoko's main offering to farmers includes automated alerts containing agrarian and economic information, sent to cellphones in the form of SMS and voice messages. The products offered include information on market prices (58 commodities in 42 markets countrywide, collected at markets daily), weather forecasts, crop price bids, and crop production protocols. Esoko also developed the first call center (called Helpline) for farmers in Ghana to improve communication and usability of the provided information. The messaging and call centers operate in English and 12 local languages (Dagbani, Mampruli, Twi, Kusaal, Frafra, Sissali, Dagaari, Wali, Ewe, Ga, Fante and Hausa). Esoko's non-mobile products include deployment support for surveys in the field (e.g., the deployment of the company's own agents), strategic planning and field training. While farmers do use these services, they are mostly directed at agri-business clients.

Most products offered by Esoko use mobile technology. In addition to its information products, it offers a number of B2B products aimed at larger, paying customers. These include marketing products, monitoring and evaluation products, as well as goods sourcing products. These products can take the form of bulk messaging, SMS polling, call center monitoring and call surveys.

Funding

The founder and the first CEO of Esoko was Mark Davies. Investors, who provided the bulk of the capital, were the International Finance Corporation, the Soros Economic Development Fund, Lundin Foundation, and Acumen. Currently, Esoko relies on a mix of donor funding and self-generated revenue from the products and services it has developed for agri-businesses, NGOs, governments and mobile operators.

Demand and Supply of Data type(s) and sources

As mentioned, Esoko was born from Ghanaian farmers' need for data on market prices and weather to help inform planting and other market-related decisions. Esoko sources this data from a variety of data suppliers, including the government, international NGOs and agri-data companies such as aWhere. Esoko Ghana also collects its own data from about 50 markets in Ghana and directly from farmers.

Open Data Use

Esoko's offerings and pricing models rely on a combination of data sources and types. Its services are based on a tiered franchise/subscriber model in several sub-Saharan countries, including Ghana, Burkina Faso, Cote d'Ivoire and Malawi.[405] The company's SMS price alerts, monitoring capabilities and information system management products are all made possible by the use of open government data.

Impact

As with the other case studies included in this series, the impact of Esoko can be measured in a number of different ways, using a variety of quantitative and qualitative information. These include:

Usage Statistics

According to its website, Esoko has reached 350,000 farmers in 10 countries across Africa. It has sent 9.5 million messages on one million prices in 170 markets collected by 150 field agents. In 2014, Esoko operated 29,344 calls in Ghana, of which 40 percent were related to weather data. Although usage is not always a perfect proxy for impact, the breadth of use and interest in Esoko's offerings is clearly evident, and points to real usefulness for the company's intended audience.

Improved Bargaining Power

A key goal of Esoko is to help farmers better navigate the complexity of global value chains, and in particular to improve their bargaining power versus some of the large, global actors in those chains. Although there have been no widespread studies of the value and impact of Esoko's service, the company has done some targeted surveys of farmers who have reported being able to negotiate prices more confidently and sell their harvests in more distant markets.[406]

One empirical research study on the impact of Esoko's market price information was conducted by Pierre Courois and Julie Subervie for the *American Journal of Agricultural Economics*.[407] Courois and Subervie set out to establish how price information affects the balance of power in the bargaining of prices. They found that farmers typically sell to traders at the farm gate rather

405 U.S. Agency for International Development, "Using ICT to Provide Agriculture Market Price Information in Africa," Briefing Paper, 2010.

406 U.S. Agency for International Development, "Using ICT to Provide Agriculture Market Price Information in Africa," Briefing Paper, 2010.

407 Pierre Courois and Julie Subervie, "Farmer Bargaining Power and Market Information Services," *American Journal of Agricultural Economics*, 97, No. 3, pp. 953–977, 2014, http://ajae.oxfordjournals.org/content/97/3/953.

than at district markets because of high transportation costs, and are thus at a disadvantage when negotiating prices because they are unaware of what prices are available in markets. The study also found that Northern Ghanaian farmers who are clients of Esoko were able to negotiate better prices for their produce. Specifically, farmers receiving market price information from Esoko received 10 percent more for maize and 7 percent more for groundnuts than those farmers who were not receiving the market price information.

Value Chain Transparency

One important effect of Esoko's activities as an intermediary in the agricultural ecosystem is to increase the transparency of the value chain. Farmers are able to compare prices at various markets in the country, and compare prices to those offered to them by traders at the farm gate. They can also better recognize the structure and the roles of other agents involved in the food production system. As a result, farmers can negotiate higher prices and discover entirely new markets—in short, they can trade more effectively. This transparency also affects the activities of other agents in the ecosystem. For instance, being aware of farmers' understanding of the ecosystem, traders modify their own bargaining and trading strategies. Because all actors are more aware of each others' positions in the ecosystem, the net result is greater transparency.

Seeding the Ecosystem

According to Andrason and Van Schalkwyk,[408] Esoko, along with similar intermediaries such as Farmerline, have stimulated the emergence of new niches in the local information and communication technology (ICT) ecosystem. At least four new (albeit interconnected) niches are identified in the study:

- First, the presence of Esoko has created room for additional research and thus the need for companies dedicated to agri-data capture and processing. Esoko seeks data that goes beyond what is currently available or provided directly from open sources present in the ecosystem. That is, it generates a need for experts, data collectors and data processing personnel.
- Second, Esoko creates a demand for a range of educational and training organizations that can interact with individuals and communities.

---

408 Alex Andrason and François van Schalkwyk, *Open Data Intermediaries in the Agriculture Sector in Ghana*, Research Paper, Washington DC: World Wide Web Foundation, 2016, http://webfoundation.org/docs/2016/12/WF-RP-Open-Data-Intermediaries-in-Agriculture-Ghana-Update.pdf.

- Third, Esoko contributes to technological innovation. By discovering more efficient means of conveying information and connecting agents in the ecosystem, it creates an additional need for technical personnel, for instance programmers and mobile-phone specialists. In fact, the efficiency of the services offered by Esoko may also contribute to a more rapid development of the mobile phone sector.

- Fourth, the emergence of Esoko enables a more adequate use or even a reuse (or relocation) of elements already present in the ecosystem. To be precise, the previously mentioned government extension agents—relatively ineffective in the traditional framework—have seen their roles and objectives reframed to ensure they are better targeted to the real-world needs and opportunities. This relocation has turned out to be successful and beneficial both for these agents themselves and for the data flow.

Risks

Open data offers tremendous opportunities, but also carries certain risks. As with all the case studies included in this series, it is important to balance the potential rewards with the challenges and pitfalls that may also arise as a result of new and potentially disruptive technological interventions.

Marginal short-term gains may jeopardize future benefits

The success of Esoko depends in many ways on balancing short-term and long-term benefits. The risk exists that some farmers may decide that information helping them accrue a 7 to 10 percent increase in farm-gate prices is insufficient to compensate for the cost of subscribing to the market price information service. Should they elect to discontinue their subscription, they may lose out on the future benefits that could accrue from new information made available by Esoko.

There does exist some evidence that non-governmental organizations subsidize the subscription costs of farmers and this lowers the risk of losing out on future benefits. However, the role of NGOs introduces secondary risks: (1) farmers rely on an organization type that in itself does not have sustainable income and may therefore have to discontinue the subsidy scheme at some point, and (2) aggregating access via NGOs may unintentionally exclude some farmers who may not be aware of, or have access to, these NGOs.

New forms of bargaining emerge that negate the benefits that some farmers enjoy

Courtois and Subervie acknowledge the possible risk that the availability of market price information is not uniform. That is, some farming communities, especially larger or otherwise privileged ones, may be informed while others are not. They describe the following scenario:

> *"Specifically, he [the trader] should seek to deal in uninformed communities when the market price is high, because in that case uninformed farmers, who systematically make incorrect estimates of the market price, agree to accept relatively low prices. On the contrary, the trader should visit informed communities when the market price is low, because it allows him to avoid costly negotiation failures."*[409]

Such a scenario does not necessarily correct the pricing information asymmetry in a food supply chain.

Personal data

Esoko collects personally identifiable data from farmers and repackages and sells this data to agribusiness. Details on the levels of aggregation and anonymization of personal data collected and shared could not be found. However, the risk remains that either Esoko or its clients (or both) may use personal data to target smallholder farmers and that any misuse of personal data in this way could damage any trust that may currently exist between smallholder farmers and Esoko. This, in turn, could reduce usage of the Esoko platform in general, and more generally lower trust in and usage of open data products.

Lessons Learned

Lessons learned can be broadly divided into Enablers (positive lessons) and Barriers (negative lessons). Both types of lessons are important in assessing the success of the project, and more generally in assessing the potential and feasibility of other open data products.

---

409 Pierre Courois and Julie Subervie, "Farmer Bargaining Power and Market Information Services," *American Journal of Agricultural Economics*, 97, No. 3, pp. 953–977, 2014, http://ajae.oxfordjournals.org/content/97/3/953.

Enablers

Existing market failures

Esoko came into being due to a propitious combination of phenomena: an inefficient agricultural information and support delivery system (extension agents); pervasive and relatively low-cost communication technologies (mobile phones/SMS); and the availability of data combined with the ongoing demand from farmers for relevant agricultural information. All these factors together created a market failure and thus a genuine opportunity, or niche, that could be occupied by an organization such as Esoko. Organizations seeking to develop similarly successful open data projects may therefore consider beginning by trying to identify similar market failures and niches.

Multi-tier business model

A further enabler was Esoko's business model of providing low-cost, affordable services to smallholder farmers and targeting established agriculture organizations to generate sufficient income to establish itself as a viable business. This mixed revenue model has enabled more farmers to access Esoko's services. It also allows Esoko to collect its own market price data (which is of value to farmers) because it can resell this data as information not only to farmers but also to its business clients.

Emerging ecosystem

Esoko is operating in a maturing ICT for agriculture ecosystem. As research by Andrason and Van Schalkwyk shows,[410] there are at least two other players operating in the same space as Esoko: Farmerline and CacaoLink, both data-driven agriculture businesses seeking to benefit farmers across many African countries. Each of these organizations has been careful to differentiate its particular niche in the Ghanaian agricultural market, but their presence is nevertheless indicative of a maturing data ecosystem.

Lastly, Esoko was endowed with an effective constellation of "capitals"— mainly economic and social—that enabled it to exploit the niche that presented itself. Specifically, reliable funding at the outset, a strong B2B business model, connections to a network of like-minded organizations and a technically proficient team positioned Esoko for success. The lesson is clear: Not all actors

---

410 Alex Andrason and François van Schalkwyk, *Open Data Intermediaries in the Agriculture Sector in Ghana*, Research Paper, Washington DC: World Wide Web Foundation, 2016, http://webfoundation.org/docs/2016/12/WF-RP-Open-Data-Intermediaries-in-Agriculture-Ghana-Update.pdf.

are equal in the ecosystem, and only some possess the requisite capital to make the most of the niches that open up in an ecosystem.[411]

Barriers

Despite its relative success, Esoko faces four main challenges: deployment costs, infrastructure reliability, information quality on the supply side and information quality on the demand side.

- **Costs:** As far as costs are concerned, deployment constitutes the bulk of Esoko's expenses (95 percent) while the actual technology only contributes a small amount (5 percent). The costs of deployment place limits on the extent to which Esoko can provide free and equal access to its information products.
- **Infrastructure reliability:** In terms of infrastructure, the access to mobile network infrastructure is at times difficult, restricting Esoko's ability to provide a reliable, real-time service to its customers. An unreliable supply of electricity places a similar burden on Esoko's operations.
- **Supply-side information quality:** The quality and timeliness of data received from the government's Ministry of Food and Agriculture can also be an issue. While the government published open data on agriculture more regularly and more frequently in the past, it does not appear to be able to sustain the publication of relevant and timely data. At the time of writing, for example, the most recent published data on market prices was for the first week of June 2014.[412]
- **Demand-side information quality:** Certain information provided by Esoko can also be difficult for farmers to understand, and this limits the usability and the potential impact of the information provided. While Esoko does provide telephonic support in local languages to help farmers use the data, providing information in formats that smallholder farmers can understand remains an ongoing challenge.

Looking Forward

The fact that Esoko currently operates in a number of African countries is indicative of the replicability of its product. In addition, the existence of other

---

411 Ibid.

412 Ministry of Food and Agriculture, Republic of Ghana, "Weekly Market Prices of Food Commodities," http://mofa.gov.gh/site/?page_id=13613.

organizations (e.g., Farmerline) offering similar products and services in Ghana suggests the existence of genuine market opportunities in the local ICT ecosystem, and perhaps a sustainable business climate for open data projects. As more data sources become available, and as the needs of smallholder farmers evolve, it seems likely that new information products that rely on data will enter the market and that value chain transparency will continue to change how prices are negotiated in the agricultural sector.

Partnerships between data intermediaries and data owners may also evolve as both intermediaries and the data owners benefit from having access to better quality data. Already Esoko is working with the Ministry of Food and Agriculture to collect data on market prices. In this case, the Ministry has access to human resources in the form of extension officers and other staff that would be financially burdensome for Esoko to retain, while Esoko has the technology and expertise to collect, curate and disseminate the data.

Conclusion

This case study on the use of open data in the agricultural sector in Ghana offers one of the few instances where solid empirical evidence is available to support claims of the positive impact of open data in developing countries. However, it is important to note that the empirical evidence provided by the cited Courois and Subervie study relies on data collected in 2012. Similarly, while the study by Andrason and Van Schalkwyk on open data intermediaries in the agricultural sector is more recent, its findings are inhibited by limited access to primary source evidence from Esoko and from the smallholder farmers themselves. Therefore, while there is strong evidence that open data can make a positive contribution to development, further research is required to build on and further validate the positive findings currently available, and to better understand the risks and barriers identified in this case study.

CHAPTER 14

Jamaica's Interactive Community Mapping

Open data and crowdsourcing for tourism

Andrew Young and Stefaan Verhulst

Summary

Like much of the Caribbean, the Jamaican economy is heavily dependent on the health of its tourism sector. Influenced by the rise of all-inclusive resorts, which create a general disincentive for tourists to stray far from a few highly-trafficked areas, tourists rarely experience much of Jamaica's unique culture, and the economic benefits of tourism tend to be highly concentrated. In order to demonstrate the potential for increasing tourism (and the spread of its economic benefits), a community mapping project launched in November 2015 sought to combine open government data with crowdsourced mapping data to enable a more participatory development of the tourism sector. Built around open tourism data and the efforts of government agencies, civil society organizations, developers, and a group of motivated community mappers, the initiative is providing early insight into how data and collective intelligence can impact an industry that in many ways represents the lifeblood of the country.

Context and Background

Problem Focus/Country Context

Jamaica is a small island nation located about 600 miles from Miami and 100 miles south of Cuba. It is a member of the British Commonwealth of Nations and has close economic ties to the United States. It gained its independence in 1962 during an era of global decolonization and still grapples with the political, economic, and social legacies left by colonization.

The Caribbean region continues to be a hotbed of tourism activity. From 2005 to 2013, tourist arrivals to the Caribbean grew by 5.4 percent, outpacing the average global growth rate (4.7 percent). In 2014, the Caribbean as a whole received 26.3 million trips (breaking the previous record set in 2013 by 1.3 million). This level of tourism activity represented 2.3 percent of total global tourism arrivals.[413] The Caribbean is also the number one cruise destination in the world.

Jamaica's economy, similar to that of the Caribbean as a whole, is heavily reliant on service industries, which, according to some estimates, makes up as much as 70 percent of the nation's GDP.[414] Most of those services are related to tourism, one of the nation's economic strengths. According to the *Jamaica Observer*, more than 3 million tourists visited the island in 2014, including those from cruise ships.[415] Jamaica has experienced year-to-year growth over recent years—a 3.6 percent increase from 2013–2014 in stopover visitors and 12.5 percent increase in cruise visitors over the same period, continuing a trend observable since 2007.

While the tourism sector is seemingly healthy and evolving rapidly, the need for a more citizen-inclusive model for tourism development is widely recognized, as is the need for a more intelligent, centralized system for collecting and managing tourism data.[416]

The all-inclusive tourism model

Over the past few decades, tourism in the Caribbean has been influenced by the rise of all-inclusive tourism offerings. The paradigmatic example of this model is a central beachside resort that offers, among other services, all-you-can-eat and drink packages for visitors, ensuring that consumers do not have to leave the grounds of the resort for any reason. These resorts tend to cater to preconceived notions held by travellers about Jamaican culture and life—relatively few visitors, for instance, ever explored Kingston beyond the sights seen from a one-day tour bus. The Trench Town Development Association, a

413 Caribbean Tourism Organization, *Caribbean Tourism Review*, 2014, http://www.onecaribbean.org/wp-content/uploads/2014TourismReviewDocumentAmendedFEB11.pdf.

414 Witherbee, Amy, "Jamaica," *Our World, Research Starters*, January 2016, EBSCO*host* (accessed September 21, 2016).

415 "Tourist Arrivals Increased by 3.6 % in 2014," *Jamaica Observer News*, February 5, 2015, http://www.jamaicaobserver.com/news/Tourist-arrivals-increased-by-3-6---in-2014.

416 Caribbean Tourism Organization, *Caribbean Sustainable Tourism Policy Framework*, http://www.onecaribbean.org/content/files/CbbnSustainableTourismPolicyFramework.pdf.

grassroots initiative, has aimed to help visitors experience the famous Trench Town neighborhood of Kingston – the home of Reggae icon Bob Marley, and the acknowledged birthplace of rocksteady and reggae music – by offering a local tour guide, featuring "a museum, a music studio, and a school, as well as interaction with artists, craftspeople, and community elders."[417] Though still wary of inner-city Kingston violence, visitors are somewhat more likely today than ever before to interact with local communities that have proven to be resilient in the face of both violence and poverty

Christopher Whyms-Stone of the Trench Town Development Association argues that while there are many benefits to the all-inclusive tourism model, "it is lazy for a country to say it is going to push this model because crime in the country is too high so we can't let the visitors go outside. ... No wonder we still have not solved crime in Jamaica.... That is the strongest word I will use—lazy. That is the easy way out."[418] Whyms-Stone is careful to point out that the all-inclusive model has very real benefits for Jamaica—including the fact that many Jamaicans are employed by such resorts, and that many visitors to the Trench Town Development Association are based at all-inclusive resorts for much of their stay. Rather than demonizing the all-inclusive approach, he argues that tourists and Jamaican citizens would benefit from additional efforts to advance community-oriented tourism initiatives rather than relying solely on the all-inclusive model.

Tourism and information

The centrality of tourism to the local economy presents various challenges for policymakers and business owners in Jamaica and across the Caribbean, particularly due to the volatility and unreliability of tourism arrivals. Recently, the need for information has become more apparent, for instance to help Jamaican tourism authorities plan their offerings as well as for tourists themselves to better understand the possibilities on offer (especially the possibilities beyond the all-inclusive resort).

Better information is seen as key to opening up new tourist activities and areas. For instance, a tourist may be more likely to engage in a community-based tour of a Kingston neighborhood if there is easily-accessible information about the unique culture, history, and people of the region. Similarly, a local entrepreneur will make more informed decisions if he/she has access to data detailing the interests and activities of tourists visiting his/her region.

---

417 Eveline Dürr and Jaffe Rivke, "Theorizing Slum Tourism: Performing, negotiating and transforming inequality," *European Review of Latin American & Caribbean Studies*, no. 93, pp. 113–123, October 2012.

418 GovLab Interview with Christopher Whyms-Stone, Trench Town Development Association, September 29, 2016.

The Inter-American Development Bank notes "a general absence of data for [tourism] benchmarking and strategic planning in the region" and argues that "the effective use of Big Data has the potential to transform the tourism sector, delivering a new wave of productivity growth and consumer surplus." As such, it recommends the development of "public policy promoting positive externalities such as knowledge sharing and addressing coordination failures so that the private sector is encouraged to innovate and upgrade, aiming for collective efficiency."[419]

Open Data in Jamaica

Open data could be critical in generating the necessary information. A recent study conducted by the Caribbean Policy Research Institute (CaPRI) concluded that an open data initiative in Jamaica could improve productivity in the tourism industry by 10 percent. Jamaica is well-aware of this potential (and of the need for better information) and has signalled its openness to open data policies and frameworks.[420] In 2014, the Jamaican government partnered with the World Bank to develop a framework for "open data development as a job creation and entrepreneurship option."[421] It is the opinion of the World Bank that Jamaica has "many of the essential prerequisites needed to support a successful program" as well as "the region's most vibrant community of people who could use" the data.[422]

Maurice McNaughton, the Director of the Caribbean Open Institute (COI), a coalition promoting open development, argues that while the Caribbean as a whole was "late to the open data, open government party," the Jamaican open data space is noteworthy in a number of ways. For instance, he notes that, "unlike many of the more celebrated instances which start with governments publishing a lot of data and then trying to simulate activity around that, we've actually started from a demand side perspective in a number of key sectors and have been working our way back towards identifying the most impactful data sources." He continues: "on the demand side, the user capacity and interest in

419 Seggitur and CICtourGUNE, *Compete Caribbean: Improving competitiveness in the Caribbean tourism sector through ICT-based innovations*, InterAmerican Development Bank, 2014, http://competecaribbean.org/wp-content/uploads/2015/04/Improving-Competitiveness-in-the-Caribbean-Tourism-Sector-Through-ICT-Based-Innovations_September_v4_docx.pdf.

420 Maurice McNaughton, "Open Government Data: A Catalyst for Jamaica's Growth and Innovation Agenda," Caribbean Policy Research Institute, October 2014, http://www.capricaribbean.com/documents/open-government-data-catalyst-jamaicas-growth-and-innovation-agenda.

421 "World Bank to Assist Jamaica with Open Data Development," *Jamaica Observer News*. December 9, 2014, http://www.jamaicaobserver.com/latestnews/World-Bank-to-assist-Jamaica-with-open-data-development.

422 Jamaica Ministry of Science, Energy and Technology, "Jamaica Receives Favourable Open Data Assessment Report," Ministry of Science, Energy, and Technology, http://mstem.gov.jm/?q=jamaica-receives-favourable-open-data-assessment-report.

open data is quite high. In fact, it was rated the highest of the 7 pillars in terms of the World Bank's overall readiness assessment."[423],[424]

The belief that the Caribbean and Jamaican tourism industry can benefit from increased open data activity is resulting in greater availability of information.[425]

Interactive Community Mapping (ICM)

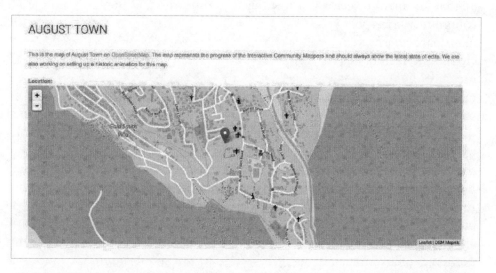

Figure 1. Digital map of August town (http://icm.msbm-uwi.org/content/august-town)

A community map is a map produced by citizens of residents of a particular area. It includes local knowledge and expertise, and is seen by some as a more democratic and people-centric response to traditional cartography.[426] [427] Changes to traditional cartography have been driven in recent years by two main forces: (1) the emergence of critical geographers who have "illuminated the map's crucial and tendentious role in shaping the world" and its relationship to power,[428] and (2) the emergence of freely-accessible data and accessible

423 GovLab Interview with Maurice McNaughton, August 24, 2016.

424 Jamaica Ministry of Science, Energy and Technology, "Jamaica Receives Favourable Open Data Assessment Report," Ministry of Science, Energy, and Technology, http://mstem.gov.jm/?q=jamaica-receives-favourable-open-data-assessment-report.

425 Gerard Best, "How Open Data Can Help Caribbean Development, *Caribbean Journal*, October 4, 2015, http://www.caribjournal.com/2015/10/04/how-open-data-can-help-caribbean-development/.

426 Brenda Parker, "Constructing Community through Maps? Power and Praxis in Community Mapping," *Professional Geographer* 58, no. 4, 2006, pp. 470–84.

427 John Pickles, *A History of Spaces: Cartographic reason, mapping, and the geo-coded World*, London: Routledge, 2004; Chris Perkins, "Community Mapping," *Cartographic Journal*, 44, no. 2, 2007, pp. 127–37; and Jennifer Shkabatur, "Closing the Feedback Loop: Can technology bridge the accountability gap?" *Interactive Community Mapping: Between empowerment and effectiveness*, The World Bank, May 2014, pp. 71–106.

428 J.B. Harley, "Maps, Knowledge, and Power," in Denis E. Cosgrove and Stephen Daniels, eds., *The Iconography of Landscape*, Chicago: university of Chicago Press, 1988, pp. 277–312; and J.B. Harley,

mapping technologies."[429] Most community mapping projects are found in developing country contexts.[430]

There are several advantages to interactive community maps. Like many community information projects, they rely fundamentally on open data. Chief among their advantages are the facts that they tend to be drawn quicker, are more dynamic, cost less to produce, and provide more granular information.[431] Successful map projects must carefully consider the particularities of a community being mapped (as well as that community's access to the resulting map, particularly in poorer, marginalized neighborhoods); the existence of civil society actors who can utilize the maps in public campaigns and activist pressure; and the government officials who service the community being mapped (taking care to include their priorities and needs in the mapping project).[432]

There are several examples of ICMs in developing country contexts. ICM efforts have been used for community-driven advocacy (e.g., in Nairobi[433]), and in responses to public health crises (Sierra Leone[434]) or natural and other disasters (e.g., Gulf of Mexico,[435] Haiti[436]). Jennifer Shkabatur, a scholar at the Interdisciplinary Center Herzliya, an Israeli research university, notes that the prevalence of ICMs in fields like disaster response is not surprising. ICM efforts are often successful in such situations because "the incentives are there, you do not have to encourage people. People know they should be there."[437] ICM in less urgent situations, however, are much harder to sustain without similarly clear incentives for participation.

"Deconstructing the Map," *Cartographica*, 26, no. 2, pp. 1–20.

429 John Pickles, *A History of Spaces: Cartographic reason, mapping, and the geo-coded World*, London: Routledge, 2004; and Brenda Parker, "Constructing Community through Maps? Power and Praxis in Community Mapping," *Professional Geographer* 58, no. 4, 2006, pp. 470–84.

430 Chris Perkins, "Community Mapping," *Cartographic Journal*, 44, no. 2, 2007, pp. 127–37.

431 Jennifer Shkabatur, "Closing the Feedback Loop: Can technology bridge the accountability gap?" *Interactive Community Mapping: Between empowerment and effectiveness*, The World Bank, May 2014, pp. 71–106.

432 Ibid.

433 Ibid.

434 Andrew Young and Stefaan Verhulst, "Battling Ebola in Sierra Leone: Data sharing to improve crisis response," GovLab, http://odimpact.org/case-battling-ebola-in-sierra-leone.html.

435 Jennifer Shkabatur, "Closing the Feedback Loop: Can technology bridge the accountability gap?" *Interactive Community Mapping: Between empowerment and effectiveness*, The World Bank, May 2014, pp. 71–106.

436 Wikiproject, "Haiti," http://wiki.openstreetmap.org/wiki/WikiProject_Haiti.

437 GovLab Interview with Jennifer Shkabatur, November 14, 2016.

KEY ACTORS

Key Data Providers

Jamaica's tourism industry is governed by the Ministry of Tourism, which maintains data on the number of visitors who enter the nation and where those visitors stay. Local mappers are also providing data in a crowdsourced manner to supplement official data sources with on-the-ground information.

Key Data Users and Intermediaries

The Caribbean Open Institute (COI) was the lead actor in the ICM effort in August Town. The COI is a "regional coalition of individuals and organizations that promotes open development approaches to inclusion, participation and innovation within the Caribbean, using open data as a catalyst." Its focus areas include spurring "awareness, advocacy and engagement with public sector stakeholders on Open Government and Open Data" and catalyzing "regional capacity building in a core set of technology platforms, tools and standards that are commonly used across the Open Data universe."[438] COI also plays a key role in regional efforts, like the Developing the Caribbean open data conference and Codesprint.

COI's Maurice McNaughton notes that, "we have been very deliberate about picking sectors that are high impact for the Caribbean."[439] As a result, COI's initiatives focus on four main sectors: agriculture, tourism, and marine protected areas.

Key Beneficiaries

The ICM effort is meant to benefit a wide range of actors, including tourists themselves, stakeholders in the local tourism industry, and the country at large, which stands to gain from the economic benefits of a more widely dispersed tourism industry. In a paper describing the initial pilot project studied here, Michelle McLeod, Maurice McNaughton, the drivers of the initiative, note beneficiaries such as, community residents; tourism businesses (to the end of improving the "technology and data literacy skills of tourism businesses to develop innovative tourism products and services); the UWI Mona Source hosting service (which stands to "become a hub for open data and ICM activities"); the Social Development Commission (a government agency that will play a key role in scaling tourism ICM efforts and gain access to new mapping artefacts); and tourism app developers, who stand to gain access to useful new maps and, potentially, new collaboration opportunities with other stakeholders in the space.[440]

---

438 Caribbean Open Institute website, http://caribbeanopeninstitute.org.

439 GovLab Interview with Maurice McNaughton, August 24, 2016.

440 Maurice McNaughton, et al., "Open Data as a Catalyst for Problem Solving: Empirical evidence from a Small Island Developing States (SIDS) context," Paper presented at the 2016 Open Data Research Symposium, Madrid, Spain, October 5, 2016, https://drive.google.com/file/d/0B4TpC6ecmrM7OEN6OVlIUXh1d1U/view.

Project Description

As the potential for crowdsourced mapping efforts (often but not always supplemented with open government datasets) continues to grow in recognition, it is seen as an important enabler of community tourism, which is a "key component of Jamaica's Tourism master plan and efforts to diversify the Tourism product."[441]

In 2015, Maurice McNaughton and Michelle McLeod of the University of the West Indies and Caribbean Open Institute (COI) began a tourism-focused ICM initiative. The project was aimed at leveraging open data and a crowdsourced ICM effort to create new tourism-focused mapping artefacts and build new mapping skills for community members. The initiative was developed to highlight "heritage, culture, ecology, and visitor-community interaction" in a way that enabled the community to generate "its own data and its own intelligence and based on its own indigenous knowledge."[442]

As McNaughton put it in a paper, underlying this initiative was the belief that:

> [C]ombining the Internet and new low-cost, interactive, map-based technologies with official Open Government data and indigenous content creates the opportunity for the active engagement of community members in the planning, development and increased visibility of the community tourism product, as well as enhances the interactions between the community, the tourism agencies, and other service providers within the sector; i.e., transportation, larger hotel chains, tour operators, and prospective tourists.[443]

To set the stage for the ICM effort, a team from COI conducted a detailed sector study, looking at the main data sets being put to use in five countries that had important tourism sectors. This effort sought to gain a greater grasp of both the supply and demand sides of the tourism open data ecosystem, the current and potential users of such data and where most of these datasets existed on the open-closed spectrum. The team found that while in some cases data are not fully open, there was "quite a lot of activity both in terms of the demand and supply side in the tourism sector" and available datasets were "being used to make critical strategic decisions in the sector."[444] For example, in an interview,

---

441 Maurice McNaughton, "Open Data and Community Tourism: A strategy for empowering local communities," Paper presented at the Third International Tourism Conference, Jamaica, November 9–11, 2014, http://ocs.msbm-uwi.org/index.php/itc/index/pages/view/abstract-mcnaughton.

442 Ibid.

443 Ibid.

444 GovLab interview with Michelle McLeod, August 24, 2016.

McLeod pointed to Barbados' use of tourist arrival data to enable targeted outreach to new airlines that could benefit from servicing the island and to adjust airline policies to enable growth. She argues that the Barbados case is only one example of how the "openness of the tourism data is critical for timely decision making and strategic adjustments in the sector."[445]

Following these initial research efforts, the ICM pilot project advanced by McLeod and McNaughton began in earnest during an initial meeting in June 2016 with partners from the Centre for Tourism and Policy Research; Mona Social Services, a social and economic development NGO; and The Source, a local resource hub. The goal was to identify potential mappers to take part in the project. The initial meeting was followed by an "intensive 5-day workshop" wherein volunteer mappers were trained on geodata capabilities and, in particular, the use of the OpenStreetMap platform. Upon completion of the workshop, the participating mappers were placed into teams and assigned to different grid areas across August Town, a neighborhood in Kingston. Over a four-week period, the participants mapped landmarks and areas of interest, tour routes and bus stops. They also collected pictures and video for inclusion in mapping artefacts made available to the public.[446]

The ICM initiative was developed with the goal of achieving four main aims. First, it set out to map points of interest and community assets around Kingston and St. Andrew. Second, it sought to provide useful data and information to stakeholders active in the Jamaican tourism sector. Third, it sought to lay the groundwork for future community mapping and community-oriented tourism activities. Finally, the effort sought to provide new skills and entrepreneurial opportunities for community members participating in the mapping initiative.[447] The first output of the initiative was a Virtual August Town tour companion app providing data-driven and community-oriented maps and suggestions for making the most out of visits to the area.

A follow-on initiative was organized shortly afterward, bringing together a number of community leaders in addition to the strategic partners and mappers. This second focus group yielded a "Tourism Related Wish List" that helped to better target the efforts of the community mappers. Some of the items on the wish list included, food festivals, youth sports facilities and local

---

445 Ibid.

446 Maurice McNaughton, et al., "Open Data as a Catalyst for Problem Solving: Empirical evidence from a Small Island Developing States (SIDS) context," Paper presented at the 2016 Open Data Research Symposium, Madrid, Spain, October 5, 2016, https://drive.google.com/file/d/0B4TpC6ecmrM7OEN6OVlIUXh1d1U/view.

447 Ibid.

community tour guides.[448] The two initial pilot mapping projects yielded a number of digital maps and tourist routes described in more detail below.

Demand and Supply of Data Type(s) and Sources

According to the Open Knowledge Foundation's Caribbean census site, a number of open data sets related to tourism are available (even if some of the data is not truly "open" by the strictest definition). Some of these datasets include: tourism arrivals ("aggregate data about tourist stop-over visits, derived from anonymized landing card data"); tourism service providers ("listing of registered service providers including Tour Operators, Transportation / Taxi service, Car rental, Adventure & Entertainment providers"); and tourism assets ("list of registered tourism assets including large/small hotel properties, attractions, craft markets").[449] These datasets represent the core public information on the sector, and provided a foundation for the ICM effort, helping to target mappers' focus toward areas of particular interest.

Funding

COI has five central partners and funders: the International Development Research Center (IDRC), Mona School of Business & Management, SlashRoots, Fundacion Taiguey and Open Data for Development Network. Specifically, the ICM effort was one of four strategic sector initiatives being implemented as part of the Harnessing Open Data to Achieve Development Results in Latin America and the Caribbean program funded by IDRC.[450]

Open Data Use

The ICM effort leveraged the open datasets available listed on the Open Knowledge portal to target mapping efforts and provide the backbone for the crowdsourcing effort. The newly generated, crowdsourced, open data was created through the OpenStreetMap platform, available for access and reuse by anyone, including other tourism-focused actors in Jamaica, demonstrating

---

448 Ibid.

449 "Caribbean Open Data Census," http://caribbean.census.okfn.org.

450 Maurice McNaughton, et al., "Open Data as a Catalyst for Problem Solving: Empirical evidence from a Small Island Developing States (SIDS) context," Paper presented at the 2016 Open Data Research Symposium, Madrid, Spain, October 5, 2016, https://drive.google.com/file/d/0B4TpC6ecmrM7OEN6OVlIUXh1d1U/view.

the value of supplementing open data with crowdsourced – and ensuring the crowdsourced data itself is made open.[451]

Impact

The Jamaican Interactive Community Mapping initiative is still in its infancy, and major on-the-ground impacts have not yet been achieved. The initiative has, however, achieved some early wins – in the form of new deliverables produced, skills provided for community members, and inspiration for similar initiatives in the region aimed at leveraging open and crowdsourced data to benefit the public good.

Encouraging More Diverse, Community-Oriented Tourism

One of the initial outputs of the project, demonstrating the utility and potential of interactive community mapping data, was the design of a virtual August Town tour companion app, which was launched at the 178th anniversary of the August Town community.[452] Some of the key points of interest include the Judgement Yard, the Bedward Church Ruins, the Berry Spring and the culminating food- and craft-focused Artisans' Village.[453] Many other buildings and points of interest are interspersed along the path.[454]

This new community-produced route for tourists stands to be a win-win situation, where tourists are exposed to points of interest that they would be unlikely to experience if they stayed on-site at their all-inclusive hotels (or, indeed, participated in a traditional bus tour), and the local community is exposed to a larger population, with the map helping "to create more business activity in the community."[455]

Skill-Building for Mappers

From the start, McNaughton and McLeod saw the digital maps as only one of the intended outcomes of the project. McNaughton describes the second

---

451 Ibid.

452 Ibid.

453 Carlos Gordon, "A Hidden Gem: August Town Tour Comes to Life!", The Caribbean Open Institute, August 2016, http://caribbeanopeninstitute.org/ATour_pilot.

454 Maurice McNaughton, et al., "Open Data as a Catalyst for Problem Solving: Empirical evidence from a Small Island Developing States (SIDS) context," Paper presented at the 2016 Open Data Research Symposium, Madrid, Spain, October 5, 2016, https://drive.google.com/file/d/0B4TpC6ecmrM7OEN6OVlIUXh1d1U/view.

455 GovLab interview with Michelle McLeod, August 24, 2016.

objective as "more of a process outcome," specifically: "How do we build capacity and a capability for the community to begin to create its own narrative and its story?"[456] As such, the ICM effort was aimed at seeding "the ability of the community to generate its own content and to anchor new tourism products and services around that open map content."[457] Such a focus is common among ICM efforts. Shkabatur notes that "the engagement itself, the skills and the tools that community members gain from the mapping exercise" are often as beneficial as the fruits of their efforts.[458] For McLeod, "It's all about community resilience."[459]

There are several indications that such efforts in Jamaica have borne fruit. McNaughton found that the mappers "developed an energy and enthusiasm and entrepreneurial spirit" as a result of their new-found skills. For example, many mappers have taken it upon themselves to create maps of nature tours, hiking trails and other potential tourist attractions. This entrepreneurial spirit has not gone unnoticed. Other communities in Jamaica with significant Tourism interests such as the Treasure Beach Cluster are keen to explore similar approaches to enhancing their community tourism product.[460] Community leaders, like the President of the Community Development Council have recognized the value and potential of such efforts, and are in the early stages of developing and implementing new opportunities for mappers to leverage their skills, with the goal of further "showcasing the heritage, the music, the art, and just that general community spirit."[461]

Scaling and Replication Across the Region

Maurice McNaughton found that "one of the major emerging insights" from the effort was the fact that the "digital asset and its openness…can be pivoted in many different directions."[462] For example, community mappers are exploring opportunities with local government agencies to support a number of initiatives, including efforts to promote school safety, improve resilience and response to Zika, and to further increase the visibility of Jamaica's tourism offerings.[463]

---

456 GovLab Interview with Maurice McNaughton, August 24, 2016.

457 GovLab interview with Michelle McLeod, August 24, 2016.

458 GovLab Interview with Jennifer Shkabatur, November 14, 2016.

459 Ibid.

460 "The Emergence of Experiential Tourism in Jamaica," Compete Caribbean, http://files.constantcontact.com/825e9e58201/9c460a8f-b801-41ad-85d9-d7a15599a398.pdf.

461 GovLab interview with Michelle McLeod, August 24, 2016.

462 GovLab Interview with Maurice McNaughton, August 24, 2016.

463 Maurice McNaughton, et al., "Open Data as a Catalyst for Problem Solving: Empirical evidence from a Small Island Developing States (SIDS) context," Paper presented at the 2016 Open

Going forward, the COI team hopes to continue to replicate and expand on the initiative across regions and sectors, with a notable focus on education.[464] Future efforts specifically related to tourism could include "spinoffs such as bed and breakfast [mapping] opportunities, and opportunities to even beautify the environment in the community."[465] Shkabatur argues that replication of ICM efforts are often quite easy in terms of technology, especially given the prevalence of OpenStreetMap, but sometimes experience challenges when there is a mismatch in social context or the strength of community groups and organizers.[466] Given the ICM interest and buy-in among both organizers and participants in the Jamaican tourism effort, perhaps these issues will be less challenging than in other contexts.

Risks

As evidenced by the example of the Jamaican ICM effort and various other case studies included in this series, open data holds tremendous potential for positive transformation. But, as we also see throughout this series, open data also poses certain risks. It is important to understand these risks in order to ensure that open data projects are implemented in a way that maximizes the potential upside and limits the downside.

Potential for Negative Publicity

While the ICM effort is premised on the belief that tourists and the Jamaican community both stand to benefit from increased interaction, the impetus for the rise of all-inclusive resorts remains a question. Poverty and crime issues are still present in Jamaica, and on top of the obvious human cost of any crime (violent or otherwise) befalling tourists using the ICM-generated artefacts, the potential negative publicity arising from encouraging tourists to venture off the beaten path could undermine these community tourism efforts.

Data Research Symposium, Madrid, Spain, October 5, 2016, https://drive.google.com/file/d/0B4TpC6ecmrM7OEN6OVlIUXh1d1U/view.

464 GovLab Interview with Maurice McNaughton, August 24, 2016.

465 GovLab interview with Michelle McLeod, August 24, 2016.

466 GovLab Interview with Jennifer Shkabatur, November 14, 2016.

Lessons Learned

Several important lessons with wider applicability emerge from this particular case study. These can broadly be categorized by considering the key enablers of the project, as well as the most important barriers or challenges to its success.

Enablers

Problem definition and context

Tourism is not one of the central areas of focus for open data initiatives in most parts of the developing or developed world. McNaughton notes, however, that while other countries are actively engaged in transportation, government budget, or agriculture open data efforts, "the Caribbean is seen as the most tourism-dependent region in the world. We thought it was important to look at tourism as one of the region's key sectors and what the possibilities or the opportunities were for open data to make an impact…Context matters."[467]

To refine and focus in on the areas of most potential impact, as described above, COI conducted detailed tourism open data and ICM scoping studies, which helped to target mapping efforts and data use. This clear, upfront problem focus also helped to identify gaps in existing open government datasets, and consider other avenues for filling those gaps. It was one of the keys to the project's relative success.

Engaging the press

Upon completion of the initial ICM effort, COI leveraged the press as a key intermediary in spreading the word about the fruits of the project. While many open data efforts—including some in this series of case studies—struggle with raising awareness, COI promoted both the output (i.e., the August Town tour) and the process (i.e., OpenStreetMap-enabled ICM) through the local press.[468] Such an effort could help to ensure that the tourism artefacts, maps and datasets are used by those who stand to benefit the most from them. In addition, such efforts can also promote the use of open data and ICM more generally, potentially pushing forward the approaches in other areas.

---

467 GovLab Interview with Maurice McNaughton, August 24, 2016.

468 Maurice McNaughton, et al., "Open Data as a Catalyst for Problem Solving: Empirical evidence from a Small Island Developing States (SIDS) context," Paper presented at the 2016 Open Data Research Symposium, Madrid, Spain, October 5, 2016, https://drive.google.com/file/d/0B4TpC6ecmrM7OEN6OVliUXh1d1U/view.

Building partnerships

Brokering partnerships with community groups, intermediaries, NGOs and government was seen as a key factor in allowing for the targeted matching of the supply and demand for data around Jamaican tourism.[469][470] COI is not only well-connected in the local Jamaican community, leading to more buy-in from government actors and volunteer mappers, but also to the global open data community, helping to enable knowledge transfer and collaboration with others doing similar work across the world.

Barriers

Resource challenges

Given the relatively limited availability of open data, as described above, it is little surprise that the availability of resources at the data supply side represented the central challenge for the ICM effort. In reference to the supply side, McNaughton notes that, "I don't think in the Caribbean we have the luxury of just opening up all data and making hundreds or thousands of data sets available and then seeing what happens. We don't have the luxury of that scattershot approach as has characterized many open data initiatives."[471] So while this project could be advanced with relatively little funding (considering the volunteer nature of the mappers and the open source OpenStreetMap platform), resource constraints at the supply side often create barriers to efforts to leverage open data in the country.

To address these types of challenges, McNaughton notes that Jamaican open data efforts often must be "very targeted, starting from sector-specific challenges and opportunities that we perceive and then working from those back towards engaging in partnerships with the supply side to get the data that is relevant to those either problem- or opportunity-centered approaches."[472] [473]

---

469 Ibid.

470 Carlos Gordon, "Enabling Sustainable Partnerships through Open Data and Interactive Community Mapping," The Caribbean Open Institute, http://caribbeanopeninstitute.org/icm_partners.

471 GovLab Interview with Maurice McNaughton, August 24, 2016.

472 GovLab Interview with Maurice McNaughton, August 24, 2016.

473 Maurice McNaughton, "Problem-Solving with Open Data: A Caribbean Perspective (Part 2), International Open Data Conference Blog, November 19, 2015, http://opendatacon.org/problem-solving-with-open-data-a-caribbean-perspective-part-2/.

Institutional culture challenges

While resource constraints create major challenges, McNaughton believes that "perhaps a larger barrier that we have encountered in much of our work is a cultural barrier to sharing data."[474] While progress is being made—students no longer need to parse static government PDF documents to pull out relevant "open" data as they previously did—shifting the culture remains a slow process with fits and starts. The growing visibility of international open data assessments and shared policies are helping to push for meaningful culture change and institutional recognition of the value of machine-readable open data, and, as a result, the opening of more useful datasets.[475] Important steps forward were taken in 2016 with the launch of Jamaica's Open Data Portal (http://data.gov.jm/) and its entry into the Open Government Partnership.[476]

Supply-side awareness building

As discussed above, the open data ecosystem in Jamaica is largely demand-driven. And while international readiness assessments like those conducted by the World Bank are helping to push forward the supply side, there is still relatively little awareness of the potential value of providing more open data to the public. McNaughton believes that making the case more effectively to government that the issues they face could help to bring more problem-solvers outside of government into the equation could help improve the supply of open data in the country. As it stands, there is little understanding of the types of problems that could be solved through open data, the benefit of allocating the time and resources necessary to make it available, and what open data can do to "enhance what we do in terms of growth and development in the region."[477]

Looking Forward

Due to the importance of tourism to the Jamaican economy, continued development and scaling of open data-driven tourism efforts is likely to continue. As Whyms-Stone of the Trench Town Development Association

---

474 GovLab Interview with Maurice McNaughton, August 24, 2016.

475 Ibid.

476 OGP Support Unit, "Leaders at OGP Summit Call for Greater Government Openness in Response to Worrying Global Trends," Open Government Partnership Blog, December 7, 2016, https://www.opengovpartnership.org/blog/ogp-support-unit/2016/12/07/leaders-ogp-summit-call-greater-government-openness-response.

477 GovLab interview with Michelle McLeod, August 24, 2016.

notes: "we are an island with not a lot of resources…Not a lot of minerals, we don't got oil. But what we do have is a place like Trench Town, a place called Jamaica that people want to come to for whatever reason."[478]

He continues that he "believes in tourism 100%…it is a source, an economy of revenue so your people can have a better quality of life, health, education, housing. And that is why I believe in tourism because it is necessary. People want to come here; we want people to come here. We need an economy, let's make it work."[479]

Current Status

The initial pilot ICM initiative has now concluded, but the insights and resources (including the tourism artefacts) it generated are being put to use in a number of ways. The project is now expanding and evolving across a number of sectors and regions, described more below.

Sustainability

Given the benefits provided to community mappers in terms of skills development, and the limited resources required for spurring an ICM effort, the continued expansion of the Jamaican tourism initiative seems promising. While there are challenges, as described above, especially around the availability of relevant open datasets, the public interest and availability of the open source OpenStreetMap platform bodes well for the sustainability of such efforts. As a cautionary note, it is worth mentioning that in other parts of the world, efforts to sustain ICM interest and engagement over a longer time period have proven difficult after the initial motivation for citizen participation (e.g., a natural disaster or the creation of a specific mapping artefact) became less urgent.[480] The ICM Tourism Pilot in Jamaica has identified the many actors that need to collaborate in order to develop a vibrant, sustainable open data ecosystem in community tourism.[481]

---

478 GovLab Interview with Christopher Whyms-Stone, Trench Town Development Association, September 29, 2016.

479 Ibid.

480 GovLab Interview with Jennifer Shkabatur, November 14, 2016.

481 "Building a Sustainable GeoData Ecosystem," Open Data for Development, Caribbean Open Institute, http://caribbeanopeninstitute.org/sites/default/files/images/Building_geoData_Ecosystem.png.

Replicability

Replicability of the ICM effort across the Caribbean is promising, given the key insights and resources developed as part of the Jamaican effort. Given resource constraints, scaling innovations across the region often rely on the availability of "common resources and common approaches," which this effort has provided.[482] Regarding the replication of the tourism ICM effort, McNaughton notes, "We have packaged it. We have developed approaches and platforms and techniques and quite interesting workshop around mapping. We can easily replicate that in many other contexts so that everybody is not reinventing the wheel, which is a challenge that the Caribbean has had in traditional endeavors."[483]

As McLeod notes, "Of course, we are divided by the sea and that is a barrier, but we want to be able to really replicate it across the islands and ensure that our region can benefit with the whole open data movement."[484]

Conclusion

While the on-the-ground impacts of the Jamaican interactive community mapping effort are still largely aspirational, the initiative provides inspiration and important lessons regarding the use of open data and crowdsourcing to create new economic opportunity and improve social cohesion. Based on a clearly defined problem – i.e., the need for more information on the tourism sector in the country to benefit local stakeholders and tourists themselves – the project organizers were able to identify useful open data sets and fill gaps in the data with a community-oriented data collection effort. By both producing new artefacts to benefit the sector and providing community members with new mapping skills, the initiative stands to create an ongoing impact for those living in the region, as well as those vacationing there.

---

482 GovLab Interview with Maurice McNaughton, August 24, 2016.

483 Ibid.

484 GovLab interview with Michelle McLeod, August 24, 2016.

Open Data's Impact on Solving Public Problems

CHAPTER 15

Nepal Earthquake Recovery

Open data to improve disaster relief

Juliet McMurren, Saroj Bista, Andrew Young and Stefaan Verhulst

Summary

After two devastating earthquakes in 2015, Nepal faced a lengthy and costly relief effort and recovery. Nepali open data activists sought ways to crowdsource and deploy open data to identify the most urgent needs of citizens, target relief efforts most effectively, and ensure aid money reached those in need. A number of initiatives created post-quake maps that were used by relief agencies, alerted rescuers to Nepalis in need of urgent assistance, provided opportunities for citizens to share feedback on the recovery with government, and ensured fiscal accountability for aid money through transparency portals. Data-driven disaster preparedness efforts and the use of local knowledge, expertise and connections greatly enhanced the success of the post-quake open data projects. Natural disasters are human and economic calamities, creating a huge drain on the resources of countries and the international community. The initiatives discussed in this case study show the potential for open data to inform crowdsourced data collection efforts, helping to save lives and make relief efforts more effective.

Context and Background

Problem Focus / Country Context

Nepal is a seismically active country: between 1900 and 2011, there were six serious earthquakes, resulting in a total of around 13,500 deaths.[485] In April and May 2015, Nepal was struck by a series of major earthquakes that killed 8,898[486] people and injured a further 22,300.[487] The first earthquake, measuring magnitude 7.8,[488] struck on April 25, 2015, with an epicenter in Barpak Village, approximately 75km from the capital, Kathmandu. The weeks that followed saw over 300 quakes greater than magnitude 4.0, including a second serious earthquake (magnitude 6.3[489]) on May 12, with an epicenter near Mount Everest.[490]

The effect of the earthquakes was devastating. Thirty-one of the country's 75 districts were affected, of which 14 were declared crisis-hit. Almost half a million homes were destroyed,[491] including entire villages near the epicenter of the earthquakes,[492] and a further 250,000 were damaged.[493] In addition, there was extensive damage to government buildings, schools, hospitals, heritage sites, transport and power infrastructure, and agricultural land. All told, almost 3.5 million people were left homeless by the earthquakes, and 8 million people—almost a third of the country's population—were affected.[494]

The impact of the earthquakes was exacerbated by Nepal's poverty and low levels of development. Although Nepal has been highly successful in reducing its poverty rate from 64.7 percent in 2006 to 44.2 percent in 2011, it remains

---

485 Wikipedia, "List of Earthquakes in Nepal," Wikipedia.org, https://en.wikipedia.org/wiki/List_of_earthquakes_in_Nepal.

486 Government of Nepal, *Nepal Earthquake 2015: Sector plans and financial projections*, May 2016, http://nra.gov.np/uploads/docs/AStGGdnejZ160823113341.pdf.

487 National Planning Commission of Nepal, *Post Disaster Need Assessment*, Executive Summary, NPC, 2015.

488 Jessica Robertson and Heidi Koontz, "Magnitude 7.8 Earthquake in Nepal and Aftershocks," U.S.G.S., May 12, 2015, https://www2.usgs.gov/blogs/features/usgs_top_story/magnitude-7-8-earthquake-in-nepal/; and Government of Nepal, *Nepal Earthquake 2015: Sector plans and financial projections*, May 2016, p. 47, http://nra.gov.np/uploads/docs/AStGGdnejZ160823113341.pdf.

489 Jessica Robertson and Heidi Koontz, "Magnitude 7.8 Earthquake in Nepal and Aftershocks," U.S.G.S., May 12, 2015, https://www2.usgs.gov/blogs/features/usgs_top_story/magnitude-7-8-earthquake-in-nepal/.

490 "Nepal – Earthquake post disaster needs assessment: sector reports (English)," The World Bank, 2015, http://documents.worldbank.org/curated/en/546211467998818313/Nepal-Earthquake-post-disaster-needs-assessment-sector-reports.

491 Ibid.

492 Sahina Shrestha, "Lang Tang Is Gone," Nepali Times, May 1–7,2015, http://nepalitimes.com/article/nation/langtang-destroyed-in-earthquake,2205.

493 https://www.worldbank.org/content/dam/Worldbank/document/SAR/nepal/PDNA%20Volume%20A%20Final.pdf.

494 Ibid.

one of Asia's poorest countries, with a GDP per capita of $2,573 in 2016.[495] The United Nations Development Program considers Nepal a low human development country.[496]

On the 2015 Global Open Data Index, Nepal is ranked 61st of 122 countries, with a score of 30 percent open.[497] The 2015 Open Data Barometer ranked Nepal 68th with a score of 13.09, well below the global average of 32.96. As of January 2017, Nepal has not joined the Open Government Partnership (OGP), though preliminary steps have been taken toward that eventual end.[498] The 2014 creation of OpenGov Hub Kathmandu, a co-working and collaboration space for open data, transparency and accountability, and civic technology organizations and startups, also points to a continued evolution of open data interest and use in the future.[499] However, Nepal's technical infrastructure and readiness remains limited. According to the ODB, for instance, Nepal has only 15 Internet users per 100 people.[500]

KEY ACTORS

Key Data Providers, Users and Intermediaries

Unlike many of the projects included in this series of case studies, where different actors assumed different roles in the open data value chain, the actors involved in this particular initiative combined roles as data collectors, providers, users and intermediaries. The focus on generating crowdsourced data and putting it to use alongside open government data blurred the lines that typically demarcate traditional roles among open data stakeholders.

With that in mind, the lead actors in the projects examined here are:

495 International Monetary Fund, "Report for Selected Countries and Subjects," IMF, October 2015, http://www.imf.org/external/pubs/ft/weo/2015/02/weodata/weorept.aspx?sy=2015&ey=2016&scsm=1&ssd=1&sort=subject&ds=.&br=1&pr1.x=34&pr1.y=16&c=558&s=NGDPD%2CNGDPDPC%2CPPPGDP%2CPPPPC&grp=0&a=.

496 United Nations Development Program, *Human Development Report 2015*, "Statistical Annex," UNDP, http://hdr.undp.org/sites/default/files/hdr_2015_statistical_annex.pdf.

497 Open Knowledge, "Global Open Data Index: Nepal," http://index.okfn.org/place/nepal/.

498 Narayan Adhikari and Pranav Budhathoki, "The OGP Process in Nepal – On the Path of Our Own Choosing," Open Government Partnership Blog, December 1, 2016, http://www.opengovpartnership.org/blog/narayan-adhikari/2016/12/01/ogp-process-nepal-%E2%80%93-path-our-own-choosing.

499 "We've Opened an OpenGov Hub in Nepal!" OpenGov Hub, May 21, 2014, http://opengovhub.org/blog/5/2014/weve-opened-an-opengov-hub-in-nepal.

500 World Wide Web Foundation, "Open Data Barometer, 2015," http://opendatabarometer.org/data-explorer/?_year=2015&indicator=ODB&lang=en&open=NPL.

Kathmandu Living Labs[501] *(KLL)*

A non-profit civic technology company working to create high impact technology to transform the ways government works.

Young Innovations Ltd[502]

A Kathmandu tech company founded in 2007 specializing in solutions for development, their goal is to establish open data as one of the priorities of the Government of Nepal.

Local Interventions Group[503]

Local Interventions Group (LIG) is a non-profit working in the global south to improve governance through data-driven solutions. Founded by participants in a student seminar at the London School of Economics, it has offices in the UK and Nepal. LIG is both data user and provider, having actively sought to expand Nepali open datasets through crowdsourcing and the conversion of static government data to machine-readable format.[504]

Open Nepal[505]

A knowledge hub and learning space for Nepali organizations and people who produce, share, and use data for development. The platform is owned by Young Innovations, NGO Federation of Nepal, Freedom Forum, and Development Initiatives, and was intended to bring together journalists, CSOs and those in the tech industry working with open data.[506]

Code for Nepal[507]

A 501(c)(3) non-profit organization registered in the U.S., dedicated to empowering Nepal through increasing digital literacy and access to open data, building apps to improve lives, service delivery to earthquake survivors and right to information.[508] Cofounded by Mia Mitchell and Ravi Kumar Nepal in 2014, Code for Nepal has pursued projects aimed at bridging the digital divide experienced by women, poor people, rural people, and ethnic minorities in Nepal.[509]

Key Beneficiaries

Most of the open data projects reviewed here were intended to directly benefit the Nepali population affected by the quakes, either through immediate relief work or through a more efficient and effective recovery. This improved efficiency, however, also

---

501 http://www.kathmandulivinglabs.org/.

502 http://younginnovations.com.np/.

503 http://www.localinterventions.org.uk/.

504 Interview with Pranav Budhathoki, CEO, Local Interventions Group, September 7, 2016.

505 http://opennepal.net/.

506 Interview with Bibhusan Bista, CEO, Young Innovations, September 12, 2016.

507 http://codefornepal.org/en/.

508 See: Code for Nepal, http://codefornepal.org/en/.

509 Code for Nepal, "About Us," http://codefornepal.org/en/about-us/.

benefited aid agencies, donors, and government, through better targeting of relief and recovery efforts and funds. Other projects were intended to reach intermediaries such as journalists, so that they could use the data to improve accountability.

Project Description

The effort to leverage open data in response to the Nepal earthquakes was diverse, and spanned a number of initiatives and organizations – with additional examples not covered in this case study involving the use of corporate datasets to inform relief efforts.[510] This case study focuses on a number of these efforts, addressing each in sequence and then trying to draw some cross-cutting lessons.

Among the most prominent of the projects, Kathmandu Living Labs (KLL), arose out of a collaborative effort in the Fall of 2013. Dr. Nama Raj Budhathoki, now Executive Director of KLL, member of the Humanitarian OpenStreetMap Team (HOT), and local organizer of OpenStreetMap, had recently completed a doctorate in crowdsourcing, open data and social and mobile media at the University of Illinois, Urbana-Champaign in 2010.[511] His co-founder, Robert Soden, was working for the World Bank in Washington D.C., and looking for a Nepali partner for a World Bank Open Data for Resilience Initiative (OpenDRI) project in 2012. Robert and Nama met in Kathmandu in Fall 2012, when Nama took on a leadership role on OpenDRI in Nepal. KLL was formed as a not-for-profit civic technology company in the fall of 2013, as a means of continuing the work after the end of the OpenDRI project.[512] This kick-off initiative brought sought to map all the "educational institutions, health facilities, road networks, tangled mesh of *gallies*, religious sites and other geographic features of Kathmandu Valley."[513]

Immediately after the earthquakes, KLL began to build on its pre-earthquake mapping work. Working from desks in the organization's parking lot—it was unsafe to go back indoors[514]—KLL members coordinated the work of about 8,000 local and international volunteers who collaborated to build a detailed map of affected areas. Online volunteers around the world used post-quake

---

510 Stefaan G. Verhulst, "Corporate Social Responsibility for a Data Age," *Stanford Social Innovation Review,* February 15, 2017, https://ssir.org/articles/entry/corporate_social_responsibility_for_a_data_age.

511 Saira Asher, "How 'Crisis Mapping' Is Helping Relief Efforts in Nepal," BBC News, May 6, 2015, http://www.bbc.com/news/world-asia-32603870.

512 See: Kathmandu Living Labs, http://www.kathmandulivinglabs.org/pages.

513 "Who We Are," Kathmandu Living Labs, http://www.kathmandulivinglabs.org/about.

514 Shreeya Sinha, "Three Ways Nepalis Are Using Crowdsourcing to Aid in Quake Relief, *New York Times,* May 1, 2015, http://www.nytimes.com/2015/05/02/world/asia/3-ways-nepalis-are-using-crowdsourcing-to-aid-in-quake-relief.html?_r=3.

satellite images to update the team's pre-quake maps, while in Kathmandu, KLL staff scraped images of damage from social media and mapped the damaged city on foot.[515] The resulting map was then used by search and rescue teams, emergency services, the Nepal Army, and international relief agencies such as the Red Cross[516] and UN[517] to plan and mobilize their resources. The volunteer mapping efforts were coordinated using the Humanitarian OpenStreetMap Team (HOT) tasking manager,[518] an open source tool that helps to coordinate large-scale mapping efforts by breaking the job into smaller tasks to be assigned to collaborators.[519]

KLL also used its data to develop QuakeMap.org, a website through which users could report their needs to emergency organizations. With phone networks largely inoperative after the earthquakes, the internet became a lifeline for many. Built on the open source Ushahidi platform that had previously been used after the Haiti and New Zealand earthquakes, QuakeMap. org invited people to contribute information in real time about immediate local needs. Observers could note where people were trapped, identify damage to infrastructure, post information on resources such as emergency shelter, or ask for assistance with necessities such as shelter, food, and water.[520] KLL had a small team of volunteers dedicated to validation of reports on QuakeMap. org, via a callback to the poster to verify the facts. The Nepal Army, which took the lead in the relief effort, downloaded reports from QuakeMap.org every two hours, passing on requests for assistance to their relief division. A second level of validation also took place within Army headquarters, where a desk was set up to verify QuakeMap.org reports.[521] Once assistance was received, the database was updated to indicate the problem was resolved and to avoid duplication of resources.[522] QuakeMap.org also included a page called Who's

515 Imogen Wall, "Could Mapping Tech Revolutionize Disaster Response? *The Guardian*, April 25, 2016, https://www.theguardian.com/global-development-professionals-network/2016/apr/25/could-mapping-tech-revolutionise-disaster-response?CMP=share_btn_tw.

516 Shreeya Sinha, "Three Ways Nepalis Are Using Crowdsourcing to Aid in Quake Relief, *New York Times*, May 1, 2015, http://www.nytimes.com/2015/05/02/world/asia/3-ways-nepalis-are-using-crowdsourcing-to-aid-in-quake-relief.html?_r=3.

517 Imogen Wall, "Could Mapping Tech Revolutionize Disaster Response? *The Guardian*, April 25, 2016, https://www.theguardian.com/global-development-professionals-network/2016/apr/25/could-mapping-tech-revolutionise-disaster-response?CMP=share_btn_tw.

518 http://tasks.hotosm.org/.

519 Nirab Pudasaini, "Open Source and Open Data's Role in Nepal Earthquake Relief," OpenSource.com, June 8, 2016, https://opensource.com/life/16/6/open-source-open-data-nepal-earthquake.

520 Saira Asher, "How 'Crisis Mapping' Is Helping Relief Efforts in Nepal," BBC News, May 6, 2015, http://www.bbc.com/news/world-asia-32603870.

521 Interview with Dr Nama Raj Budhathoki, Executive Director, Kathmandu Living Labs, September 10, 2016.

522 Siobhan Heanue, "Nepal Earthquake: How open data and social media helped the Nepalese to help themselves," ABC News, August 17, 2015, http://www.abc.net.au/news/2015-08-16/nepal-earthquake-how-open-data-social-media-helped-rebuild/6700410.

Doing What Where, to help relief agencies view activity in the field and direct their work more effectively.

Open Nepal and Young Innovations

A second prominent initiative, the Earthquake Response Transparency Portal,[523] was launched by Open Nepal and Young Innovations, two organizations involved in technology and development. Soon after the Haiti earthquake in 2010, more than 40 countries ratified the International Aid Transparency Initiative (IATI)[524] standard for publishing development-related data (including budgets, annual reports, and strategic documents for country plans). In 2012, Young Innovations launched AidStream,[525] a platform to help aid organizations publish data in the IATI format, which uses XML.[526] Since then, the format has been adopted by more than 470 organizations, including Oxfam, the Red Cross, and the Bill & Melinda Gates Foundation.[527]

Before the earthquakes, few organizations within Nepal had adopted the standard.[528] However, within 24 hours of the first earthquake, Open Nepal, an online and offline development data knowledge hub, and Young Innovations had partnered to produce the Earthquake Response Transparency Portal, a portal that tracks national and international donations (both cash and in-kind) to earthquake relief efforts. As Bibhusan Bista, CEO Young Innovations, put it:

> *Immediately after the earthquake there was a self-ignited, organic movement among youth in different sectors… to provide whatever assistance they could to earthquake victims. On April 26, the day after the earthquake, five or six of my colleagues and I gathered in the carpark at our office, since the ground was still shaking and we couldn't go inside. And we asked ourselves: what can we do? Instead of rushing to the field, where a lot of people are already active, can we do something based on our expertise? So… we said, let's start tracking the resources coming into Nepal.*[529]

---

523 http://earthquake.opennepal.net/.

524 http://www.aidtransparency.net/.

525 http://aidstream.org/.

526 Jennifer Rigby, "A Year After the Devastating Earthquake, Nepals Young Are Rebuilding Their Country," Quartz.com, April 27, 2016, http://qz.com/670197/a-year-after-the-devastating-earthquake-nepals-young-are-rebuilding-their-country/.

527 "Who's Using It?" AidStream, https://aidstream.org/who-is-using.

528 Amrit Sharma, "Where Is All the Aid Money for Nepal Going? Open data could help lift the veil," Takepart.com, August 6, 2015, http://www.takepart.com/article/2015/08/06/open-nepal-earthquake-aid-money.

529 Interview with Bibhusan Bista, CEO, Young Innovations, September 12, 2016.

The group began with United Nations Office for the Coordination of Humanitarian Affairs (OCHA) Financial Tracking Service (FTS) data, but then began scraping, cleaning and standardizing data as it was reported in the national and international media, as well as from government and non-government sources, to create a centralized portal. As Bista said: "There were a lot of questions being asked: do we have enough resources? Are those resources being used appropriately? We needed a common, accessible repository to track those data."[530]

The portal's intent was "to support the accountable and effective use of funds that are available for relief and reconstruction activities." To achieve this goal, it sought to (1) establish the traceability of funds from donors to intermediaries to implementing organizations; (2) enable inquiries about results of specific relief efforts and projects; and (3) provide a country-wide view of relief efforts to avoid duplication. Attempting to provide a holistic view of relief efforts and their finances, the portal shows both data from primary and secondary sources on funds given and received by all national and international entities, as well as how funds were used by these organizations.[531] Data used to build the portal is available for download in csv format.

The data used for the Earthquake Response Transparency Portal had to be scraped, cleaned and standardized before it could be used. Much of the data came from press releases issued by donors and was in unstructured text format, which had either to be manually entered or scraped using purpose-built tools. Data from the UN was machine-readable, but not fully open. Double counting was common in the days after the earthquake, with numbers reported from donors and implementing agencies working on the same project being added together.[532]

Bista observes that the portal was intended to reduce friction and overcome some of the delays inherent in IATI reporting. In addition, the portal was also designed to address irregularities that often plague the aid and donor ecosystem. Bista notes that irregularities are apparent just by looking at the data at the macro level. For example, he said that despite a promised $4.4 billion in aid, the data only accounted for some $3.85 billion.[533] The Earthquake Response Transparency Portal sought to address such shortcomings by tracking pledge money as it passed from the donors through intermediaries, and by

---

530 Ibid.

531 Young Innovations, "Earthquake Response Transparency Portal," http://earthquake.opennepal.net/about.

532 Interview with Bibhusan Bista, CEO, Young Innovations, September 12, 2016.

533 Amrit Sharma, "Where Is All the Aid Money for Nepal Going? Open data could help lift the veil," Takepart.com, August 6, 2015, http://www.takepart.com/article/2015/08/06/open-nepal-earthquake-aid-money.

independently verifying aid money's use for intended projects in an open manner. In the process, Young Innovations hopes to improve accountability by uncovering instances of corruption or inefficiencies leading to money failing to reach its intended beneficiaries. "Independently verifying that the pledged money was delivered to the intended project is the biggest challenge for transparency and accountability today," he says. "We want to prevent the Haiti mistakes and serve as a model for how technology can help facilitate transparency and accountability."[534]

The main users of the Earthquake Response Transparency Portal were data-using intermediaries such as journalists. After the post-disaster needs assessment and the donors' conference, as donor pledges began to flow in, media reporting often failed to make a distinction between pledges, commitments and actual disbursement. As Bista put it: "There were reports in the media saying, this is the amount that has been given by India, or the UN. We wanted to educate intermediaries that we have actually not received that money. The pledge has to be converted to commitment, the commitment then has to be converted to disbursement, the disbursement then has to be converted to expenditure on an actual project."[535]

In addition to data intermediaries, Bista identifies three other potential target audiences: the donors themselves, to hold them accountable for gaps between pledges and actual disbursement; CSOs and NGOs, who could use the portal both to investigate donor resources and areas of interest for potential rebuilding projects, and to "follow the money" to ensure projects were carried out; and government policymakers, to enable planning of government contributions to the rebuilding.[536]

Code for Nepal

A third series of projects were launched by Code for Nepal, a Nepal-based nonprofit that seeks to leverage innovation, data and training efforts to improve public life. Soon after the first earthquake, Code for Nepal was looking for ways to provide a humanitarian response in badly affected regions outside Kathmandu. To do this, the team used a low-tech form of crowdsourcing, hoping to encourage the widest possible participation.[537] Within 36 hours of

---

534 Ibid.

535 Interview with Bibhusan Bista, CEO, Young Innovations, September 12, 2016.

536 Ibid.

537 Femke Mulder, et al., "Questioning Big Data: Crowdsourcing crisis data towards and inclusive humanitarian response," *Big Data and Society*, August 1, 2016, http://bds.sagepub.com/content/3/2/2053951716662054.

the earthquake, Code for Nepal developed an open Google document to enlist information about relief agencies, volunteers and victims.[538]

Additionally, Code for Nepal carried out two surveys of earthquake survivors to seek feedback on the kind of aid they had received. Rahat Payo[539] (a Nepali term meaning "did you get relief?") and the Kobo Toolbox[540] surveys were carried out in two phases. The first phase surveyed 776 affected Nepalis in 40 locations across five districts in August 2015. A second phase, conducted in December 2015, focused solely on residents of the village of Barpark, the epicenter of the first major earthquake. The preliminary findings were published on the Code for Nepal website and the data shared in an open format.[541] The results of the surveys were published in the media, and were shared with non-profits working in the field, providing a granular, on-the-ground perspective of the effectiveness and reach of aid distribution. Ravi Kumar reports that more surveys are planned, probably in online format.[542]

Local Interventions Group

Local Interventions Group, governance-focused non-profit with offices Nepal, also used open data to address the post-earthquake situation. This work was built on the foundations and experience of earlier projects in the areas of open governance, crowdsourcing, and smarter city solutions. In particular, the organization had built projects to help Kathmandu citizens report complaints concerning local police; crowdsourced grievances with government in two remote regions of Nepal; and worked with Google to create GIS maps of human trafficking hotspots and routes.

Within 24 hours of the earthquake, Local Interventions Group began partnering with the Nepali Home Ministry to digitize information collected by its post-earthquake emergency telephone hotline. It partnered with Accountability Lab, an incubator aimed at "strengthening systems of accountability,"[543] to send out Mobile Citizen Help Desks into affected areas, identify local needs and linking affected communities to resources. Over subsequent weeks and months, as the recovery progressed, this work developed into #quakeHELPDESK, a four-part earthquake response strategy that not only allowed users to track aid

538 Interview with Ravi Kumar Nepal, September 9, 2016.

539 http://codefornepal.s3.amazonaws.com/rahatpayo/index.html.

540 https://1s3ej.enketo.kobotoolbox.org/webform.

541 Interview with Ravi Kumar Nepal, September 9, 2016.

542 Ibid.

543 http://www.accountabilitylab.org/.

data use, but also provided "a platform for affected communities, emergency responders, and volunteers to report gaps at the last mile."[544]

The other components of the project included citizen perception surveys conducted for the UNOCHA InterAgency Common Feedback Project[545] (an open data platform designed to improve the responsiveness of the relief and recovery effort); the Open Mic Project,[546] a partnership with Internews which sought to track and counter earthquake rumors and misinformation; and Follow the Money, an aid tracking and accountability program.[547] All these projects helped the Local Interventions Group close the feedback loop through a communications campaign with the UN, in which town hall meetings with local political representatives to discuss grievances raised through the #quakeHELPDESK were broadcast on local FM radio.[548]

Who's Doing What Where

In addition to these projects, various other organizations also sought to use data to introduce new efficiencies and greater transparency into relief efforts. One notable example arose from the Humanitarian Data Exchange (HDX),[549] an open platform managed by the UN OCHA for sharing humanitarian data to drive analysis. The HDX team set up Nepal—Who's Doing What Where (Housing Recovery and Reconstruction) (HRRP 4W). This tool inventories relief housing efforts in the 14 districts most severely affected by the earthquakes according to what, where, when, and by whom projects are being planned and carried out. Data is supplied every two weeks through self-reporting after training by over 350 partner organizations working in housing recovery and reconstruction. The data are then compiled and cleaned at a national level, and used to develop reports.[550] The current database shows data from January 1, 2016 to the present, and reports continue to be filed as of late August 2016.

Funding

The projects had varied sources (and amounts) of funding. The Earthquake Response Transparency Portal was funded entirely by Young Innovations

---

544 "Our Mission," #quakeHELPDESK, http://www.quakehelpdesk.org/what.php.

545 http://cfp.org.np/.

546 http://www.quakehelpdesk.org/openmic.php.

547 Local Interventions Group, "Interagency Common Feedback Project: Nepal earthquake 2015," http://www.localinterventions.org.uk/programmes.php?post=32.

548 Interview with Pranav Budhathoki, CEO, Local Interventions Group, September 7, 2016.

549 https://data.humdata.org/.

550 Humanitarian Data Exchange, "Nepal—Who's Doing What Where," https://data.humdata.org/dataset/160625-hrrp-4w-national.

from the proceeds of its more commercial activities.[551] Most of the projects, however, were heavily dependent on grants from aid agencies such as the United Nations. Quake Map and the perceptions surveys that formed part of #quakeHELPDESK were both UN funded, for example.[552] The work of Code for Nepal was funded largely through donations, although the second Rahat Payo survey was supported by George Mason University and Tufts University.[553]

Impact

Indicators of success and impact can be divided into two broad categories: metrics and stories of use, and changes to organizational, political and social culture or behavior.

Given that the projects in Nepal emerged from a crisis, efforts to track site metrics or analyze use or traffic were seldom made at the time, although some of those interviewed said that they intended to do so in the future. As a result, it is necessary to rely on more qualitative accounts to gauge the use made of these various projects. It is important to keep in mind that even such accounts are incomplete and conjectural, however, since we can only speculate on how the relief effort would have been different if, for example, KLL's OSM project had never taken place. Nonetheless, the below attempts to assess some illustrative examples of impact across the different initiatives.

Metrics and Stories of Use

Before the earthquake, Dr. Budhathoki and a dozen student interns collectively mapped every educational institution, health facility, road network, and religious site of the Kathmandu Valley, adding these and other important geographic features to OpenStreetMap. The team also gave mapping workshops to university students, government officials, the tech community, NGOs, and youth groups, recruiting volunteers to join their mapping efforts.[554] Through their pre-earthquake efforts, they had collectively created the most detailed map of the Kathmandu Valley available in the country.[555]

---

551 Interview with Bibhusan Bista, CEO, Young Innovations, September 12, 2016.

552 Interview with Pranav Budhathoki, CEO, Local Interventions Group, September 7, 2016.

553 Interview with Ravi Kumar Nepal, September 9, 2016.

554 See: Kathmandu Living Labs, http://www.kathmandulivinglabs.org/pages.

555 Shreeya Sinha, "Three Ways Nepalis Are Using Crowdsourcing to Aid in Quake Relief, *New York Times*, May 1, 2015, http://www.nytimes.com/2015/05/02/world/asia/3-ways-nepalis-are-using-crowdsourcing-to-aid-in-quake-relief.html?_r=3.

After the earthquake, Dr. Budhathoki went from managing a small team of between seven and 100 local volunteers to coordinating the efforts of 9,000 remote volunteers from a situation room. A week after the first earthquake, the team had been able to map 70 to 80 percent of the earthquake-affected areas.[556] International media reported that the OSM map was being used by relief agencies such as the Red Cross. According to Adele Waugaman, a former fellow at the Harvard Humanitarian Initiative, KLL's efforts to map all the health facilities in Kathmandu Valley before the earthquake would "undoubtedly help the relief workers' ability to deliver supplies and help save lives."[557]

QuakeMap.org received 2,035 reports, of which 978 were verified by volunteers and 551 required action.[558] Calculating the true value of the portal is more complicated, however, than looking at the metrics. As Dr. Budhathoki put it: "How many lives were saved by it? How much human suffering was relieved by the use of QuakeMap data? I don't know. I can't give any quantified data about that."[559]

Changing Culture and Behavior

Although the Earthquake Response Transparency Portal had no use case before its launch, Bista's hunch that the target market would be the media proved correct. Within Nepal, the portal has been used by national journalists to provide evidence for their write-ups. Bista reports that international media such as the BBC have also used the portal to track governmental use of funds.

Young Innovations also found an audience among journalists. It found itself being asked to provide training in data journalism to members of the media wanting to know how they could make better use of the platform. In addition, some surprising uses also emerged. For instance, the Nepalese diaspora in the US, which was actively generating and gathering funds and resources for the relief effort, used the portal to screen NGOs to decide where to contribute. There were also requests for increased granularity of data by district, by users who were interested in tracking geographic distribution of aid, although the nature of the data reporting made this difficult to supply.[560]

---

556 Ibid.

557 Ibid.

558 Nirab Pudasaini, "Open Source and Open Data's Role in Nepal Earthquake Relief," OpenSource.com, June 8, 2016, https://opensource.com/life/16/6/open-source-open-data-nepal-earthquake.

559 Interview with Dr. Nama Raj Budhathoki, Executive Director, Kathmandu Living Labs, September 10, 2016.

560 Interview with Bibhusan Bista, CEO, Young Innovations, September 12, 2016.

Improving IATI

The experience of the Earthquake Response Transparency Portal has also illuminated some of the limitations of IATI reporting in emergencies, and in the process perhaps contributed to future improvements in the system. The portal met a clear need by several audiences for immediate, centralized reporting of structured and standardized data during a crisis and its aftermath; these were benefits existing IATI reporting mechanisms could not provide. Bista has been able to feed this experience back into the IATI ecosystem through participation in international conferences on humanitarian data, such as the World Humanitarian Summit in Istanbul in May 2016. "Through this, we are also contributing to the discussion on how data on global humanitarian aid should be standardized," he said. IATI now has a team working on data standardization, including representatives from Young Innovations.[561]

Risks

The proliferation of open data projects in the chaotic environment after a natural disaster presents opportunities to help, but also introduces the possibility of greater confusion and chaos. Untrained volunteers keen to help may swamp relief agencies and hamper their efforts; even where their help is welcome, as with KLL's QuakeMap work, managing volunteers requires the commitment of staff time. Unconscious duplication of effort may also occur: several perception surveys of earthquake survivors were carried out by those organizations interviewed, for example, with surveyors sometimes unaware of one another's work. Finally, crowdsourced emergency information platforms can add to confusion among survivors and waste time among rescuers if information is not carefully verified. Platforms such as Open Mic, which counter rumor among survivors, provide a tool to combat misinformation.

Lessons Learned

Several important lessons with wider applicability emerge from this particular case study. These can broadly be categorized by considering the key enablers of the project, as well as the most important barriers or challenges to its success.

---

561 Ibid.

Enablers

Learning from Haiti

Several of the projects were very consciously built on the experience of Haiti's devastating earthquake of January 2010. Those involved were well aware of the pitfalls of poor preparedness and a lack of transparency for a poor, earthquake-prone country, and sought to find ways to improve the outcome for Nepal, either before the earthquake or immediately after it.[562] This awareness of previous efforts, and willingness to build on lessons learned, was one of the key enablers that contributed to the impact and success of Nepali efforts.

The experience of Haiti motivated Dr. Nama Budhathoki to return to Nepal to begin mapping the country. During his studies, he had observed how open mapping was used to aid relief efforts during the Haiti earthquake. Aware that a serious earthquake would one day hit Nepal,[563] and conscious of the poor quality of Nepal's existing official maps,[564] some of which had not been updated for between 10 and 25 years,[565] he had returned to Kathmandu after graduating to begin building an open mapping community in Nepal. "Nepal sits in one of the most risky zones for earthquakes and other disasters. In Haiti they made [the map] after—I wanted to make the map before the earthquake."[566]

The creators of the Earthquake Response Transparency Portal were also acutely aware of the problematic history of the Haiti earthquake appeal. Nepalis had been concerned about reports of discrepancies in the reporting policies of international aid organizations, particularly after it was revealed that $500 million was missing from Red Cross funds earmarked for Haiti's earthquake recovery. According to Bibhusan Bista, CEO of Young Innovations, "[The portal] empowers people with a snapshot of how money is flowing into Nepal's rebuilding and reconstruction projects and promotes transparency at a time of great need.... We don't want to repeat the mistakes of Haiti."[567] He continues:

---

562 Amrit Sharma, "Where Is All the Aid Money for Nepal Going? Open data could help lift the veil," Takepart.com, August 6, 2015, http://www.takepart.com/article/2015/08/06/open-nepal-earthquake-aid-money.

563 Shreeya Sinha, "Three Ways Nepalis Are Using Crowdsourcing to Aid in Quake Relief, *New York Times*, May 1, 2015, http://www.nytimes.com/2015/05/02/world/asia/3-ways-nepalis-are-using-crowdsourcing-to-aid-in-quake-relief.html?_r=3.

564 Saira Asher, "How 'Crisis Mapping' Is Helping Relief Efforts in Nepal," BBC News, May 6, 2015, http://www.bbc.com/news/world-asia-32603870.

565 Interview with Dr. Nama Raj Budhathoki, Executive Director, Kathmandu Living Labs, September 10, 2016.

566 Saira Asher, "How 'Crisis Mapping' Is Helping Relief Efforts in Nepal," BBC News, May 6, 2015, http://www.bbc.com/news/world-asia-32603870.

567 Amrit Sharma, "Where Is All the Aid Money for Nepal Going? Open data could help lift the veil," Takepart.com, August 6, 2015, http://www.takepart.com/article/2015/08/06/open-nepal-earthquake-aid-money.

After Haiti, there were a lot of concerns about the relief and rehabilitation funds being misused and misallocated. To avoid that, it is critical to first see who is giving what money to whom. To us, that was an interesting case to be made, that openness could avoid the mistakes that were made in Haiti. That was, for us, the internal incentive to go on with the project.[568]

Permission to innovate

The government also played a central role in the success of these various Nepali open data projects. Immediately after the earthquake, Bista says that crucial government actors including the National Planning Commission and the then Prime Minister of Nepal embraced the importance of transparency and accountability. Crucially, they supported such efforts not merely within the government, but also through independent, non-state initiatives like the Earthquake Response Transparency Portal.[569] This type of high-level buy-in can play a key role in pushing forward innovation and experimentation with open data.

International organizations and tapping into existing ecosystems

Many of the projects discussed in this case also relied on data and infrastructure provided by international organizations like UN OCHA. This case demonstrates the importance of such organizations in enabling open data efforts in developing countries through access to tools and funding, and in helping to fill gaps in national government databases by opening relevant datasets in their possession.

Pranav Budhathoki also points to an existing ecosystem of data users as a potent enabler in gaining the necessary traction to get results from the data they collected and opened. Because of their funding connections within the UN, they were connected to an international open data system that responded quickly and enthusiastically to their bulletins.[570] Activating this global, distributed network of problem-solvers brought to bear a diversity of skill and experience that would otherwise have remained untapped.

---

568 Interview with Bibhusan Bista, CEO, Young Innovations, September 12, 2016.
569 Ibid.
570 Interview with Pranav Budhathoki, CEO, Local Interventions Group, September 7, 2016.

Relationships, trust, and access

Several interviewees commented that Nepal is a highly hierarchical society in which relationships, and the nature of those relationships, strongly condition access to people and institutions. Making effective use of data may involve creating relationships with key actors before a disaster strikes, when, as Dr. Budhathoki notes, government agencies and relief organizations may have no time or inclination to meet open data groups, no matter the potential value of their data. Demonstrated expertise, and a product in hand, are also helpful in putting to rest doubts. Dr. Budhathoki found his past career in government mapping, his expertise with OSM, his publications, and his qualifications helped overcome institutional suspicion and mistrust of crowdsourced data, while the map data OSM had already generated in Nepal allowed him to demonstrate its value and robustness.[571]

Pranav Budhathoki, CEO of Local Innovations Group, noted that the organization made a point of hiring the most senior journalist they could find as district coordinators for #quakeHELPDESK, since these people would already have unfettered access to government agencies and established relationships with decisionmakers. Social connections with legislators were even more helpful. "That's the sort of access we needed to ensure the information we produced got the audience that so many other agencies were struggling to get."[572] At the same time, Budhathoki cautions that depending too much on personal connections—and perhaps becoming too cozy with those in power—can hamper the ability to effect real change on the ground.[573]

Volunteers: Both barrier and enabler

Several of the interviewees spoke of the benefits of working with local volunteers. Once trained, a team of committed volunteers can take possible projects beyond the means of a relatively poor country, as Nepal's OSM community has shown. For crisis mapping, local volunteers bring a depth of detailed knowledge that remote contributors, however experienced or careful, cannot.[574]

At the same time, training volunteers represents a significant and uncertain investment. There is no guarantee that, once trained, volunteers will continue to participate, as life circumstances change and interest wanes. Sometimes the

---

571 Ibid.

572 Interview with Pranav Budhathoki, CEO, Local Interventions Group, September 7, 2016.

573 Ibid.

574 Interview with Dr Nama Raj Budhathoki, Executive Director, Kathmandu Living Labs, September 10, 2016.

supply can be overwhelming, as Dr. Budhathoki describes in the aftermath of the earthquakes, when he found himself managing thousands of remote crisismappers. "There was chaos on the ground, but the chaos was also there in the online community," he says. "How do we effectively coordinate and channel that desire to help Nepal?"[575]

Nonetheless, Dr. Budhathoki believes that Nepal was better positioned to harness the potential of mapping than previous countries in crisis because of the existence of a robust and skilled group on the ground, who were able to direct, coordinate and guide international volunteers, and ensure that efforts went where they were most needed. "Without that local knowledge—the in-country capacity—[remote mapping] doesn't take us too far."[576]

Barriers

Connectivity and tech literacy

As with many case studies in this series, a lack of technical capacity and readiness was one of the most commonly cited barriers to success. Many of the intended beneficiaries and users of these portals lacked even a simple Internet connection. Adele Waugaman, a former fellow at the Harvard Humanitarian Initiative, notes that a tool's capacity to function offline can make the difference in determining its usefulness in hot zones during a crisis.[577] One doctor interviewed by the *New York Times* working in Gorkha District said he would have used the work by Code for Nepal and Kathmandu Living Labs if he had Internet connectivity. For those like him without a reliable connection, use may be impossible, or limited to screenshots of maps for later use offline.[578] The production of the maps also relies on a viable Internet connection, since even pencil and paper maps must be uploaded to OSM at some point.[579]

Those with an internet connection must also be comfortable using technology. Dr. Budhathoki observed a certain discomfort with the technical aspects of mapping among potential volunteers.[580] As Code for Nepal has noted, there is a clear digital divide in Nepal that negatively affects the capacity

---

575 Ibid.

576 Ibid.

577 GovLab interview with Adele Waugaman, September 16, 2016.

578 Shreeya Sinha, "Three Ways Nepalis Are Using Crowdsourcing to Aid in Quake Relief, *New York Times*, May 1, 2015, http://www.nytimes.com/2015/05/02/world/asia/3-ways-nepalis-are-using-crowdsourcing-to-aid-in-quake-relief.html?_r=3.

579 Interview with Dr Nama Raj Budhathoki, Executive Director, Kathmandu Living Labs, September 10, 2016.

580 Ibid.

of women, poor people, rural people, and Nepal's ethnic minorities to partake in the benefits of the Internet.[581]

Data creation vs. data use

Dr. Budhathoki observes that one of the barriers confronted was a preoccupation with simply creating data rather than with ensuring that data is actually useful or used. "We need to emphasize the use of the data from day one," he says. "It's very important not just to create the data, to make maps, but to ensure that the data is being used by relief organizations. ... Creation is the easy part. The harder part is to talk to the relief organizations and ensure they use the maps."[582]

Institutional culture

Institutional culture—in government, in civil society, among the public— always plays a key role in determining whether open data projects are successful or not. Bista reports that his organization would like to increase the granularity of its data to show giving at different levels. For instance, he says it would be helpful to show how money is apportioned to secondary donors who subsequently disburse it to others. However, this kind of granularity is not supported by current reporting practices or by an institutional culture, both of which have yet to embrace openness and transparency. "The organizations are not responsive," he said. "They feel their obligation is to their donors and to the government authorities and what they demand, instead of feeling that they need to release data for public consumption. That lack of accountability and transparency, to me, is the biggest challenge—and it's not just people in Nepal, it's international organizations."[583]

Ravi Kumar agrees that institutional and political culture is a major brake on the impact of open data in Nepal:

When there's a lack of capable, responsive institutions on the ground, there's only so much you can do to leverage open data, civic tech, or ICT4D. Nepal hasn't had local elections in more than a decade. There's no local capacity—or if there is local capacity, they were not ready to be responsive, equitable and fair. Even though we have the results, we can't get a response to these things.[584]

---

581 Interview with Ravi Kumar Nepal, September 9, 2016.
582 Ibid.
583 Interview with Bibhusan Bista, CEO, Young Innovations, September 12, 2016.
584 Interview with Ravi Kumar Nepal, September 9, 2016.

Looking Forward

Current Status

Most of the projects were short- or medium-term, and were not intended to persist beyond the relief or recovery phases. The relief projects, such as QuakeMap and Code for Nepal's Google Doc, have largely been shut down. QuakeMap.org is no longer actively soliciting new reports as of July 13, 2015, although new reports could still be filed and would be followed up. Dr Budhathoki reports, however, that the site is being held in readiness in case it is needed for future emergencies.[585]

Those projects tracking the experiences of survivors through the recovery period are still ongoing, although surveys occur less frequently. Interviewees from LIG and Code for Nepal hope to continue their respective surveys into a third phase if funding permits.

As of September 2016, the Earthquake Response Transparency Portal continues to be active. "The rebuilding and reconstruction will go on for the next five years," says Bista. He adds: "After the early, chaotic relief and rescue phase, we are moving towards a tangible reconstruction effort and structured rebuilding of schools and health centers. If we can structure the data and get it into the portal, 'follow the money' activities become much easier. As we see it, this is where the real value of the portal [lies], and centralized open data on fiscal flows for rebuilding and reconstruction becomes even more crucial."[586]

Sustainability

The projects surveyed are, with few exceptions, supported by commercial ventures or aid funding and carried out by teams of paid staff, sometimes with volunteer help. Furthermore, Nepal's recovery and reconstruction is the nation's highest priority, so demand for projects to facilitate the process continues to be high. Bista emphasizes the sustainability of his project will depend on maintaining both supply and demand sides—the openness of the data from the government side, and the community of users—but the project's funding has been provided by Young Innovation's commercial projects, whose profits are reinvested to support its civic tech activities. Bista hopes, however, that it will be possible to sync the portal with other projects on evidence for development, and in the process diversify its funding sources.[587]

---

585 Interview with Dr Nama Raj Budhathoki, Executive Director, Kathmandu Living Labs, September 10, 2016.
586 Interview with Bibhusan Bista, CEO, Young Innovations, September 12, 2016.
587 Ibid.

Replicability

Many of the projects use platforms or models that have been successfully deployed after disasters in the past, and clearly could be again. For example, OSM HOT and Ushahidi-based crowdsourcing platforms were both used successfully after the Haiti and Christchurch earthquake, and are now an established part of the humanitarian open data toolbox.

Bista feels that the experience of the Earthquake Response Transparency Portal would be highly replicable in other places. "We would need to do a little work to create an open source model, because the software we've created is not quite ready to just take and use elsewhere," he says. "But the concept itself is highly replicable." Bista says Young Innovations are currently in discussion with the UN OCHA FTS about the possibility of incorporating some components of the portal's software into FTS. "[R]eplication could involve not just using the software as a whole, but the standards and the concepts that we have could be brought in to make another system that's working elsewhere even better," he says.[588]

Surveys of the kinds carried out by LIG and Code for Nepal could also be successfully deployed in other locations to oversee the responsiveness and accountability of the recovery process. Their efficacy would be greater, however, if agencies conducting such surveys carried out environmental scans to ensure they were not duplicating one another's work. Currently, there is no equivalent of Ushahidi's crowdsourcing platform for humanitarian surveys. The emergence or creation of a dominant technology might help reduce such duplication.

Conclusion

The response of Nepal and the international community to the earthquakes of 2015 was greatly enhanced by the efforts of its open data community. In some cases, their activities provided vital information that would otherwise have been unavailable to rescuers, as with KLL's OSM work. In other cases (QuakeMap.org and Code for Nepal's Google doc) the work they did offered a lifeline to survivors, who could use the new platforms to reach out for assistance.

All this work continues to be significant through the recovery phase, as organizations like LIG, Young Innovations, and Code for Nepal seek to ensure that survivors' voices are heard, that their needs are met, and that donor money

---

588 Ibid.

is received and responsibly spent. Despite the important role such institutions played in enabling the projects discussed in this case study, interviewees often spoke with frustration about the challenges a lack of responsiveness from international organizations and national government could introduce into open data efforts. These experiences make clear that although open data can have major impacts in crisis relief efforts, open data proponents must continue to advocate for open governance to obtain the full benefit of humanitarian open data.

CHAPTER 16

Paraguay Dengue Prediction

Forecasting outbreaks with open data

Juliet McMurren, Andrew Young and Stefaan Verhulst

Summary

Dengue Fever has been endemic in Paraguay since 2009. Recognizing that the problem was being compounded by the lack of a strong system for communicating dengue-related dangers to the public, the National Health Surveillance Department of Paraguay opens data related to dengue morbidity. Leveraging this data, researchers created an early warning system that can detect outbreaks of dengue fever a week in advance. The data-driven model can predict dengue outbreaks at the city-level in every city or region in Paraguay—as long as data on morbidity, climate and water are available.

Context and Background

Problem Focus / Country Context

Paraguay is a tropical to subtropical country of 6.7 million inhabitants, of whom almost a third live in the capital, Asunción.[589] Following several decades of rapid economic growth, the 2015 UN Human Development Index classifies it as a country of medium human development,[590] and the World

---

589 Wikipedia, "Paraguay," https://en.wikipedia.org/wiki/Paraguay.

590 United Nations Development Program, "Human Development Index," *Human Development Reports*, http://hdr.undp.org/en/content/human-development-index-hdi.

Bank now considers it an upper middle income nation.[591] The percentage of the Paraguayan population living below the poverty line has declined sharply over the last two decades, from 49 percent in 2002 to 22.2 percent in 2015.[592]

While most of Paraguay's urban population has access to clean drinking water, rural and/or indigenous communities are frequently reliant on surface or rainwater, raising the risk of water- and mosquito-borne disease.[593] In 2013, the Millennium Development Goals Fund reported that only 6 percent of Paraguay's indigenous households had access to drinking water, and only 3 percent had adequate sanitation. Furthermore, only 10 percent of Paraguay's sewage was treated.[594]

Dengue is a mosquito-borne tropical infection caused by four viruses (DENV-1, DENV-2, DENV-3, and DENV-4) in the *Flavivirdae* family. These viruses are transmitted by infected female *Aedes aegypti* and *Aedes albopictu*s mosquitoes that feed diurnally both indoors and outdoors, and breed in settings with standing water (including in puddles, water tanks, containers and old tires), poor sanitation, and a lack of garbage collection. The mosquitoes that transmit dengue are endemic in parts of Central and South America, Africa, Asia, and Oceania, with most cases occurring during the rainy season or warmer months in urban and suburban areas.[595] Up to 100 million people worldwide contract dengue each year, with 500,000 developing severe illness and 22,000 dying. Some 2.5 billion people live in dengue-endemic areas. Worldwide, cases of dengue have increased thirtyfold since 1960, driven by urbanization, population growth, increased international travel, and climate change.[596]

Dengue fever is asymptomatic in as many as 50 percent of those infected, while a further minority, particularly among the young and those contracting dengue for the first time, experience an undifferentiated fever only.[597] Symptoms of dengue, which appear four to seven days after a bite, include a sudden high fever lasting two to seven days; headache and pain behind the eyes; muscle, joint, and bone pain; and skin rash and bruising. Treatment

---

591 World Bank, "World Bank Country and Lending Groups," https://datahelpdesk.worldbank.org/knowledgebase/articles/906519.

592 World Bank, "Data: Paraguay," http://data.worldbank.org/country/paraguay.

593 Natalia Ruiz Diaz, "Paraguay: Clean Water Out of Reach for Native Peoples," *Inter Press Service*, June 29, 2010, http://www.ipsnews.net/2010/06/paraguay-clean-water-out-of-reach-for-native-peoples/.

594 Millennium Development Fund Achievement Goals, "Paraguay," http://www.mdgfund.org/country/paraguay.

595 International Association for Medical Assistance to Travellers, "Country Health Advice: Paraguay," https://www.iamat.org/country/paraguay/risk/dengue.

596 Wikipedia, "Dengue Fever Outbreaks," https://en.wikipedia.org/wiki/Dengue_fever_outbreaks.

597 Centers for Disease Control and Prevention, "Clinical Guidance: Dengue Virus," Updated September 6, 2014, http://www.cdc.gov/dengue/clinicallab/clinical.html.

consists of supportive care, and no antiviral treatment is available.[598] In severe cases, patients may progress to Dengue Hemorrhagic Fever (DHF), with severe abdominal pain, vomiting, diarrhea, convulsions, bruising, and uncontrolled bleeding. Complications can lead to potentially fatal circulatory system failure and shock, also known as Dengue Shock Syndrome (DSS). Dengue infection confers immunity to future infections with the same virus serotype, and a transient immunity to other serotypes. Once that transient immunity passes, however, patients contracting other dengue serotypes are at increased risk of developing DHF.[599]

Dengue has been declared endemic in Paraguay since 2009.[600] The Pan American Health Organization reported that there were over 173,000 probable cases of dengue for the year 2016, with 48 cases of severe dengue and 16 deaths.[601] The Direccion General de Vigilancia de la Salud (DGVS) (National Health Surveillance Department of Paraguay) heads up the country's prevention and response efforts.

Open data in Paraguay

Paraguay ranked 62nd in the 3rd Open Data Barometer, ahead of Venezuela but behind the majority of Latin American countries, including Argentina (52nd), Peru and Costa Rica (44th), and Colombia (28th). Paraguay's ranking is largely the result of low scores regarding government policies and government action related to open data.[602] The Open Knowledge Foundation's Open Data Index ranked it 50th worldwide in 2015, moving down from its previous ranking of 41 in the 2014 Index. Its open data on procurement tenders and government budget information received high marks, but many other datasets from sectors like the environment and company registers were non-existent or low quality.[603]

---

598 International Association for Medical Assistance to Travellers, "Country Health Advice: Paraguay," https://www.iamat.org/country/paraguay/risk/dengue.

599 Ibid.

600 Juan Pane, Julio Paciello, Verena Ojeda, Natalia Valdez, "Enabling dengue outbreak predictions based on open data," Open Data Research Symposium Draft Paper, October 5, 2016, https://drive.google.com/file/d/0B4TpC6ecmrM7Q1lpQ0xoNlJnZlU/view.

601 "Number of Reported Cases of Dengue and Severe Dengue (SD) in the Americas, by Country: Figures for 2016," Pan American Health Organization, World Health Organization, February 6, 2017, http://www.paho.org/hq/index.php?option=com_docman&task=doc_download&Itemid=270&gid=37782&lang=en.

602 World Wide Web Foundation, Open Data Barometer, Third Edition, WWWF, April 2016, http://opendatabarometer.org/3rdedition/regional-report/latin-america/.

603 "Paraguay," Global Open Data Index 2015, http://index.okfn.org/place/paraguay/.

KEY ACTORS

Key Data Providers

Direccion General de Vigilancia de la Salud (DGVS) (National Health Surveillance Department of Paraguay)

DGVS is the agency responsible for the prevention and control of epidemic disease in Paraguay. It collects and publishes data on disease outbreaks and morbidity.[604]

Key Data Users and Intermediaries

Juan Pane

A researcher at the Facultad Politecnica-Universidad de Asuncion with an interest in open data and open government, Juan Pane leads a team seeking to develop data models to provide early warning of dengue outbreaks in Paraguay. He also works for a democracy initiative funded by USAID assisting the Paraguayan government with transparency portals. Paraguayan by birth, Pane completed a doctorate in computer science at the University of Trento, Italy in 2012, followed by a postdoctoral fellowship. He returned to Paraguay with his family in 2013, just as the country was experiencing a dengue epidemic, with 150,000 reported cases and 233 deaths.[605] Pane reports that the probability of acquiring dengue in some Asunción neighborhoods that year was as high as one in four, a rate that filled him with alarm for his family, but also motivated him to find ways to address the problem of dengue.[606]

Iniciativa Latinoamericana por los Datos Abiertos (ILDA)

ILDA, a network of NGOs and research organizations focused on Latin America, played a key enabling and funding role for the initiative studied here. ILDA's "overarching objective" is to "strengthen the accountability and legitimacy of public institutions, improve public services, and fuel economic growth in Latin America and the Caribbean through research and innovation on open data initiatives."[607]

Key Beneficiaries

The direct key beneficiary was DGVS itself, since the data model provided an early warning system of future demands on the healthcare system. Beyond that, Pane intended to help the people of Paraguay: "Dengue doesn't distinguish between a government minister and my child. Mosquitoes don't care who they bite. I don't want *anyone* to get dengue."[608]

---

604 Juan Pane, Julio Paciello, Verena Ojeda, Natalia Valdez, "Enabling dengue outbreak predictions based on open data," Open Data Research Symposium Draft Paper, October 5, 2016, https://drive.google.com/file/d/0B4TpC6ecmrM7Q1lpQ0xoNlJnZlU/view.

605 World Bank, "The Dengue Mosquito Bites and Makes Latin America Sick," *World Bank News*, April 7, 2014, http://www.worldbank.org/en/news/feature/2014/04/07/dengue-en-latinoamerica.

606 GovLab interview with Juan Pane, September 9, 2016.

607 "About ILDA," Iniciativa Latinoamericana por los Datos Abiertos, http://idatosabiertos.org/about-ilda/.

608 Ibid.

Project Description

Initiation of the Open Data Activity

DGVS collects and publishes incidence and morbidity data on dengue outbreaks in Paraguay. Despite the presence of this data, DGVS lacks an automated predictive tool to enable it to predict dengue outbreaks. In 2013, shortly after returning to Paraguay from his doctoral studies in Italy, researcher Juan Pane and his colleagues at Facultad Politecnica-Universidad de Asuncion noted that there was no open source tool available that could be adapted for this purpose by DVGS, nor had any work been done to examine the correlation between incidence of dengue in Paraguay and variables such as climate, cartography, and population.[609]

Pane's initial hope was to build dynamic maps using the published data to show the origin and spread of outbreaks. He quickly found, however, that the available data would not support this type of granular geospatial tracking.[610] Looking to other dengue-affected countries in Latin America for examples of disease modeling, he found that the few other countries where data was collected, such as Brazil, had similar problems with inadequate granularity and comparability of data, creating major obstacles to longitudinal analysis that could inform predictive modeling. He successfully applied to Iniciativa Latinoamericana por los Datos Abiertos (ILDA), a Latin American open data research, funding and advocacy network, for a research grant to study data modeling of dengue. He and his colleagues then defined the required epidemiological variables and co-variables such as climate, geographic and demographic information, and surveyed 30 dengue-affected countries to assess the availability and format of published dengue data, as well as relevant government agencies responsible for publishing such data.[611] Pane and his team surveyed the reporting forms used throughout Latin America, identifying 285 variables collected across the 30 countries. Finally, Pane's team reviewed literature to identify those variables necessary to model dengue incidence.[612]

Pane's team then correlated the dengue incidence data with open climatic, geographic, demographic, and sanitation data, and produced a prototype model which was shared with DGVS. The open source web application allowed DGVS

---

609 Juan Pane, Julio Paciello, Verena Ojeda, Natalia Valdez, "Enabling dengue outbreak predictions based on open data," Open Data Research Symposium Draft Paper, October 5, 2016, https://drive.google.com/file/d/0B4TpC6ecmrM7Q1lpQ0xoNlJnZlU/view.

610 GovLab interview with Juan Pane, September 9, 2016.

611 GovLab interview with Juan Pane, September 9, 2016.

612 Ibid.

to incorporate collected data on a weekly basis and produce early warning maps of predicted dengue incidence for the following week.[613]

Demand and Supply of Data Type(s) and Sources

Pane's team used existing DGVS data on dengue incidence. The data, which was being collected on forms to report confirmed or probable cases of notifiable diseases to DGVS for subsequent reporting to the World Health Organization, provided information on number of cases, incidence of the four dengue serotypes, and demographics and location of patients. Some of this data was published in PDF format on a weekly basis, but was spread across multiple documents and tables, and did not follow a standard format in each publication. In order to access the raw data, Pane made an agreement with DGVS to supply them with the data model and training in data collection in exchange for granting his team access to the data itself.[614] This arrangement demonstrates how a clear problem definition and understanding of specific datasets that could help address the problem can enable progress even while government open data efforts lag behind standards and expectations.

Funding

As noted, the project was partially funded through a research grant from Iniciativa Latinoamericana por los Datos Abiertos (ILDA). Aside from this funding, however, the project has been conducted entirely on of the university research team.

Open Data Use

Data on dengue morbidity that feeds into the prototype application was already opened by DGVS. Additional data accessed by the research and development team was also opened as part of the process of developing the data model. Additionally, all source code used to build the predictive tool is open on. As described above, however, much of the data was provided to the researchers in a reciprocal arrangement, rather than broadly opened to the public by the government itself.

---

613 Ibid.
614 Ibid.

Impact

The dengue prevention tool exists as a prototype and proof of concept on how open data can be used to inform the fight against dengue in Paraguay. As such, the principal success indicator to date is successful prediction of future outbreaks, with a secondary indicator of adoption of the data model by the intended key user, DGVS.

Accurate Forecasting

The research and development team's preliminary results indicated that the open data-driven model was able to predict dengue outbreaks a week ahead with an accuracy of 94.78 percent.[615] The prototype data model was given to DGVS after the first round of research to enable their uptake of the tool and its continued development. The follow on impacts of providing this type of predictive capacity to the government entity responsible for managing dengue prevention and response remains to be seen. As of early 2017, there is little indication that this new predictive capacity has fundamentally shifted the intervention strategy at DGVS, but with this newly developed and demonstrably accurate tool in their dengue-prevention toolkit, there is significant potential for impact going forward. Any such impact, however, will be largely dependent on DGVS's responsiveness, especially in the form of a commitment to act on insights generated through the tool; readiness for change and commitment to ensuring sustainability for the effort through consistent resource allocation and data provision.

Risks

The potential for privacy harms is likely the central risk of the use of open data to predict dengue outbreaks in Paraguay. As is the case with any data-driven efforts focused on public health concerns, the possibility exists for personally identifiable information to made accessible, open information to be mashed up with other accessible datasets to create new privacy concerns and disease history to inform future decisions (e.g., insurance, housing or hiring) in an unacceptable way.

Additionally, countries affected by dengue are tropical and subtropical, often with a substantial economic dependence on tourism. As a result, they

---

615 Juan Pane, Julio Paciello, Verena Ojeda, Natalia Valdez, "Enabling dengue outbreak predictions based on open data," Open Data Research Symposium Draft Paper, October 5, 2016, https://drive.google.com/file/d/0B4TpC6ecmrM7Q1lpQ0xoNlJnZlU/view.

stand to see their economies suffer as a result of full disclosure of the true incidence of dengue and other mosquito-borne viruses. Many of the data-driven efforts to fight dengue and mosquito-borne illnesses focus on mapping high-risk areas and encouraging additional vigilance.[616] Although important for minimizing the spread of such diseases, such interventions could lead to a downtick in tourism and greater reluctance to inform this type of openness from government.[617]

Finally, the initiative is being driven by a small team and championed by a single individual. While this structure helped enable agility in the project development, the project's large dependence on one individual introduces risks to its longer-term sustainability.

Lessons Learned

Several important lessons with wider applicability emerge from this particular case study. These can broadly be categorized by considering the key enablers of the project, as well as the most important barriers or challenges to its success.

Enablers

Leveraging existing relationships

The research team behind the effort found success not only thanks to data science capabilities, but also the ability of Pane to leverage contacts from his various professional roles as a researcher and transparency consultant to the Paraguayan government to advance the project. For example, Pane's ability to broker an agreement with DGVS to access their unpublished data, despite their initial concerns about the privacy status of the data, was critical to the tool's launch; he was only able to reach such an agreement because of his preexisting relationship of trust. Dedicated data champions outside government (the demand side of open data) can play a central role, especially if they are able to leverage pre-existing relationships, networks and associations within government.

---

616 Andrew Young, David Sangokoya and Stefaan Verhulst, "Singapore's Dengue Cluster Map: Open data for public health," GovLab, http://odimpact.org/case-singapores-dengue-cluster-map.html.

617 GovLab interview with Juan Pane, September 9, 2016.

Clear problem definition and understanding of data needs

As described above, important data that feeds into the prototype dengue prediction tool was only made available to the researchers as a result of a reciprocal data-sharing arrangement. While this arrangement would likely not be possible were it not for the existing relationships just discussed, the clear problem definition and granular understanding of the specific datasets that could be brought to bear to help solve the problem also played a key enabling role. Rather than being driven exclusively by the data already available, the university research team developed a clear understanding of the objective of their data use (i.e., a longitudinal understanding of incidences of dengue in Paraguay toward the development of a predictive tool for DGVS), which led to a clear understanding of which datasets needed to be accessed and the development of a strategy to loosen the government's grip on them.

Barriers

Reluctance to share

Pane identifies an unwillingness to share data—manifested both as data hugging and exaggerated fears about personal privacy violations—as the single greatest barrier to the project's success.[618] Before he built his tool, the data published by DGVS was in static rather than machine readable format, and was of limited usability for automatic data processing.[619] Better, more complete and more usable data existed, but was being withheld. "The biggest issue is not the technology: it's convincing people to do transparency based on open data," says Pane. [620] Pane also adds that the World Health Organization and Pan American Health Organization could play a more pro-active role, arguing that they too sometimes withhold or otherwise restrict the free flow of data.[621] "We need good data," he says. "The more people publish the data, the better we all collectively will be."[622]

---

618 GovLab interview with Juan Pane, September 9, 2016.

619 Juan Pane, Julio Paciello, Verena Ojeda, Natalia Valdez, "Enabling dengue outbreak predictions based on open data," Open Data Research Symposium Draft Paper, October 5, 2016, https://drive.google.com/file/d/0B4TpC6ecmrM7Q1lpQ0xoNlJnZlU/view.

620 GovLab interview with Juan Pane, September 9, 2016.

621 Ibid.

622 Ibid.

Other mosquito-borne priorities

The dengue data model benefitted in part from growing awareness of and concern about not just dengue, but a host of related mosquito-borne illnesses, such as Zika and Chikungunya. On the other hand, the rapid emergence of these multiple illnesses, with often overlapping symptoms, has also created challenges for the team. For example, Pane reports that DGVS is currently withholding data updates while it struggles to come to terms with the impact of Zika on its dengue data. He adds that the new viruses make identifying and modeling dengue much more complex, in large part because the symptoms being reported that previously indicated probable cases of dengue are the same as those for Zika and Chikungunya.[623]

Looking Forward

Current Status

In 2016, Pane's team released preliminary results and a prototype open source web application that makes use of their data model as proof of concept. In collaboration with another group of researchers, Pane is currently modifying the existing model to enable it to predict the number of dengue cases. The current model merely predicts whether there will be an outbreak or not, but Pane is dissatisfied with the subjective nature of the prediction, since there is no accepted definition of what constitutes an outbreak other than disease incidence beyond what would normally be expected.[624]

Pane notes that the rules of engagement have changed dramatically since the emergence of two new mosquito-borne viruses, Zika and Chikungunya. "The world changed. We don't have just dengue now," he says. "Here we have two more diseases that we don't understand."[625] For example, he says that in the past, if a region had 10 confirmed and 40 probable cases of dengue, it was reasonable to assume that the probable cases were also dengue. That assumption can no longer safely be made. Pane and his team are now trying to determine whether to continue to attempt to model dengue, or to attempt to model the suite of symptoms common to all three viruses.[626]

---

623 Ibid.
624 Ibid.
625 Ibid.
626 Ibid.

At the same time, Pane acknowledges that the crisis of Zika may catalyze change, forcing the Paraguayan government and other affected countries to embrace greater openness in order to contend with the threat the disease poses. "We should use this momentum to boost the conversation about openness," he says.[627]

Sustainability

The project's results are preliminary, but the fact that an apparently successful open source model has already been developed suggests that it is sustainable. Future use would depend on the development of an immediately replicable open source model.

Pane identifies a number of potential risks to the project's longevity. Like other open data projects, the Paraguay data model is being driven by the passion and conviction of a single individual, and could therefore fall victim to changes in his time and circumstances. Pane also acknowledges the possibility that his model could fail to attract international attention, languishing in obscurity while other researchers attempt to produce similar models. In an attempt to prevent this, he has spoken about the project at several international open data conferences, and all the source codes are open, so that other researchers can benefit from the work already done.[628]

Replicability

Although it is not yet ready for immediate adoption elsewhere, Pane's intent is to produce an open source model that can be readily adapted for use in other countries and with other diseases. Within Paraguay, he hopes to extend its use beyond dengue to include other mosquito-borne viruses such as Zika and Chikungunya.[629]

Potential barriers to replicability outside Paraguay foreseen by Pane include national data privacy legislation; varying definitions of dengue infection; lack of technical infrastructure and national data collection and management; and political reluctance to jeopardize tourism revenue by exposing the true incidence of dengue. [630]

---

627 Ibid.

628 Ibid.

629 Ibid.

630 Juan Pane, Julio Paciello, Verena Ojeda, Natalia Valdez, "Enabling dengue outbreak predictions based on open data," Open Data Research Symposium Draft Paper, October 5, 2016, https://drive.google.com/file/d/0B4TpC6ecmrM7Q1lpQ0xoNlJnZlU/view.

Conclusion

While it remains a work in progress, Pane and his team have demonstrated that it is possible to use open health data to build a highly accurate early warning system for dengue. Although its continuance has been cast into doubt by the confounding variables of Zika and Chikungunya, Pane remains optimistic that these challenges can be overcome, and that his predictive model could be useful both within Paraguay and abroad.[631]

Pane has sometimes been exasperated by the reluctance of Paraguayan authorities to share data with his team of researchers. He emphasizes the need for governments to consider the usefulness of the data they publish—and withhold: "If there's a message I could send to disease authorities around the world, it is that you are not on your own. There are people around who are smart, who could help you understand what is going on. But for that to happen, you need to publish your data in a way that is actually useful for researchers."[632]

---

631 GovLab interview with Juan Pane, September 9, 2016.
632 Ibid.

PART 3
Conclusion

CHAPTER 17

Leveraging Open Data as a New Asset for Development

The preceding discussion has relied on a wide variety of emergent evidence to better understand how, when, and under what conditions open data projects succeed and fail in developing economies. Our goal, as indicated at the outset, has been neither to champion nor denigrate the potential of open data. The available evidence indicates a mixed picture, with open data resulting in meaningful impact in some cases, and less so in others. Identifying the signal in current research and practice is challenging since the field is still largely built around a belief in the potential of open data and a few compelling yet anecdotal success stories. Our effort here has been to understand specific pathways—using a logic model—by which open data operates in developing economies. This logic model can inform future research and evidence gathering toward a more conclusive understanding of open data's true impacts on development.

Our broad conclusion, supported by the literature, stories, and examples contained in the case studies, are that the theory of change being advanced in the field of open data for development is built around the premise that open data can:

- *Improve governance*, specifically by enhancing transparency and accountability, introducing new efficiencies into service delivery, and increasing information sharing within government departments
- *Empower citizens* in developing countries by improving their capacity to make decisions and widen their choices, and also by acting as a catalyst for social mobilization
- *Create economic opportunity*, notably by enabling business creation, job creation, new forms of innovation and more generally spurring economic growth
- *Help solve complex public problems* by improving situational awareness, bringing a wider range of expertise and knowledge to bear on public problems, and by allowing policymakers, civil society, and citizens to better target interventions and track impact

Again, none of these impacts are inevitable; they are currently better understood as intended rather than realized impacts. As part of our broader logic open data model, we have identified a number of enabling conditions and disabling factors—phenomena or aspects that may spur the potential of open data in developing economies. In particular, the impact of open data in developing economies depends upon:

- *Problem and Demand Definition*: whether and how the problem to be addressed and/or the demand for open data are clearly defined and understood
- *Capacity and Culture*: whether and how resources, human capital and technological capabilities are sufficiently available and leveraged meaningfully
- *Partnerships*: whether and how collaboration within and, especially, across sectors using open data exists
- *Risks*: whether and how the risks associated with open data are assessed and mitigated
- *Governance*: whether and how decisions affecting the use of open data are made in a responsive and legitimate manner

The accompanying Periodic Table of Open Data Impact Elements, outlined in Part II details the enabling conditions and disabling factors that must be taken into account. The list can be used as a checklist of elements that are essential to keep in mind whenever designing or funding open data projects since they may determine the difference between success and failure.

We conclude this book with six takeaways and subsequent recommendations for open data practitioners and decision makers, such as donor agencies, on how to leverage open data as a new asset for development. They represent an initial effort to operationalize the above discussion, and are derived from the empirical evidence in the case studies conducted as part of this project. Considered together, they amount to something of a "roadmap" of open data project design, implementation, and monitoring within developing economies.

Focus on and define the problem, understand the user, and be aware of local conditions. The most successful open data projects are those that are designed and implemented with keen attention to the nuances of local conditions, have a clear sense of the problem to be solved, and understand the needs of the users and intended beneficiaries. Projects with an overly broad, ill-defined, or "fuzzy" problem focus, or those that have not examined the likely users, are less likely to generate the meaningful real-world impacts, regardless of funds available. Too often open data projects have less impact because they are overly focused on leveraging newly available technology or datasets rather than being problem- and user-focused.

Recommendations for open data practitioners

- Articulate the issue to be addressed with as much granularity as possible.
- Identify and seek to understand the needs of the intended users and beneficiaries (including data intermediaries/partners such as NGOs or journalists) of the open data effort (potentially using user-centric design methods).
- Clearly define why the use of data for addressing the problem matters.
- Explore existing work that seeks to address the problem (locally or otherwise) and how your open data efforts are complementary.

Recommendations for decision makers (including donor agencies)

- Seek to promote problem- or demand-focused open data policies and strategies where open data can provide value.
- Seek ways to strengthen the capacity toward problem definition and user-centric research, for instance, by developing common problem definitions or user research tools and decision trees that can be used by practitioners.
- Develop and integrate—or ask your partners or grantees to conduct— regular exercises that identify how open data could contribute to the problem(s) one seeks to address (as to generate a data-demand culture).
- Invest in research that maps and seeks to create a better understanding of the demand side of data that can or could be matched with the current or future supply side of open data (including, for instance, a list of questions and problems that can complement the list of data-sets released).
- Invest in the development of data-capturing tools that can be used toward specific ends (such as opening information on results-based financing efforts) but have the flexibility to be applied in varied contexts.
- Require grantees to complete a "canvas" or diagnostic of open data project design to demonstrate that the problem and theory of change have been well-defined and to provide the basis for conversation between donor and recipient about the use of data.

Focus on readiness, responsiveness, and change management. Implementing open data projects often requires a level of readiness among all stakeholders, as well as a cultural transformation in the way governments and institutions collect, share, and consume information. For development funders, this important determinant of success can imply difficult decisions regarding high-potential open data initiatives in developing economies that lack clear institutional readiness or demonstrated responsiveness to feedback. The existence of a robust ICT4D sector, such as that found in Ghana, can act as a catalyst for the quick and effective development of open data capabilities. Moreover, commitment and buy-in from international development agencies themselves can play a key role in establishing the readiness necessary for impact, as evidenced in cases like Burundi's Open RBF efforts.

Recommendations for practitioners

- Consider the institutional culture(s) and "readiness" of the relevant data providers, data intermediaries, and data users that may impact both the supply of data and the response to or use of the insights generated.
- Explore partnerships with providers, partners, or intermediaries with capabilities that could help fill existing capacity gaps.
- Develop internal data literacy training opportunities.

Recommendations for decision makers (including donor agencies)

- Develop and/or fine-tune data-readiness assessment tools that can help determine the true potential of releasing and leveraging open data in developing economies.
- Invest in the generation and dissemination of evidence that can strengthen the value proposition of open data toward increasing political will to open up datasets.
- Invest in or develop coaching efforts that can nurture data-readiness and a data-driven culture at the supply, demand, and use sides of the open data ecology.
- Consider the creation of new "data intermediaries" and/or seek to support existing intermediaries (such as journalists or libraries) that can bridge the data-gap.
- Develop roadmaps to prevent or address the growing divide between those who have access and capacity to leverage data and those who do not.

Nurture an open data ecosystem through collaboration and partnerships. Data does not exist in isolation. The success of open data projects relies on collaboration among various stakeholders, as well as collaboration with data scientists and topic or sector experts. During the problem definition and initial design phase, practitioners and funders should explore the types of collaborations that could increase uptake and impact. Such partnerships could, for example, take place with other data providers (perhaps from different sectors), like-minded international or local organizations, as well as established intermediaries such as journalists or industry groups.

Recommendations for practitioners

- Conduct due diligence on important actors in the field relevant to the initiative.
- Explore, in particular, private-sector data holders that could be incentivized to participate in a data collaborative (complementing open government data).
- Build bridges with cross-sector stakeholders in the problem and solution (i.e., open data) spaces, for example, by attending conferences or meetups.
- Establish mechanisms and agreements to enable ongoing collaboration between identified partners.

Recommendations for decision makers (including donor agencies)

- Promote collaboration and dialogue among and between the supply (including national statistical agencies and corporate actors) and demand side of open data.
- Develop methodologies that can help identify different demand segments and/or constituencies that can leverage open data toward their mission.
- Invest in "labs" and creating those structures in which different partners can freely collaborate and exchange expertise toward solving hard problems.
- Develop and/or strengthen problem-solving and expert networks seeking to address sustainable development challenges with open data.
- Develop and/or fine-tune common agreements that can accelerate partnerships and exchange of data and expertise.
- Support the organization of and participation in events where different actors (global, regional, and national) can connect and identify common solutions toward improving the open data ecosystem.

Have a risk mitigation strategy. Open data projects need to be mindful of some of the important risks associated with even the most successful projects. Notably, these risks include threats to individual privacy (for example, through insufficiently anonymized data) and security. Funders should ensure that projects dealing in information that is potentially personally identifiable (including anonymized data) have audited any data risks and developed a clear strategy for mitigating those risks before proceeding with the partnership.

Recommendations for practitioners

- Assess how the data will be accessed and used, including ways that might not represent the central intended use case(s).
- Conduct a data inventory to determine how the data will be stored and monitored, and who can gain access to the data.
- Consider risk-producing scenarios or use cases to help target a mitigation strategy.
- Develop risk counter-measures based on these scenarios, such as data handling policies, training, technological solution (for example, to de-identify personal information) and a data ethics framework.

Recommendations for decision makers (including donor agencies)

- Seek ways to complement the value-proposition of open data with a broader awareness of the risks involved— for instance, through an effort to collect (learn-by-failure) case studies or stories that illustrate what can go wrong.
- Support or develop "data responsibility" models, including decision trees or expert systems that enable responsible decision making at each stage of the data life cycle (collecting, processing, sharing, analyzing, and using);

Secure resources, build evidence, and focus on sustainability. Open data projects can often be initiated with minimal resources, but require funding and additional sources of support to sustain themselves and scale. It is important to recognize that access to funding at the outset is not necessarily a sign that open data projects are destined for success. A longer term, yet flexible, business model or strategy is a key driver of sustainability, and should be developed in the early stages of the design process.

Recommendations for practitioners

- Identify local and international funders active in the sector or vertical problem area to be addressed, or in the use of data and technology to solve public problems.

- Determine how long current funding streams will be sufficient for sustainability.
- Explore and learn about additional funding or revenue generation options (e.g., tiered pricing models for open data-driven business offerings).

Recommendations for decision makers (including donor agencies)

- Develop assessment methodologies that can help identify the cost and resources necessary to sustain open data initiatives, such as the World Bank's Open Government Data Toolkit, the Open Governance Costing project being advanced by the World Bank and Research Consortium on the Impact of Open Government Processes.[633]
- Coordinate and increase funding resources—for instance, by allocating an (open) data line in each budget proposal.

Build a stronger evidence base and support more research. This book sought to capture the narratives, practice, and evidence around open data's uses in developing economies. Although there are some early, often muted signals pointing to the impacts of open data for development, the field is still largely built on a belief that open data is creating demonstrable positive outcomes. To move to a more evidence-based understanding of open data in developing economies, we distilled a theory of change and analytical framework informed by the current practice, not to further entrench faith in the positive narrative surrounding open data, but to create a flexible analytical framework that can inform future research and impact assessment. We identified a number of premises—in the form of apparent enabling conditions and disabling factors for open data initiatives—but these premises need further study (and scrutiny) by the research field to determine whether or not they hold water in practice. Thus we end with a call for more research; if open data is to reach its significant, and much-discussed, potential for spurring development, we need to move beyond ideology to create a systematic understanding and evidence base regarding what open data's impacts have been to date and how positive impacts can be enabled.

---

633 Stefaan Verhulst, "Research Consortium on the Impact of Open Government Processes," *The GovLab Blog*, February 11, 2016, http://thegovlab.org/research-consortium-on-the-impact-of-open-government-processes/.

Recommendations for open data practitioners

- Embed research and analysis of what works in the design of the open data initiative allowing for both more iterative approaches and long-term insights into how to improve certain variables.
- Integrate lessons learned and research findings into the design and development of open data initiatives (toward a more evidence-based design process).

Recommendations for decision makers (including donor agencies)

- Support more research and the further development and implementation of assessment frameworks (as provided in this book) that can help identify what works and what doesn't; as well as what can be used to scale open data initiatives across developing economies (including the possible creation of "what works labs" in different regions).
- Seek ways to translate and disseminate existing research and evidence into an "open data canvas" (akin to the GovLab Public Projects Canvas[634]), using the Periodic Table we developed in this book, that can guide more informed approaches to leverage scarce resources and ensure that interventions do not reinforce existing power or economic inequities.

Finally, given the nascent nature of existing open data initiatives, the signals of open data's impact in developing economies are still largely muted, as evidenced in the examples discussed in our paper. Our goal in this book was not to use these examples as the ultimate proof of open data's importance for development; rather, we have picked up these signals and placed them into an analytical framework to enable further practice and analysis going forward. It is only with this type of structured analysis that we can gain a systematic and comparative evidence base of whether and how open data is meaningfully impacting on-the-ground conditions in developing economies.

Remaining Questions and Evidence Gap

Although much research has contributed to our understanding of how and when open data works, there remain several questions that could benefit from more evidence and research. For instance:

---

634 The GovLab Academy Canvas, http://canvas.govlabacademy.org.

- Matching supply and demand:
  - How can we identify and unlock currently closed datasets that are likely to have a real-world impact, while avoiding "open-washing"— i.e., the tendency of governments to characterize data releases of questionable impact as examples of "open data" as a means for improving reputation?
  - How can we better match the supply of open data to the demonstrated demand for data among communities of use, and, as a result, minimize instances of scarce resources being used to open data with low potential for use and impact?

- Building capacity and an institutional open data culture:
  - How can developing countries build open data capacity, e.g., technical readiness, culture change, and training, necessary to maximize positive impacts and avoid potential harms?
  - How does the average cost of building open data capacity differ between developing and developed countries?
  - How does one establish a data-driven mindset and sense of responsibility among decision makers in developing economies that would generate a commitment and willingness to act upon the insights gained from open data?
  - How can development agencies accelerate the supply and responsible use of open data and share their own data with a broader range of constituencies, including governments, NGOs, educational institutions, business hubs, and other donor organizations?
  - How can we strategize and implement institutional and cultural change, including within international development organizations, to amplify the impact of open data in developing economies?

- Building an open data ecosystem:
  - How can we better capture the direct effects of impact enablers—like intermediaries—to help practitioners target efforts?

- Risks and challenges:
  - How can we avoid entrenching existing power asymmetries and inequalities—both socioeconomic and digital—when much of the marginalized community in developing countries is not represented in official datasets?
  - How can we minimize the potential privacy and security harms resulting from the opening of more government data?

Interviewees

Experts and stakeholders interviewed during the development of the 12 Open Data in Developing Economies Case Studies:

- Bibhusan Bista, Young Innovations
- Nama Raj Budhathoki, Kathmandu Living Labs,
- Pranav Budhathoki, Local Interventions Group
- Penhleak (Pinkie) Chan, Open Development Cambodia
- Dr J. Cunningham, Doctor in the Public and Private Healthcare Sectors, South Africa
- Aidan Eyakuze, Twaweza
- Adi Eyal, Code for South Africa
- Miryam Patricia Guzmán García, Fedearroz
- Dr R. Henry, Doctor in the Public Healthcare Sector, South Africa
- Elena Ignatova, BlueSquare, Belgium
- Priya Jadhav, Assistant Professor, Indian Institute of Technology—Bombay
- Daniel Jimenez, International Center for Tropical Agriculture (CIAT)
- Vincent Kamenyero, Burundi
- Verena Luise Knippel, World Bank
- Swheta Kulkarni, Research Associate, Prayas Energy Group
- Antoine Legrand, BlueSquare, Belgium
- David Lemayian, Code for Africa
- Anca Mantioc, The Engine Room
- Michelle McLeod, Caribbean Open Institute / University of the West Indies
- Maurice McNaughton, Caribbean Open Institute / University of the West Indies
- Arnold Minde, Developer of Shule.info
- Oscar Montiel, Open Knowledge International
- Mulle Musau, Elections Observation Group (ELOG), Kenya
- Ravi Kumar Nepal, World Bank, Code for Nepal
- Dr. Etienne Nkeshimana, Burundi
- Jean Claude Nshimirimana, Open RBF Programs, Ministry of Health, Burundi

272

- Muchiri Nyaggah, Local Development Research Institute, Kenya
- Juan Pane, National University of Asunción, Paraguay and Latin American Open Data Initiative
- Esteban Peláez Gómez, Coordinator of Social Projects, Fundación Corona
- Ashok Pendse, Authorised Consumer Representative with the Maharashtra Electricity Regulatory Commission (MERC)
- Mor Rubinstein, Open Knowledge International
- Priyadarshan Sahasrabuddhe, Vishwadeep Pressparts Pvt. Ltd
- Fabrizio Scrollini, DATA Uruguay
- Jennifer Shkbaktur, IDC Herzliya
- Simone Soeters, Cordaid, The Netherlands
- Thy Try, Open Development Cambodia
- Daniel Uribe, Fundacion Corona
- Samhir Vasdev, ICT Sector Unit, World Bank Group
- Adele Waugaman, USAID
- Christopher Whyms-Stone, Trench Town Culture Yard

Open Data in Developing Economies Advisory Committee

- Izabela Corrêa, Former Coordinator for the Promotion of Ethics, Transparency, and Integrity, Directorate for Corruption Prevention, Brazil
- Elena Ignatova, BlueSquare
- André Laperrière, Executive Director, Global Open Data Initiative for Agriculture and Nutrition (GODAN)
- Maurice McNaughton, Director of the Centre of Excellence for IT Enabled Innovation, Mona School of Business and Management, University of the West Indies, Jamaica
- Jean Philbert Nsengimana, Minister of Youth and Information Communication Technology, Rwanda
- David Selassie Opoku, Open Data for Development (OD4D) Africa Lead, Open Knowledge International
- Fernando Perini, International Development Research Center, Canada
- Nii Narku Quaynor, Chairman, Network Computer Systems, Ghana
- Nicole Stremlau, Programme in Comparative Media Law and Policy, University of Oxford, UK

Recognized Peer Reviewers of the Open Data in Developing
Economies research

- Patrick Enaholo, Pan-Atlantic University, Nigeria
- Sara Fernandes, University of Minho and United Nations University
- Claudia Frittelli, Carnegie Corporation
- Silvana Fumega, University of Tasmania, Institute for the Study of
  Social Change
- Shurland George, World Wide Web Foundation
- Felipe Gonzalez-Zapata, University of Manchester
- Julina Hooks, Teachers College Columbia University
- Alicia Johnson, San Francisco Emergency Management
- Antonio Almansa Morales, Diputación Provincial Málaga (Málaga City
  County Council)
- Freddy Oswaldo, Independent Consultant
- Iris Palma, DatosElSalvador
- Mohamed Salimi, HCP
- Juliana Taylor, Start Smart
- Julia Roberto Herrara Toledo, Red Ciudadana
- Mariam Rafique Vadria, Delivery Associates
- Christopher Wilson, University in Oslo
- Ken Zita, Network Dynamics Associates

Participants to Workshop at the International Open Data Conference in
Madrid, Spain (Wednesday, October 5, 2016) on "Getting to Grips with the
Impact of Open Data" (The Open Data in Developing Economies Project)

Facilitator: Stefaan Verhulst, The GovLab
Participants:
- Laura Bacon, Omidyar Network
- Mark Cardwell, USAID
- Patrick Enaholo, Pan-Atlantic University, Nigeria
- Adi Eyal, Code for South Africa
- Feng Gao, Open Data China
- Silvana Fumega, University of Tasmania, Institute for the Study of
  Social Change
- Mohammad Hossein Ichani, Open Data for Iran
- Michael Jelenic, World Bank
- Michelle McLeod, University of the West Indies
- Maurice McNaughton, University of the West Indies

- Indanna Minto-Coy, University of the West Indies
- Jean Claude Nshimirimana, Ministry of Health, Burundi
- David S. Opoku, Africa Lead, Open Data for Development, Open Knowledge International
- Juan Pane, National University of Asunción, Paraguay and Latin American Open Data Initiative
- Alán Ponce, University of Southampton
- Brandon Pustejovsky, USAID
- Lorna Seitz, Legis Institute
- Tanya Sethi, AidData
- Ilham C. Srimarga, University of the Western Cape
- Kat Townsend, MCC
- Mireille van Eechoud, University of Amsterdam
- Roza Vasileva, World Bank
- Julian Walcott, University of the West Indies
- Natalie Widmann, Max Planck Institute for Intelligent Systems